Hanover rail station where
Luftwaffe guards save our lives

Three engines shot out by enemy fighters

Flight path surviving planes fly
to target—JU-88 aircraft
plant at Oschersleben

THE FLAME
KEEPERS

THE FLAME KEEPERS

The True Story of an American
Soldier's Survival Inside Stalag 17

Ned Handy AND **Kemp Battle**

HYPERION

NEW YORK

*To the prisoners of all nations who
entered the gates of Stalag XVII-B.*

They endure.

ACKNOWLEDGMENTS

First thanks go to the "kriegies" of Stalag 17 who, knowing about this project, backed it and, in so many ways, provided its life's blood. Particular thanks to the ten of you who are part of the story and who provided input, in some cases heavy-duty, to make that possible: Tom Barksdale, Bill Clarke, Frank Grey (with ongoing help from his noble wife, Dorothy), Rich Hoffman, Ed McKenzie (Stalag 17 historian and major contributor to the book in unending ways), Gene Meese, Tony Saccomanno, Stoop Morrissey, George Saccomanno and Bob Watson.

Thanks also to you other Stalag 17ers who—often with your wives as well—gave us solid, ongoing support: Oren Albright, Charlie Belmer, Bill and Anne Caruso, Les Jackson (current Stalag 17 historian and now, too, Executive Director of American Ex-Prisoners of War), Roy and Doris Livingstone, Moe Molen, Ralph and Pat Moulis, Walter Pawlesh, Ed Sexton, and Native American Chief Arthur Silo. And special thanks to those kriegies who shared their

viii   • ACKNOWLEDGMENTS

combat and Stalag 17 stories with us at the Branson and San Diego reunions.

Key help was also given by "Kurt" Kurtenbach, Stalag 17's outstanding leader, who now belongs not to us but to the ages. Ralph Orlando, Air Force pilot and nephew of the Tedrowe crew's tail gunner, provided crew photos and much other help. Steve Tedrowe and Chester Shattuck Jr. told us about their fathers' lives after World War II. Steve Firestone helped with information about his father, Captain Clinton Firestone Jr.—pilot of Tony Saccomanno's crew.

We are particularly grateful to two brave kriegies, Ben Phelper and Bernie Resnicoff, for the photographs of Stalag 17 included in this book. These rare images were taken with a smuggled camera at great risk and first privately published in 1946. Their very existence is a testament to the devotion these kriegies had for their comrades-in-arms and to their deep sense of history.

To the readers who read the manuscript with such care and offered such invaluable editorial insight—Carol Bundy, Margaret Handy, Joshua Horwitz, Glenn Koocher, Candy Lee and (as always) Carolyn Slaughter—we are indebted. Particular appreciation to Frances Schaefer, Karin Galloway and Alex Hoyt for launching us, Gretchen Young at Hyperion for having faith and both Natalie Kaire and Zareen Jaffery for keeping us on track. Thanks to the libraries at the Century Association, Massachusetts Institute of Technology, Harvard and Princeton universities and to the Library of Congress. Much gratitude for the great illustrations provided by Chris and Amy Hughes and for their genuine interest in the project.

Kemp's own deep thanks to Logan Fox, Lindsay McGowen, John Battle, Bill Stoehr, Caroline Seebohm, Elaine Pagels, Als, TC, Emily, Joe and his crew (Steve, Jesse, Conor, Brian and Frankie) and special gratitude to the three great American warriors in his life, Hyman L. Battle, James F. Calvert and Samuel Hynes. And Ned's special thanks for support in abundance from his daughter/writer

Jenifer and her husband, Steve Pittman; from his brother, Jack; from his sisters and so many others in his immediate family; from his cousins Mary Margaret, John and Harriet Chapman; from Joe Basile, Rudy Colaluca, Ed MacNeal, Tim Foley, and Conevery Bolton Valencius; and from the countless supporters—key were Georgia Bowman and Jane Maguire—among his own professional colleagues.

THE YEAR OF FIVE SEASONS

> *There is a destiny that makes us brothers,*
> *None goes his way alone.*
>
> —EDWIN MARKHAM

NORTHWEST OF VIENNA, past the farms and vineyards that lie along the Danube, just beyond the town of Krems, runs a road that climbs up into blue hills and winds like memory to a village called Gneixendorf. There is little sign that in this place, nearly sixty years ago, sprawled Stalag XVII-B, Nazi Germany's third largest, and most notorious, prisoner-of-war camp. There are still locals who remember that their village was once home to a vast patchwork of raggedly wrapped barbed wire compounds, grim acres of grassless dirt. They recently erected several modest monuments to commemorate the prisoners who suffered and died there between 1939 and 1945. Determined visitors, knowledgeable of the ground's heritage, might unearth a strand of wire or a scorched brick; they might even see, if the light is right, the grass-covered scar of the main street that ran through the American compounds. They will find little else. Between the last two springs of World War II, in a year that spanned five seasons, I was a prisoner in Stalag XVII-B. In the six decades I have lived since leaving that camp, I have learned that the past can be unforgiving when unshared, and that some memories, when suffered alone, weaken the spirit.

So I choose to remember it all again.

STALAG XVII-B (WE SIMPLY CALLED IT STALAG 17) had been built in 1939 by the Wehrmacht, the German army, as a dulag—a transition camp—for the Polish and French prisoners captured before they'd had time to become soldiers. Following the Blitzkrieg, the biggest dulags were quickly converted to oflags (for officers) and stalags, permanent camps to collect the residue of the Nazis' fast-defeated enemies. French, Poles, Russians, Greeks, Serbs and Italians were routed into already crowded, pitiful facilities and left to rot. By 1943, Stalag 17 would claim as many as sixty-six thousand prisoners, though about half of them at any given time were farmed out to satellite work camps to feed the Nazi war machine.

When the first American prisoners (all American fliers) arrived in the fall of 1943, transferred from Stalag 7A in Moosburg, Germany, they were greeted by lice-filled, rat-infested compounds that had sheltered Russian prisoners only hours before. I was not there then, but I heard about it. The Americans were stunned by the facilities and justifiably worried about the resources they would be given to survive Stalag 17. These "kriegies" (a shortened form of *kriegsgefangenen*, the German word for prisoner of war) quickly recognized that to manage life within the wire they were going to need careful organization to steward limited resources, maintain discipline and safeguard morale. They understood that though the Germans could be resisted, even occasionally outwitted, suffering would be inevitable.

So the kriegies went to work. They built within the wire a world that could sustain and discipline morale; it became the Americans' experience of Stalag 17. They knew that order and management would have to depend on something other than rank, and the best available methodology in a camp full of sergeants was also the most natural: democracy. They voted for their leaders at all levels. Governance depended first upon group leaders, individuals who represented the needs of several bays within a barracks. (Each barracks was divided into ten bays and held about 150 men.) The group leaders reported to their barracks chief, whose job was to help his men with problems at all levels as needed. The barracks chiefs—there were eight barracks in each compound—reported to the five compound leaders who in turn acted as the central operational arm of the camp's elected senior manager, a capable sergeant named "Kurt" Kurtenbach. He had been a tail gunner on a B-17 and was shot down in France in December of 1942. Six of his crew had managed to get back to England, but Kurtenbach and his ball turret gunner had wandered across France avoiding capture until the Gestapo caught them on a train at Dijon. He passed through five prison camps before ending up at Stalag 17, where the Germans accepted him as an American-designated "Man of Confidence." The Germans used him as their principal contact in the camp and considered him the lead voice on behalf of the American prisoners. Kurtenbach was tough and fair, spoke German and knew the rules of the Geneva Convention in detail. He was our constant advocate and a shrewd adversary of our German captors.

About 3,100 Americans had been brought to Stalag 17 in 1943. The next crop of prisoners (of which I was one) arrived in April of 1944. None of the roughly 1,200 of us who straggled into Stalag 17 knew how lucky we were to be alive. We would later learn that out of every ten-man crew shot down, only four would survive. In the last weeks of March 1944 and the first weeks of April, the U.S. Eighth Air Force sent thousands of planes over Germany from its English bases. The bombers were a critical part of the plan that culminated in the landings on the Normandy beaches at Omaha, Utah, Juno and Sword. The 466th Bomb Group, to which I belonged, would, in less than three weeks, lose upward of half its crews.

The Americans already in Stalag 17 were glad to see us, fresh (they hoped) with news from home. They branded us the "new kriegies," the "hairy-assed boys" who, they liked to tell us at every turn, had it easy.

We resented their resentment and thought it unfair given our own recent privations and brush with mortality, but in some profound ways, they were right. By the time we stumbled bewildered and bruised into the stalag, the old kriegies had wrought ingenious solutions out of horrific circumstances, had established rhythms and rituals where there had once been only confusion and fear. There was a system we could join, an order that we could rely on. We were not the first Americans, and if imprisonment was new to us, at least we did not have to face it as they had: alone.

For old and new kriegie alike, imprisonment was a shock. We had wondered occasionally at the idea that we could be shot down and killed, but none of us had ever imagined that we would end up prisoners of war. We were trained to be invulnerable, inspired by a sense of adventure and destiny. Most of us were somewhere between the ages of eighteen and twenty-one, and our journey in life had barely begun. I was fortunate and had seen something of the world. The second son of a Massachusetts family of six children, my early years were marked by changes in scenery and circumstance. My father had done well in the 1920s as an importer and had taken us from one home to another, even to live in Europe on one of his long business trips. Not without ups and downs, our family life during the "Roaring Twenties" was one of much privilege, and my parents had reasonable expectations that their children's future would include the benefits of private schools, fine colleges and successful careers. The Great Depression changed all that. In 1936, while we were living in Bedford, New York, on a thirty-acre heavily mortgaged "farm" (I was almost fourteen), my father's business fortunes finally collapsed, along with most notions of a secure future. Evicted by the local sheriff, we moved to our ancestral home in Barnstable Village on Cape Cod, where for the next year my mother met adversity with that towering strength reserved for women. She ran an in-house school, organized us into effective indoor/outdoor work crews, immersed us in literature and music, and brought us to an all-time peak of family grit and solidarity—meanwhile giving massive support to my father, still struggling to earn a living as his health declined. The next year that health gave way and we split up to live with caring relatives hundreds of miles from one another. My brother and I lived with our paternal grandmother and went to nearby Milton Academy on full scholarships. Though on graduating in 1940 I was accepted at MIT, there was no money to pay the costs. College would have to wait. And then along came the war.

My early life, informed as it was by the gifts of prosperity and an equally valuable though unexpected adversity, prepared me well for survival at Stalag 17. By the time I entered the Army Air Corps at nineteen, I was equipped with a kind of self-sufficient stubbornness that served me well. At its best, it had taught me to keep my own counsel; at its worst, I could be quick to judgment with an impetuous sense of right and wrong. I had much to learn, and Stalag 17 would be my unrelenting teacher.

Among the stalag's first, most immediate lessons was how to live with less. Less food, less comfort, less certainty. We were forced to master the art of managing with far fewer resources than we had ever thought possible. On the day I took off on my last mission, for example, I was wearing two layers of fresh laundered clothing under an electrically heated flight suit, headgear with a fleece-lined hood and two pairs of socks under electronically heated slippers inside fleece-lined boots. I carried a hastily packed flight bag with a steel helmet, flak vest, electronic gloves and liners, throat microphone and oxygen mask with a built-in microphone. Months later I would manage the brutal winter of 1944 at Stalag 17 with a pair of pants, wooden clogs, two shirts, an old army coat and a cap. I needed nothing else.

Other changes, however, were less easy to manage. The guards at Stalag 17 made it clear with their shouting, their endless disruptions and total disregard for our sense of place that we were of no account at all. Prisoners reacted to their calculated intrusions in very different ways. Some sat glassy-eyed on the edge of their bunks or drifted about the compound, their self-confidence trailing away behind them. Not knowing what the future held was, for these men, unbearable, and they seemed oarless boats on a shoreless lake.

All the American prisoners (as well as the British and French) understood that bad as their circumstances and prospects were, there were others nearby who were far worse off. The treatment of prisoners at Stalag 17 depended entirely upon nationality: the American and British prisoners were protected, to a great extent, by the standards of the Geneva Convention of 1929. We were entitled to a modicum of Red Cross supplies, mail (when it could get through), medical attention and sparse materials to pass the time (including outdated books, rudimentary musical instruments and worn sporting equipment). We were also guaranteed that as noncommissioned officers, we would do no manual labor. If the French were treated shabbily, victims of their fast defeat and quick absorption by the Nazis, the Russians (who were not signatories to the Geneva Convention) and their Slavic brethren were shoved right down to the gates of hell. The Germans loathed them and, for the most part, ignored their diseases, their starvation, their relentless dying. Most all of the deaths in the stalag were Russians. When an American or British prisoner died (or was killed), he was given a coffin and a burial; the Russians were carried out in paper bags and dumped into a mass grave. Those who survived Stalag 17 (and there are, every day, fewer among us) were exceptionally fortunate, and not simply because we avoided the sad fate of our Russian comrades. We know now what none of us could have imagined then: that those who shuttled us in boxcars to Stalag 17 routed millions of others to the death camps. Unlike those doomed souls, we had a measure of control over our own survival. Luck counted for something, but we were still soldiers in an army that by mid-1944 seemed on its way to victory. If we kept our wits and stuck together, the odds of survival were in our favor; we could safeguard a sense of hope. By the time Allied troops tore down the gates of camps like Auschwitz, Dachau, Bergen-Belsen and Buchenwald, hope for their prisoners had long since turned to ash. We were ignorant of the terrible history being written and focused solely on our own survival.

We were young, had all lost comrades on the journey to Stalag 17 and could not be sure we would survive. If we were determined and full of cocky humor, we were also starving and somewhat scared. If we knew, as did our captors, that the Allies now might well win the war, we did not know what victory could mean to our fate. Many feared the Nazis would kill us long before any liberation, a final act of vengeance for their failed war. The simple truth was that every day we had to fight for mastery over our fears, our bodies, our hearts. We dug our tunnels, survived our pistol-whippings and listened long into the night to one another's memories of home. For that one long year, the year I turned twenty-two, every moment seemed a test that required nothing less than everything.

The experience each of us had at Stalag 17 depended entirely on the barracks to which we belonged, perhaps even the bay in which we slept. We did not socialize in large groups, nor did we move through one another's private domains unless specifically requested. As a result, you knew fewer people than might be imagined. You kept to your own. An escape attempt hatched in one bay might not be discovered by the men in an adjacent bay until a stalag reunion fifty years later. You did not ask too many questions; you did not interfere in the plans of men you did not sleep and wake with every day. It is one of the points of pride within 32A, however, that almost all 143 men in that barracks contributed one way or another to the tunnel we built in that summer and fall of 1944. A tunnel that would save the lives of men we did not even know.

We were to learn many lessons in Stalag 17, but the deepest and most important one was how to manage under relentless pressure, to cultivate and nurture the delicate space of our own imaginations; how to keep ourselves alive to the possibility that one day we would go home. At Stalag 17, I measured my life not in hours or days but in the stories I heard, the lessons I learned, the seasons that passed. The links from one moment to the next were forged in response to danger, the need for strength, the gift of life, and bore no relation to clock or calendar. One story told in the dark could stand for a hundred such stories; the memory of one intense hour would outlast the memories of a month. So be it. What is more important than the chronology of the heart?

THIS IS THE STORY OF MY own journey through World War II and about the unexpected detour it took through Stalag 17. With my friend and coauthor Kemp Battle, we returned together to the story I had lived but had not fully reconsidered. We walked a path of memory and research, revisiting a life lived six decades ago. His questions summoned lost events, evoked forgotten characters, tapped into wellsprings of old feeling. We talked with my comrades, pieced together mysteries of days and nights barely recalled and relived incidents still as immediate and clear to me as if they had taken place this very morning. We found, in our unique collaboration, the vivid landscape of a remembered life. We both saw that much was learned in that journey sixty years ago.

The memories that follow offer little perspective as to the overarching view of war as our civilization's greatest disaster, or on the tragedy of lives cut down in their prime, unfairly closed out forever. There was little time for dwelling on such thoughts back then. It would take me some years to come to the full understanding that nothing is more important than to eliminate war as the chief tool in accomplishing national objectives. Further, there is little sense or evidence in the coming pages of everyday, human fear. Young men lacking the wisdom to grasp the tragedy of war often lack, too, a mature grasp of danger. Only years later do they come to understand; only then do they wake up in a cold sweat remembering what, like animals, they did without fear.

Life in the stalag certainly made us stronger, but surviving the stalag did not of itself make us men. Ready or not, we had become men long before we ever saw that camp. We had become men while preparing to fight our enemy, while watching our crewmates and friends die, while nearly dying ourselves. Manhood comes with responsibility and the composure one develops in the face of chaos. Stalag 17 was to be something else altogether, something deeper and more mysterious to us than the flame and fury of war. I did not know it then, but passing through the gates of Stalag 17, I was to learn the hard, beautiful lessons that were to serve me well for the rest of my life.

PART I

SPRING

> *I have a rendezvous with Death*
> *When Spring brings back blue days and fair*
> —ALAN SEEGER

"TIME'S RUNNING OUT," yelled our navigator, "Germany's dead ahead. Get those goddamned guns working." The calmest of our crew, Lieutenant Brown had never been so tense. He had reason to be. Only three days earlier, we'd lost six crews on a mission to Brunswick—fifteen crews overall in our first eight missions—150 of our 500 men lost in just nineteen days. Each of our eight guns was key, and when we had test-fired them over the English Channel, four had malfunctioned. Keith Thompson, our First Armorer, was still working on my top-turret "twin fifties." The two fifty-caliber machine guns were in parts on the radio-room floor, just below the top turret, when Brown came by. Thompson was methodically reassembling them and I was handing him each part as he called for it. I was immediately grateful that in aerial gunnery school we had learned to break guns down and put them together again blindfolded.

By the time Thompson had reassembled and installed the guns in my turret, we were already well into Germany. I test-fired the fifties and the sharp burst of fire comforted us all. Thompson returned to his own fifty-caliber waist gun on the starboard side of the plane. Tucked once again inside the top turret, I lost no time putting it into "slow-switch" 360-degree rotation. This was per Eighth Air Force orders, and it allowed me a look at all points of the compass every fifty seconds. We had been trained to use clock positions, not compass readings, along with "high," "low" and "level," in calling out the direction of attacking fighters. "Three o'clock high" crackling over the intercom meant trouble from above, off our starboard wing. At present the skies were bright and empty.

We were at about 24,000 feet and it was getting cold. I connected my electric flight suit to the aircraft power system to warm up and continued scanning the blue spring morning. For the moment, all was well; no fighters from above, no flak from below. The one blind spot lay dead ahead in the morning sun. The Luftwaffe liked to wait high in the blinding sun for a moment's advantage and though we knew it, there was little we could do. Our best defense were our own ferocious watchdogs, the American P-51 Mustangs and the P-38 twin-boom Lightnings that patrolled the skies around us. We could not see them, but like the Luftwaffe, they were out there.

We had learned that morning at the briefing that our mission was to be a strike against a military factory near Brunswick. The names of the German cities were becoming increasingly familiar to me. Our targets were military and/or industrial and always located outside those cities, but we identified them with the closest city's name. It was my fourth mission and we were flying group lead, a coveted position despite the Luftwaffe's zest for disrupting formations by attacking the lead planes.

I had heard nothing on the intercom as to our progress. First Lt. Thaddeus Tedrowe, our pilot, couldn't have kept us informed even had he wanted to—he had to maintain coordination with the fleet of bombers and their escorts to ensure that everyone got to the target intact and on time. The first milestone was the "initial point," or "IP," the place where a bomb run actually begins. In order to keep the Germans uncertain of our final destination as long as possible, we each flew to the IP from a different direction. At the IP, we would make a sharp turn and then fly straight and true toward the target, whatever the welcome, flak or fighter. Tedrowe may have advised us that we were now approaching the IP, but if he did, I did not hear him. I strapped on my oxygen mask, knowing that once the flak started or the Luftwaffe came, there would be no time.

On my turret's back swings, looking back over our tail and twin rudders, I was amazed by the immense and disciplined migration of bombers fanned out behind us in multiple formations. Some bombers held their noses proudly and bore through the sky while others scrambled into place like stragglers at a great parade. They all shone in the morning light. It was a majestic vista, and though I was not a frequent churchgoer, it made me feel part of a cathedral congregation singing a great hymn in full voice. The Eighth Air Force, headquartered in England, had twenty-six groups of B-24s and B-17s, and each group had at least fifty crews. I wondered how the Nazis could withstand the single-minded purpose and fury of all those gleaming bombers coming at them day after day.

Our two wing planes were so close I could see the pilots through their windows. To starboard, they were busy adjusting something above their heads like a pair of mechanics flipping levers; to port, the copilot's head tilted jovially toward his pilot, as if midway through a story. I relaxed for a moment to the soothing drone of our engines. My suit was warming up nicely, my turret's full-circle rotations continuing to give me a sense of a mission going well. And then, deafening explosions rocked our plane. At the same moment, I saw both those wing planes burst into flames and drop straight away like dead birds. The sight was mesmerizing, and for a split second I was knifed through with grief. The planes, and the twenty men inside them, were gone in an instant.

We had been hit hard but were somehow still flying. As the crew's flight engineer, my job was to immediately assess the damage to our plane and its ability to stay airborne. Getting down from the turret while disconnecting oxygen, heat and intercom, I heard our tail gunner, Alfredo Orlando, yelling in his distinctive Italian accent an excited account of a dogfight in the skies behind us—our fighters tangling with the dozen or more Luftwaffe pilots. They had come head-on out of the sun, riddled our three Liberators and swung under us, all in a matter of seconds.

I had to get to the cockpit fast. Manning the top-turret guns, I was almost right over Tedrowe. I dropped down past Dailey into the radio room. He was busy hunched over his radio but turned and pointed toward the bomb bay behind him. It was a shower of spraying gasoline. The bay's starboard bomb door was shattered and this let fresh air in, but not enough to clear the heavy vapor. Any spark would blow the plane apart. I still had no parachute on, but no time to think on that. Through the spray I could see heavy shrapnel damage to gas lines running along the top of the bomb bay to the radio-room fuel gauges. There were many things about a B-24 its flight engineers needed to know and didn't, but we *had* been shown how to shut down those lines. Getting a bath of gasoline, I worked my way along the bomb bay's catwalk to where the shutoff valves could be reached and closed them off. If I was afraid, I did not have time to feel it.

Back to the cockpit for engine check-out, I got into my slot between pilot and copilot. I looked out across them to our wings. It was a galvanizing moment. Both engines to port were dead, their black propellers frozen against the sky. Feathered, too, our outboard propeller to starboard. Only "Number Three"—our right wing's inboard engine—was still turning over. I was thunderstruck. Out the cockpit windows I could see that we were now alone, heading away from the sun, back toward Holland, but with only one engine still alive. The engineer's job was to report all problems, but Tedrowe would now want only what was needed to manage this fast-falling plane.

That last engine—how was it doing? A look at the instruments showed right away that its fuel pressure was down to thirteen. Sixteen was standard. At *eight,* flight engineers were taught, the engine would fail. Had ours stabilized at thirteen, or was it still on its way down? It was still falling. The altimeter showed we had already dropped five thousand feet. Our speed—normally 175 miles per hour—was down to 110, not much above our stalling speed of 90. It was time to talk with Tedrowe. He had gotten us out of the formation safely with three engines dead and headed us back toward Holland, but now looked exhausted. He was using all his strength and concentration to fly the plane. I could see the rising tendons on his wrist, and his knuckles were white as he gripped the steering column. The physical stamina needed to fly a B-24 was substantial even with all engines and other systems performing well, but under these circumstances keeping the plane on course required almost superhuman strength.

Pilots and engineers were always close and had their own shorthand language. We traded a few words. He wanted the crew prepared for a crash landing, as near the Holland border as we could get, but learning that our last engine would fail unless its pressure stabilized, he wanted the plane and men prepared for a bailout, too. I told him the damaged bomb doors had to be opened some for that.

"You and Thompson try to get those doors open," he said very calmly, almost quietly. "Then, if you can, get the bombs out. I'm going to fly this plane as far as I can. Let's try to lighten it."

I worked my way back to see what could be done about opening the bomb doors to get the bombs out and to bail through if it came to that. Thompson met me on the catwalk. Tedrowe had reached him by intercom.

"The doors are jammed!" he shouted.

"The hydraulics can't budge them," I shouted back. The wind was roaring. "We can use the crank. Get the crank." We rigged the crank, and though turning it took all our strength, we got ourselves an opening of about two feet on the starboard side. This would work for bailing, we thought, and for the bombs, which we now pushed out one-by-one over the open countryside we could see far below. It was good to see them go; neither of us liked the idea of crash-landing with a full payload. We talked for a minute before heading back to our posts. Thompson was in good shape and confirmed that Orlando and Mintz, our tail and port waist gunners, were, too.

Back to the cockpit. I checked our Number Three's fuel pressure. It had gone down further. I relayed this to Tedrowe but said it might still stabilize above the eight-pound shutdown level. There was now a growing thickness to his voice.

"Pass the word that if Number Three holds we might make it to Holland. It's a hundred miles to the border."

Lieutenant Brown must have reported that by intercom. I had no idea we were so close, but knew with our plane now at fifteen thousand feet and dropping five hundred feet a minute, we'd hit the ground well short. An east wind might get us nearer Holland, but westerlies were the rule. Even so, once on the ground we'd have to make it some distance on foot to the border.

"How're we doing?" Tedrowe asked quietly.

"Ten and a half; we're still going down but maybe it'll stabilize." Neither Tedrowe nor his copilot commented. We all understood that with Number Three's fuel pressure continuing to drop—and having dropped that far—only a miracle could save the engine now. Still, the drop was gradual and slow; there was room for hope.

I knew, as Tedrowe surely did, that setting down—crash-landing— a B-24 with only one engine could well be a disaster and that we would have to give all the rest of the crew the choice of bailing out rather than hanging in for a crash landing. If and when that last engine failed us, we'd *have* to get everyone out. With all engines gone, Tedrowe might or might not be able to maneuver the plane down to a dead-stick landing. He would have to alternately dive to develop maximum safe flying speed and then level off for a low-angle glide until just above stalling speed. Failure on either count could tear off our wings or put us into a spin from which no one could bail. If we even got positioned to land, we would have no choice of terrain—a grim bet and certainly a blind one. With little or nothing to gain from it, Tedrowe would be taking his crew on an engineless plane ride down to a near suicidal landing. If the bad news came—Number Three *was* going to fail—it would be vital that I give Tedrowe, likely the last one to bail, time to get out before the engine died altogether.

Meanwhile our gunners scanned the sky for the predictable Luftwaffe fighter plane that would be dispatched to use us for target practice—to play with us as a cat does a mouse. Dailey's radio scanned the airwaves for messages that might warn us. Lieutenant Brown tracked our progress westward on his navigation maps. My eyes were glued to the instruments, praying we'd stabilize above that eight-pound shutdown level. We flew on alone, dropping fast but free of enemy fighters.

At nine pounds Number Three sputtered and caught again. The pressure kept falling. There would be no miracle. It was a flight engineer's high noon. We were going to have to get out of the plane. We hadn't been trained to bail and were going to have to learn on the job. At eight and a half pounds, there was no more margin. It was time.

"This is it," I said to Tedrowe. "Get the crew out." He did not hesitate: he gave the order over the intercom and hit the bailout alarm. Concentrating on his flying, staring straight ahead, he said: "Go. You and Dailey, go. Bail." Time was now our last, most dangerous, enemy.

I put on my chute.

Dailey was in the radio room. He had heard the alarm and Tedrowe's command to bail. Lieutenant Levins, our bombardier, had also come up from down in the nose of the plane. What Tedrowe had in mind was that the men in the cockpit/radio-room compartment would bail through the opening in the bomb bay doors. Down in the nose compartment, Lieutenant Brown and George Saccomanno, our nose-turret gunner, had their own escape hatch in the floor of the compartment. The two waist gunners and Orlando, our tail gunner, had three ways out: an escape hatch on the waist floor, through the waist windows or through the bomb bay opening the cockpit/radio-room crew would use. Tedrowe and his copilot would wait until they were satisfied that the time was right for them—assuming that the engine hadn't cut out, which would make it essential for them to bail immediately. The bailout would proceed simultaneously from the nose, the radio room/cockpit and the waist gunnery area.

Several men were near the entrance to the bomb bay, where the backup crank had opened up the damaged bomb doors enough to let us work our way between them and the starboard side of the catwalk. Levins was closest to the bomb bay and said to Dailey and me, "Men before officers." He seemed quite cool and collected, so that was probably standard procedure for commissioned officers, though it certainly was news to me. Dailey was ahead of me, so I told him to bail. He turned and asked me to bail first. He was a tall, lanky fellow, and I could see how he would have wanted to be certain that someone could get through those mangled bomb bay doors. I got down onto the catwalk where the wrecked bomb bay doors gave me a view of the sunlit land miles below. Where were we? We had been flying for about twenty minutes at about 110 miles an hour. *Not far enough,* I thought. Although the opening was small and jagged, I realized we were all going to have to get through it with a jump. You couldn't work your way out a little at a time or the slipstream would cut you to ribbons. Crouching low on the catwalk, I looked one last time at my crewmates. It occurred to me with a sudden satisfaction that before my first flight into Germany I had written a "good-bye" letter to my mother and had sent it in a sealed envelope to my oldest sister in case I didn't return, and then I jumped. The slipstream struck me hard and almost knocked me out. We had had no training in bailouts, but before pulling the red-handled rip cord I did remember to count to ten as we'd been told. A little pilot chute whipped out and, following it, a billowing main. After an enormous jolt as the main chute took hold, I found myself right-side up, swinging away in the wind.

I rested for a moment, drifting through an azure spring sky with, at a distance, white billowing parachutes patterned against its infinite blue. Its beauty was overwhelming, but more so its awesome silence. For years the roar of engines had surrounded me. Twenty-four hours a day, wherever I was, their mighty chorus sang to me from hangar tarmacs and runways, from above in the sky or out on the wings of our own plane as we flew our missions. The thunder of those engines had become my tie to the love of flying and the inspiration it provided. Now all of that was gone. As I floated through spring's silent blue morning, below me a quilt of farmland with the midday sun melting streams to gold, I sensed that one kind of life had ended and a new one was coming at me, ready or not. For a moment I thought of our two wing planes and our twenty comrades who had no chance at that new life.

Suddenly I was aware that I was falling fast toward a good deal of trouble. Now a mile or so above the ground, I could see that a strong wind was moving me sideways at a good clip, carrying me right toward a large body of blue water. Having never been in a parachute before, I was finding my first jump likely to drop me in the middle of that lake. No one had trained me on how to land, much less on how to land in water. I began to probe my harness to figure out how to get unhooked fast. If I could get out of the chute before I hit the water, timing the release right before impact, I wouldn't drown in a tangle of cords and harnesses. Seaside summers had made me something of a fish, and that thought helped. The closer I got to the ground, however, the faster my chute seemed to be moving sideways. Soon enough the wind pulled me clear of the lake and toward some freshly plowed fields. They came up at me fast. At impact, I was on a backswing, so I landed more or less like an airplane, my legs sliding onto the ground before my waist and shoulders. The trouble came once I was on the ground and the chute, swelling with the strong wind, dragged me fast over the field. I knew my body couldn't take too much of that, particularly if I hit a large stone or two, so I hauled hard at the silk. After a hundred yards or so, the chute collapsed and I came to a stop, facedown on German soil.

I started to roll over and felt the bite of iron in my sides. Rolling a bit farther, taking it nice and easy, I came face-to-face with a farmer whose pitchfork pressed against me. He seemed nervous and determined. I stopped the rollover. Behind him stood a grinning German soldier in a green uniform. He held a large pistol aimed directly at me and made it clear he wanted me to get up and pull in the chute. Slowly wrapping the silk, I had a moment to look around at the crudely plowed field that ran to the horizon. All around me dark figures, mostly elderly men and women, stooped or moved slowly behind wooden carts. I had not noticed any of them from the air. There were also a number of German soldiers, guns slung easily over their shoulders. I wondered where I was and whether or not this was some kind of work camp.

To my surprise and relief, Dailey had landed in the same field, though still some distance from me. Several soldiers hustled him over to me, accompanied by a small crowd of men. We acknowledged each other with a nod but were both trying to assess the situation. Other farmers gathered. They carried an array of implements: mostly the handles of farm tools and large pieces of wood, though some men, I noticed uneasily, carried large stones. They all seemed angry and significantly outnumbered the few soldiers who gathered to round us up. Spotting a small pamphlet sticking out of Dailey's flying suit vest pocket, one of the farmers pulled it out with a sneer and handed it to a lanky farmer in soiled overalls. He considered the pamphlet for a moment and then began to translate it aloud to the others. He hadn't spoken more than a few sentences when five or six of the men came at us. I had no idea what had caused them to beat us with their sticks of wood and tool handles, but while the soldiers just watched, we both took some hard, bloody blows. Then, to our astonishment, the beating stopped. The women, hefty and craggy-faced beneath their kerchiefs, were yelling at the men to stop. The men sheepishly obeyed and backed off, giving the bemused soldiers the opportunity to take over. The women paid us no mind but continued growling at our attackers and moving them back into the fields. Clearly, the Geneva Convention was of little importance to these soldiers. No doubt many unlucky Allied airmen suffered from such indifference and were left to the fate of furious locals determined to fight their own kind of war. It was a confusing turn of events; only ten minutes on German soil, and I'd been saved by the very people I had come to fight.

The soldiers shouted and gestured and made it clear to us by motions and shouts that they wanted us to walk to a dike that ran through the fields. On the top of the dike was a road that carried straight toward a distant village of low buildings. Carrying our bulky chutes, we walked along the road in front of our captors, leading a growing crowd of people who followed behind us and alongside in the field below. As I was walking along, I heard a voice to my right and I looked down to see a well-dressed little boy—he might have been about six or seven—trotting below me in the field. He seemed the picture of the Hitler youth we had seen back home in the newsreels—blond hair, square face, black shorts and a white blouse, strangely out of place in these fields. I must have been walking at a pretty good clip because he had to trot to keep up. When he caught my eye, he said with a smile, "Heetlair ees a beeg monkey, eesn't he?" I was stunned. I wasn't sure I had heard him, and he said it again. Perhaps the soldiers behind were not listening—had they overheard him, I thought, they surely would have shot him on the spot. I had prepared myself for a war against people who hated Americans and worshipped a madman, so I wasn't sure what to make of the boy's good-natured poke at the Führer. I did not respond, nor did I see him again, but the incident stayed with me. I wasn't at all certain what to make of it.

In due course we got to the village, and it seemed to me a place out of another age. The buildings rose up out of the pavement; there were no trees, no front yards, just stone walls, windows and narrow cobblestone streets. We were taken to a building that turned out to be the burgermeister's offices. He was sitting behind a desk, and as we crowded into his office surrounded by soldiers, he did not look up. His glasses had slipped to the end of his long nose, and his hair, white and wispy, was uncombed. He seemed preoccupied. Then, as if satisfied with whatever he saw on his papers, he stood and greeted us in a very friendly manner. He even asked if we had any cigarettes. An infrequent smoker, I didn't have any, but Dailey still had some in his flight suit, and he passed them over. As the burgermeister lit a cigarette, he offered us each one. With more than a little uneasiness, we both declined. He spoke to the German soldiers in a very soft, unthreatening voice, and whatever he told them resulted in their taking us across the street and into a narrow house. We were led up a flight of stairs and into a small room. There was no furniture in it other than two chairs, one in each corner, and two windows, one on each exposure. The soldiers indicated that we should each sit in a chair facing the wall and that we were not to speak to each another, an order that seemed absurd to us given that following it they left the room altogether. My head hurt from the beating.

"What the hell was in that pamphlet?" I asked Dailey.

"My mother sent it to me," he said sheepishly. "It was a religious tract justifying the bombing of Germany as God's will." The concept was troubling, and I winced with a moment's sympathy for our attackers. The door opened again; this time it was not the soldiers but a young woman who peered in. After looking around the room, she entered with enthusiasm and was soon followed by another family member. Before long, a whole family had come in that room: nine or ten people, including elders, early teenagers, even a woman with a newborn baby. Two young children were posted to peek between the shades and warn the family if the soldiers returned.

Dailey and I turned our chairs around and were encouraged by their bold gestures and recognizable phrases *("Kommen zie hier!")* to join them. They brought in food and water for us and treated us as guests. I was thoroughly confused but faintly charmed by it all. There was only one man of military age, and he was a soldier on leave who was stationed in France. A tall, thin man with sad blue eyes, he spoke French and acted as our interpreter. I had grown up speaking French so we talked. A fierce-looking elderly woman, apparently the leader of the clan, interrupted him. She wanted to talk and insisted that the soldier translate for her. Her hostility surprised me; she didn't seem to like me at all. In the middle of many questions about the United States, the old woman challenged me with a bony finger: "Is it true," she said, "that all people in Chicago are gangsters? Are you a gangster?" She seemed proud of these questions, as if she already knew the answers. My appearance must have inspired her question. Two months before, tired of my ongoing demerits for unmilitary hair, I had gone to the air-base barbershop and demanded a singe cut, a high heat process that burns the hair right down to the scalp and guarantees little growth for months. My shaved head must have made me look every bit the part of a Chicago mobster.

The matriarch was the only one to treat us badly. Even the German soldier (he may have been her son or grandson) conveyed in his cool and formal way an appreciation that we were fellow soldiers. Several elderly men were also respectful, but it was the younger women and children who seemed most determined to befriend us. Both Dailey and I were moved by their laughter and their excitement. After talking for some length with the young mother, I pulled back the left sleeve of my flight suit and took off my watch. On my last home leave my mother had given it to me, along with her faith that it should protect me throughout the war. It was a flier's watch made by Abercrombie and Fitch, and she had paid a king's ransom for it with money she had set aside, I would later learn, to pay the month's rent. As it was, the watch had already become important to me as a tie to her. Certain that the Nazis would soon claim the watch for themselves, I asked the young woman if she would take the watch for her baby. To my disappointment, she graciously refused.

While everyone talked at us, they also monitored the two boys who were peering out the window watching the streets. Twice a signal was given and twice the family cleared out very quickly. Moments later a soldier would come in the door and find Dailey and me doing what we had been told: facing opposite walls in silence. Satisfied, he would leave and we would hear his boots on the stairs. Then the door would ease open and the family would pile back in.

A couple of hours passed while the women continued to bring us food to eat and water to drink. Then the signal was given a third time and everybody cleared the room. Several soldiers came, and they shoved Dailey and me out of the house and into the back of a truck. There were already two or three other aviators in there, though none from our crew. We drove out of the town. I saw none of the family that had treated us so well and I was sorry not to say good-bye to them.

We stopped several times, and one by one, my crewmates were thrown into the back of the truck. Tedrowe and Leve, our co-pilot, climbed wearily into the back, Saccomanno grinned briefly when he saw us, an annoyed Thompson and an intense Levins hauled themselves into the back under the glare of the German guards. Before long, we had everybody except Orlando and Mintz, our port waist gunner. We also picked up two survivors from another lost Liberator and an American fighter pilot shot through the thigh. He was an articulate, almost jovial officer with no apparent sense of rank, and I liked him right away. I didn't know many fighter pilots, though I knew they were very different from the heavy bomber pilots. The latter tended to be responsible and serious and meticulously well organized, whereas the former were like mischievous kids, irreverent and impetuous. Right away, though, we appreciated his humor and grit. He was badly wounded but indifferent to our offers of help. Furious that he had been shot down, he kept swearing and shaking his head.

"It was such a fucking lucky hit," he said to us as if we were skeptical. "The goddamn Luftwaffe ain't worth a shit. One of the bastards snuck up on me!" As for my crewmates, I felt great relief to see them. Thompson caught us up on what he knew about our two missing crewmates. They had been with him at the bailout signal but not sure how to get out the waist window. The plane had been losing altitude fast. Shouting to them to hurry, he had led the way and bailed. Thompson had been pretty well banged up, hitting the plane's tail as he went out. Preoccupied with his own injuries and shock, he wasn't sure whether they had gotten out. He had not looked for or seen their parachutes.

"I saw the plane, though," he said sadly. "Going down in a hell of a spin. Last engine must have finally quit. It was a long way off, but I could see the smoke from the crash." Everyone was quiet after Thompson spoke, thinking about Orlando and Mintz. Where were they? Had they gotten out? Had they met their fate at the hands of another mob of angry farmers? Perhaps they were already on the run and headed home. In my own way, I hoped and prayed.

"What the hell happened up there, Skipper?" Sac asked Tedrowe, who was rubbing his knees tenderly. Tedrowe was quiet for a moment, weighing, it seemed, what he wanted to say.

"Our second fighter escort group was late. The Luftwaffe caught us unprotected, a matter of a minute, two at most."

We all knew how the escort system worked. The bombers required separate groups of fighter escorts, two to four depending upon how far the mission went into Germany. No single group of fighters had the fuel to patrol the skies and protect a formation all the way to the targets and back, so fighter escort groups would meet with the bombers at pre-arranged times and places and cover them until replaced by fresh escorts. Planning was carefully calibrated to a fighter's fuel supply, and the escorts flew in a beeline from their base right out to meet the bombers going to, or coming back from, their targets.

"I expected we'd have coverage all the way without much problem," he recounted in his soft, patient voice, "but the second group wasn't where we thought they'd be. The first fighters stayed in contact with us for as long as they could, but finally broke off saying their fuel tanks were already too low. I hope they made it back home—they cut it close. As for the Luftwaffe, I barely saw them. They came out of the sun, hit us and were gone in a matter of seconds." He was quiet again, as if reconsidering what he might have done differently. "They made the most of the opportunity," he added.

"Our guys got there, though," said Levins. "Orlando sounded on the intercom like he was ringside to one hell of a fight . . ."

"Better late than never," said Tedrowe.

"It was all so fucking fast," said Thompson. "Did anybody even get a shot off?"

"My fifties were right on them. I got off a few rounds, but I don't know that I hit them bastards."

I knew there had been no time for Sac to hit them hard, if at all, and simple math told the story. The Luftwaffe had learned that head-on attacks were their best bet. Coming out of the sun, they were nearly invincible. If we were approaching our target at about 200 miles an hour and they came at us at about 400 miles an hour, the rate of closure would have been 600 miles an hour, or just a little under 300 yards a second. With the sun behind them, from the time we saw those fighters until the time they hit and passed us, it would have been, at most, three seconds. The only way we could have had any hope of nailing them was, on the very first pass, to have lucked into having our guns aimed directly at them. We should have been taught to aim our guns at the sun and fire at whatever came into view.

We all sat in that truck for some time, each man replaying the events up there, trying to piece the action together. I looked at their haggard faces. A terrible fatigue was falling over us. The fighter pilot was no longer talking, and he cursed softly as someone tried to make him comfortable. He was losing a lot of blood and his face was pale.

It was well into the afternoon when we came to a sudden stop. The Germans had us climb out and walk into a field to pick up a large metal container. We recognized it immediately as the wing tank from an American fighter, typically released when empty to allow for greater speed. Many hands made it light and we hauled it into the truck. The pilot saw it and perked up. "It must be getting tougher for the bastards," he cracked, "if they're tryin' to recycle my metal." Hearing him wise-crack again lightened our mood.

Within an hour we came to what turned out to be a small Luftwaffe air base on the outskirts of the town of Hamelin. I remembered the Pied Piper of Hamelin, but I had never known there was a real town. We were unloaded into a building and each put into a small room, six by twelve feet with bare wood walls, floor, ceiling and a wooden bunk without any mattress or blanket. Though the outside looked like any building, it must have been some kind of prison because the window had bars on it. They brought me a piece of dry sausage; Dailey and I were lucky to have eaten so well earlier in the day, but the sausage was edible. Night came on and it got cold fast.

I lay down and, lying on the wooden bunk, had my first chance to think hard about what had happened. I sorted through all the unaccountable moments of good luck that had conspired to keep me alive. The day had begun with a near disaster: although our own four squadrons assembled behind us in smooth order, a B-24 from another group had angled past us, and its powerful turbulence flipped our plane nearly belly-up. Tedrowe was so cool under pressure that he righted us almost instantly, and other than for some bruises and a sense of shock, we were all fine. Near our target, we'd been struck by enemy fighters but, unlike our wing planes, had come through without engines on fire and with an inboard engine still turning over. We'd gotten safely out of the formation. We'd been given twenty minutes to get back over open land. No Luftwaffe fighter had showed up to finish us off. We had bailed safely. I realized that only two weeks before, we had been told that we would no longer carry pistols (a deal worked out with the Luftwaffe to stop their pilots from killing us in our parachutes). What would those guards have done if I'd landed with a Colt six-shooter at my waist? And then I remembered my parachute. Several days before, I had been on a training mission (on the days that you weren't on a combat mission, you went up to practice). In the radio room, a friend of Tedrowe's—a copilot from another crew who had come along for the ride—had seen me going by without my chute on. Everyone was supposed to wear a chute when flying. The pilots had backpacks; the rest of us were assigned the chest type—a boxy, bulky thing about twenty inches long and ten inches in diameter. So this lieutenant had said curtly, "Sergeant, why aren't you wearing your parachute?" Hearing my explanation, that wearing it made my job unworkable, he said, "Well, let me see how you put your chute on." Getting it out of the corner of the radio room, I pulled its two snap hooks down over my harness rings, as you'd hook the painter of a boat at the dock. He frowned. "Hell, do that and you'll go down headfirst. Get this straight, Sergeant. You pull the snap hooks *up* into those rings. Up, not down." A moment's exchange only days before had saved my life. Was there some message for me in all these moments of luck or grace? Had I really been given a whole new life or just a little more time? I had no answers at the moment. I only knew I needed rest and determined to think more on all of it tomorrow. Bone-weary, I fell into a dreamless sleep.

The next morning I woke to the sound of the bolt being pulled on my cell door. It was food. I was given small boiled potatoes that I ate skin and all. My grandmother had taught me that the skin was the most nutritious part of the potato, and I knew I was going to need all the nutrition I could find. The guards thought it revolting—apparently Germans always peeled their potatoes. They conducted quite an excited conversation and I could tell they had decided I was something of an animal for eating the skin.

Before long our crew was taken on another truck, along with two more badly wounded American fliers. The two new fliers were heavily bandaged and we helped them as best we could. Our smart-talking fighter pilot was gone, and I wondered if he had survived. We were taken to the railroad station in the city of Hanover. Unloading, we looked around in bewilderment at a landscape almost annihilated by Allied bombers. I thought of the map on the briefing room wall and how I had imagined the great industrial city of Hanover, a place of teeming avenues, vast factories and the spokes of a hundred rail yards. If there ever was such a city, it was gone. Instead, men and women walked along rubble-strewn streets as if unaware of the roofless build-ings and standing walls; white curtains blew through burned-out windows and smoke hung over it all like acrid bunting. People carried bags, held the hands of young children, hurried to appointments, so many utterly ordinary scenes of city life, except for the desolation that surrounded us all. The station itself had an arching metal framework to support a canopy of glass, but there was not one pane left. Bright sky above the ruin. We were herded out onto the platform between the tracks. The Wehrmacht soldiers had turned us over to two armed, blue-clad Luftwaffe soldiers who were to take us to yet another train.

With the wounded airmen we were now ten, and we made a ragged band waiting for the train to come. Dailey poked me. "We got visitors." A crowd was gathering. At first it looked like we were a curiosity. More and more came, and whispers passed through the crowd, soon getting louder, surlier. They began to press us closer to the edge of the platform. Within minutes, there were more than fifty people in a closing semicircle, and if they were simply curious, the accessories they carried—nightsticks, knives and pistols—suggested otherwise.

"Wish we had those old ladies right now," whispered Dailey, and for the second time, I prepared to defend myself. And then the two Luftwaffe guards stepped forward, kneeled and swept their rifles slowly across the chests of their countrymen. The crowd was incensed and began to curse them, but the guards remained calm, almost impassive. Neither showed the slightest worry nor acknowledged the other in any way. They offered that mob the simple eloquence of their rifle muzzles. They stayed that way for almost an hour. The physical strain on them had to be great. It struck me that if either one chose to take a break to relieve himself, the other would be easily overwhelmed, the ten of us would be quickly dispatched and no one would be the wiser. The two guards stood their ground.

To our relief, the train eventually arrived. It was a magnificent French train of a type that I had never seen before. The luxury of it was far superior to any of the high-class Pullman cars I had seen back home. As the train pulled out of the city, the silhouette of Hanover's jagged skyline seemed something like an explanation of that mob's fury. We rode for many hours, mostly in silence. At some point someone speculated on the conduct of our Luftwaffe guards. I mentioned my experience with the guards who were utterly indifferent to the beating that Dailey and I had taken the day before.

"They weren't going to stop anybody from killing us out in that field," I said. "So what gives with the guards at the station?"

"The Luftwaffe are fliers and so are we," said Tedrowe. "Fliers look after one another." I didn't know if that was true, but it made some sense. Why else would they have safeguarded us so well? Tedrowe tilted his head back and closed his eyes. His hands were folded in his lap and he seemed, in that moment, the picture of repose. But the lines of fatigue on his face and the shadows that sagged below his closed eyes reminded me again of our ordeal. He had kept us together over these hard hours, and though we were no longer in his plane, his authority was undiminished. We were all glad he was our skipper, for unlike many of the bomber pilots, most of whom were just out of flight school and a brief four-engine training, Tedrowe had flown three years with the Army Air Corps before his four-engine bomber training. A graduate of Purdue, he was steady, fair and possessed of a quiet toughness. He was a pilot in the classic mold, an ace who never used one word more than was necessary. Though he seemed the age of our fathers, he was barely twenty-six.

It was very late at night when the train came to a stop. They took us to a little wooden shed with benches on a dirt floor and a table up front. We sat on the benches, five in the front row and five in the second. A German major strolled in. Affable, a study in charm, he no doubt had the job of putting us at ease, and he did it well. We were each asked to give our full name and we did so, though with a trace of defiance. When he got to George Saccomanno, our Second Engineer/Gunner who hailed from Brooklyn, the major looked up in surprise when he heard Sac's name.

"Saccomanno!" he shouted. "Have you a brudder in de Air Force?"

Sac turned to us, called a little huddle, and whispered, "Remember I told you guys about Tony? What do I say?" We all remembered. Sac had a little brother in the Air Force. He had told us how, a couple of weeks before we had headed overseas, he had been given leave because his father had been critically ill. His younger brother was home on leave, too, and soon enough they had gotten into a violent argument. Though hit with polio as a boy, Tony had wangled his way into the Army Air Corps and, to Sac's dismay, was now a gunner on a Flying Fortress also about to be sent into combat. With their oldest brother already fighting in the Pacific—and Sac on the verge of leaving for England—he told Tony that their mother could not face all three sons at the front at the same time. He told his kid brother to go back to his base and reveal the polio he'd hidden to get in, and to use that for a desk job behind the lines. Tony had replied, "Fine, you're right; one of us has to stay behind. *You* be the one. Remember that malaria you caught when the Army had you in Panama? It just about killed you and it could get you again. So *you'd* better stay home." The argument had revved up from there, Sac said, and they left with no decision—each telling the other to think hard and make the right move. Sac had ended his account with a confident summary to us: "I'm not worried. I'm six years older than he is and he'll do what I tell him." We had all been instructed to give the Germans no information beyond our name, rank and serial number, but it was late at night after a long day, and our sense of it was that no harm could come from saying yes. So Sac turned to the major and said "Yeah." The major, who until now had seemed to be working from a prepared script, demonstrated a genuine, spontaneous moment of pleasure. He beamed at all of us and said in a thick accent, "*He* is here!"—trying to say, it seemed, that before the war's end Germany would have *every* American flier either captured or killed. Sac shook his head and muttered, "Oh, boy, Mama's gonna be pissed."

We were ushered out of the interrogation shed and Tedrowe pulled Sac aside. "There's a bright side to this, Sac," he said, almost with affection. "You'll be able to keep an eye on your kid brother." We didn't know it at the moment, but we would not see Tedrowe and the other officers again for the rest of the war.

After spending a night in a wooden enclosure slightly larger than the one in Hamelin, I was woken the next morning by the sound of a little door in the wall being popped open. Through this porthole came a bowl. Moments later I heard the creak and rumble of a wagon and then the little door swung open again. I pushed the bowl out and it came back filled with a kind of foul-tasting oatmeal. Not having eaten anything since the potatoes the day before, I did not hesitate to eat it all. I licked the pottery dish absolutely clean, though remembering that my mother would have been horrified by such behavior. She had taught the six of us not to waste food, but she drew the line at licking bowls and dishes. An hour later, the little porthole opened up again, and I handed the empty bowl back out. Instantly I overheard a heated barking between the guards, and to my surprise, a second bowl of porridge came back through the little door. I was dumbfounded but not about to call attention to their mistake; when I had handed them back my empty bowl, it was so clean that they must have thought the porridge wagon had bypassed me altogether. I had no problem eating that second bowl, a most unexpected bonus despite its awful taste.

Belly full but exhausted by three nights of little sleep, my best bet was to bear down and get some rest. But I was too keyed up for that. Pacing the little cell, I caught sight of a small nail. Holding it in my hand, my thoughts swung back to a makeshift indoor baseball game we had played as kids on rainy summer days. Carefully prying off a sliver of wood from the rough-sawed wooden bunk and pushing the nail through it so that it made a smooth propeller, I had the equipment I needed. I scratched sectors into the wood floor (ball, strike, out, home run) and then, anchoring the nail between the floorboards, I started a game. Innings came and went, but the game was soon called by a German soldier who unlocked the door and hustled me out to a nearby interrogation room.

The interrogating officer was another who spoke English well—I was surprised by how many soldiers could speak my language—and he told me that he had been educated at the University of Chicago. I wanted to ask him about it, but I kept silent and he didn't go into any further details. Telling me that he was a Luftwaffe Major, that I was now at the Dulag Luft interrogation center for captured flyers, and that for me "the war was over," he wanted to know two things. The first was about a "black box." He asked me dozens of questions about this black box, which I later gathered was some sort of recently developed high-tech equipment for B-24s leading a group or even an entire mission. I knew nothing about it, had never even heard of it. Then he asked me whether I knew anything about a plane that had flown across northern Germany several days ago and dropped bombs over farmland. I knew that several days before, on Easter Sunday, we had flown a mission deep into northeastern Germany. Our target had been an aircraft factory located in Tutow. We had flown by way of the North Sea and had even passed over the Kiel Canal that I had read about as a boy. Though we were very near the target, the cloud cover was heavy and our squadron was ordered home. During the long return flight to England, Tedrowe gave the order to get rid of the bombs and lighten the plane—wanting to cut our risk of going down in the Channel, gas tanks empty. We could clearly see the farmland below—there were no civilians out there on Easter afternoon—so Lieutenant Levins, using his controls in the nose compartment, had opened the bomb bay doors and released the full load. I told the officer I knew nothing about the bombs. He didn't tell me why he had asked or whether the bombs had hit anyone.

As he shuffled some papers, I thought back to that particular mission, and not simply because of the Kiel Canal or the fact that we had flown the whole way home without fighter escort. I had been working my top turret, slowly revolving, watching the sky, when directly above me a small plane appeared above our formation. It was an odd thing to see—clearly not a fighter plane. As it came closer, I could see it was dragging a heavy steel cable from its belly. Swinging at the bottom of the cable was an old metal stove. We had heard talk of such things. Germany was running short of pilots, planes and fuel. The plane was maneuvering around in such a way that the cable, pulled tight by the heavy stove, might catch a bomber's propeller or wing. Before I could say anything on the intercom, we had passed the cable and the stove itself missed us by about a hundred feet.

The interrogation officer asked me whether there was anything I would like. I said, "Well, you know, I'd like a book or two to read." "Okay," he said wearily, "we'll bring you some books." Having gotten nothing from me (and apparently having been fully prepared for little), he dismissed me and sent me back to my cell. Not very long after they had locked me up again, the porthole opened and a couple of books were shoved in (Agatha Christie and a book about Dick Whittington and his cat).

Later the next day they let us out for some exercise in a wide, grassless compound. While I was out stretching my legs, I ran into Thompson, who asked me about my interrogation. Some guys were getting it rough, some not.

"They know a lot," he said with some surprise. "They know our mothers' maiden names and who we flew with and where we trained. It kind of throws you. Where do you suppose they get all that stuff?" I shrugged. I had no idea and I could not imagine why the Germans cared to track such details. Soon enough, we were rounded up and taken back to our cells.

The following day we were brought out into a compound where there were hundreds of other prisoners, and before long we were taken to another railroad siding. By the time the boxcar train arrived, our numbers had swollen to more than a thousand airmen. It appeared that only the noncommissioned airmen were here—more sergeants than any of us could have imagined and a terrible sign as to the number of crews we were losing. I lost track of my crewmates, though occasionally I would catch a glimpse of one or another in the crowd. Someone told me that the officers had been shipped to an officers-only prison camp as required by the Geneva Convention. A brief moment of hurt and loss for me as to Tedrowe. Would we ever cross paths again?

It was a confused crowd, and soon we were loaded onto the boxcars. We crouched or stood on some hay. "Where the hell are we off to now?" asked a blond kid with an ugly, open wound across his neck. He was frightened. None of us answered him because none of us knew what to say.

The doors rolled shut and we stood shivering in a rank, smelly dark. There were more than fifty of us crowded into two-thirds of the car, and either you leaned against the next guy or tried to squat with your knees under your chin. We tried as best we could to make room for the wounded and sick, but we could do very little for them. I recognized no one in my car; there was very little talking. One badly injured fellow spoke feverishly to no one in particular, and after a while he, too, grew quiet. Three or four guards lounged in the open third of the car, their rifles and a machine gun at the ready; there was a pail of water from which they regularly drank. They took turns napping but were always certain to have several barrels aimed in our direction. They did not need much to guard us at that moment. We were worn and miserable. Many of us had not slept for several days, and all were exhausted. We had neither food nor drink. In the gloomy light of their oil lamp, we couldn't tell if the guards were young or old, but it figured to be pretty grim duty. The body odor of men who had been frightened and on the move for several days was nothing compared to the smell of the piss and crap pots that quickly filled to capacity. We rolled on for many hours.

The train lurched to a stop and everyone stirred. Where were we? The guys closest to the doors or the cracks in the car walls were pelted with questions, but they couldn't see anything. It was night and there were no lights out there. With a loud crack, the doors were drawn back and the guards shouted at us to climb down. We spread out over the tracks to relieve ourselves. The guards made us dump the pots and then we all sat about on the grass and tracks for a few welcome minutes.

"Look at the bastards," said a guy near me, nodding at a group of villagers who had come out from the shadows to peer at us while the guards stretched and smoked. "Ain't they never seen no one shit before?"

We reboarded. I found myself standing next to the boxcar door that, to my surprise, our guards had left ajar, though with several chains draped across the narrow opening. No doubt the cold night air was a welcome relief from the smell, and they had rightly recognized that none of us was in any shape to leap from this train into a stony dark. I watched the German countryside pass under the faint light of a half-moon and could see the land for what it was—not a target to be bombed, but a place where life went on as it had for generations. We passed darkened farmhouses, small villages with shuttered houses and lonely crossroads, faintly silvered by the moonlight. I saw no sign of people, and from time to time, we passed through stands of trees, many of which were barely budded. Spring was coming to Germany. I had almost forgotten the seasons. A long winter's training in the Texas desert followed by wet weeks in England had dimmed any memories of wildflowers and newly sprung life. Despite the bite of the cold and the stench of the men, I liked the view of the countryside by moonlight and let my mind wander, buoyed by the passing trees and lakes, villages and occasional farmhouses.

"Where are we? Where are we going?" moaned the blond kid. He lay with his head on the grimy lap of a bucktoothed crewmate.

"Shhhh," said the bucktoothed man. "I'll tell you when we get there."

The sun was barely up, but already the shadows were drifting off the hills. It was going to be a pretty day. We had stopped a number of times, the train slowing to a crawl before stopping altogether, but the guards did not stir and we knew we weren't getting out. Fast-moving trains passed us, but we could not see them and did not know what cargo or persons were being carried past us. We knew we were the least of Germany's worries at the moment. I had been watching a broad river for some time before I realized it must surely be the Rhine. A fellow nudged me and nodded toward the other shore where high above the riverside cliffs perched a forbidding ruin of a castle. Below it, on the bank of the river, was a magnificent chalet, with a single sunlit tower. With steep walls marked by narrow windows, it seemed right out of a history book. "I don't suppose that's where we're going," said a large man behind me. He was powerfully built with a nose that had been broken a long time ago, a wide jaw, massive forehead and a dark bruise over his left eye. His voice was husky.

"Not likely," I said.

A guard saw us watching the landscape. "Dürnstein," he said haughtily. The name meant nothing to me. We looked at that castle for some time together before the train curved away from the river and into the forest. Though I had not seen him before, the big man continued to speak to me as if I were waiting for him to finish a story he had been telling me.

"When I got to that fucking interrogation center," he said, "they put me in this room with a Kraut officer. He was a little guy and his uniform was so goddamned clean it was like it come right off the rack. While he was asking me all kinds of dumb questions, the air raid alarm goes off. He walks to the window and watches through the slats. 'Look at this,' he tells me. I walk over and look out and can see the bombers and the lights and all the antiaircraft fire. It's unbelievable. A bomber blows apart and all these fiery pieces are falling through the sky. I got sick thinking of them guys dying up there. I was standing so close to him I could hear him breathing. I could smell him. He was small and he had a revolver on his belt. I knew I could snap his chicken neck before he ever saw it coming. And then, in this dreamy fucking voice, looking up at the bombers, he says, 'We kill you. You kill us.' It was like he was reading my mind. There was music playing somewhere, a woman singing a real sad song. Then he turns to me with this smile and says, 'Cigarette?' " The big man paused.

"You shoulda killed him, Beast," said a voice in the dark.

He looked out the open door and said softly, "Yeah. Maybe so."

Much later, I heard a whimpering on the other side of the car, a pitiful sound. I winced, remembering where I had heard something like it before. On our way to England by the southern route, we had landed in Brazil. The planes were in great shape and we were ready to take them into combat. We were to fly to Africa at dawn. One of the guys stationed at the airfield in Fortaleza came into the barracks with a little monkey. We were all fascinated by the monkey's facial expressions, by his alert, comical humanity. He loved his owner and swung around him with a commanding ease. Someone offered him a cracker and the monkey took it in one of his hands. The fellow gave him another and the monkey took that one with equal ease. He held both and ate neither. Offered a third cracker, the monkey paused, his head tilted in good-natured curiosity. Then, gingerly, he passed one of the crackers he held to his left foot and took the cracker with his free hand. He was pleased. When a fourth cracker was offered (we were all watching now), the monkey, knowing what was required, sat down on his owner's lap and carefully repeated the task, using his right foot. Now he had four crackers, one in each hand and each foot. He was an amusing sight. But then, and I don't know why, the fellow offered the monkey a fifth cracker. The monkey's surprise and confusion were transparent. He was puzzled, then frustrated. He swung his arms and legs around with the crackers. It was clear that he couldn't figure out what to do about that fifth cracker. And then, to our amazement, the poor little monkey began to cry just like a baby. We all felt bad for him, as though he were one of us.

As I thought about that monkey on this train trip to nowhere, I wondered about the journey ahead. We had all managed what we could, taken on what was thrust at us, surviving with whatever tools we had, but I began to think about that fifth cracker. What would come our way that we couldn't handle and what would we do when that moment came? I did not think long on this—I knew these thoughts would do me no good at all. Instead, I concentrated on stretching my legs and tried not to listen to the soft sobbing that still came from the other side of the car.

I WOKE. EVERYONE WAS IN VARIOUS states of pain and discomfort. Some leaned against the walls or one another, others stooped or squatted like beggars. Proximity was no cure for isolation; everyone was alone and worn, rattled by fear. We had grown used to the smell, and accustomed now to the train's endless lurch and halt, we no longer worried that each stop was the overture to some final disaster. We simply lumbered on, deeper and deeper into exile.

I tried to determine from the sun which way we were headed, but I couldn't get a fix, as the tracks wound around pine-crowded ravines, crossing forests and fields. I had rotated away from the door sometime in the night so that others could get air, but a sizeable crack in the wall offered me another slice of German rural life: no lonely crossroads now but passing towns, trucks and farm wagons, and fields littered with cattle. Under different circumstances, I might have thought this an agreeable and picturesque landscape, but now I was struck by how normal everything out there seemed, so unaffected by a world at war. We passed a group of farmers leaning against their wagon, talking animatedly with one another. They paid us no mind at all. Would they have cared if they had known that this train hauled hundreds of bruised, battered men who just days before had been on their way to bomb their factories and cities, where maybe their own friends and families worked? Would it have mattered to us if, before we dropped those bombs, we could have seen these men swapping stories just as we did at home? They looked like the same farmers who had wanted to beat Dailey and me to death, but we probably had more in common with them that any of us could have imagined.

We rumbled over a broad, slow-moving river, and it caught the sun in a spasm of brilliant morning light. I tried to remember the other great rivers in Germany and wished I had been more diligent studying the maps in geography class. The train slowed to a crawl, the cars groaning and creaking along the rails. And then, with a queer abruptness, it stopped. Everyone stirred. One of the wounded groaned. Growing commotion outside and energy from our once lethargic guards suggested something more than a relief stop. The guards brushed themselves off, gathered their lamp and water pail, and, as if it were an afterthought, threatened us with their gun muzzles while peering toward the door. We had definitely arrived somewhere. "Can you see anything?" guys from the middle of the car whispered. I could see that the immediate space around the train was filling with guards and prisoners.

The sunlight blinded us as the doors were pulled back. Some men paused, intimidated by the brightness and the uncertainty. *"Raus! Raus!"* barked the guards like junkyard dogs. We climbed out, our legs numb and weak. We were in some kind of a freight yard. We carefully lifted the wounded out of the cars, but the guards were impatient, imperious. They began to shove us angrily toward a swelling crowd of prisoners. Luftwaffe guards, with guns at their waists, stood at the front, authoritarian and sure, their blue uniforms almost crisp. Off to the side, surly civilians glowered at us, and it occurred to me that they had seen men like us before. With shouts and threats, the guards rounded us up alongside the track. We were being formed for a march. I saw one guy looking back anxiously at the train with a kind of regret. I understood his feelings for a moment. It was not lost on me that as grim as the previous hours had been, we had been relatively safe aboard those cars. Now we were leaving this train for good. For some, uncertainty gave way to outright anxiety. They cried out, "What is happening? Where are we? Where are we going?" Rumors were noisy, repeated, exaggerated— we were going to board another train, we were being shipped to Poland, we were going to be executed. Before long, news was passed back to us that seemed plausible: we were in Austria and were being marched to a nearby prison camp. Loosely formed into columns, we shuffled down what seemed a major thoroughfare, with many shops and commercial buildings. That night, others told me that they had seen their images in the shop windows and had barely recognized themselves. I had seen nothing at all. Trying to prepare myself for a walk that was likely to take some time, I stretched and shook my legs. It was a glorious morning. Despite the rigors of the previous days, I felt my body responding to the effects of fresh air. Nature's open, easy breezes reminded me I was alive.

Though the guards tried to move us with some semblance of order, we straggled out of the city and up a steep hill at our own stubborn pace. As we climbed higher I could see the town stretch out behind us and, in the distance, a river shining in the afternoon sun. It was a welcome sight. Life nearby. I could feel the warmth of spring on bones too long in England, too long cooped up in planes and boxcars.

We were tired, and some men pulled out of line and collapsed. Others talked or argued over things that helped them pass the time and keep their nerves steady. Most just focused on each step as it came. The prisoner next to me caught me looking at his pockmarked neck and cheek. "You know what that is?" he said with a grin. "It's typhus." I was startled and he quickly laughed. "Naw, don't worry. It ain't contagious, and if you were gonna catch it, you'da caught it by now. It's just flak, just good old Nazi flak. I got it on my first mission." We walked on.

Near the top of the hill, off to the side of the road, I was startled to come across a large boulder. Carved on it was one word: BEETHOVEN. I would learn years later that the stone marked the site of his rural workshop—a cabin he escaped to during his Vienna years where he composed some of his greatest music. But at that moment, I didn't ask myself why it was there. Seeing it, my thoughts flew back to the year when a dozen or so Victrola records were all our family had—and to the three among them that were Beethoven's *Pastoral* Symphony, Violin Concerto and *Moonlight Sonata*. They had become almost a part of religion for me from that year on, as perhaps also for my brother and four sisters. Stopping for a moment, I remembered why it was that we had so few records then—remembered the day the sheriff had evicted us from our unpaid-for home and we had made the long trek back to our ancestral digs with the few possessions we could salvage. My father had suffered setbacks during the Great Depression and had finally met with near ruin. Beethoven's music now in my thoughts was poignant with the inspiration of those days, when—led by my mother—we pulled together and made the "worst years" our best years. But it also brought sadness with the thought that either Jack, my brother now with the Tenth Mountain Infantry, or I, or both of us, might never again be part of that once-inspired family. I was not one for frequent bouts of longing, but there on the hill before that stone, I longed for them deeply.

Up ahead, the march was halted. The guys in front had stopped altogether, and despite the impatient commands of our guards, those of us in the rear soon crowded the crest of the hill. Men were looking down in dumb silence, and I shouldered my way forward. The ground sloped back down again toward a sprawling patchwork of compounds, decrepit black buildings, towers looming over double barbed wire. A prison camp. It was a horrific sight. Chilling. Men shouldered one another in fear. Below, inside the wire, thousands of men milled about, and from the hillside above, they seemed small, without purpose or energy. At that moment, the spring I had only just discovered stepping out of the boxcar seemed to utterly vanish. Someone behind me whistled softly; another simply whispered, "Shit."

STALAG 17 WAS AUSTERE AND FORMIDABLE. The towers maintained their spidery command over a tangle of wires, and I noted they all housed slouched shadows, leaning over rifles. Luftwaffe guards paced parallel walls of wire, dogs straining at their leads. Down in the valley to the north of the camp there was an airfield with a Nazi flag flying; cars, trucks, artillery pieces and gun emplacements were scattered about. Overhead a plane circled lazily, its engine droning monotonously. Even if the war seemed far away, the mood among us was uneasy, expectant with danger.

None of us knew anything about Stalag 17. It would have made little difference to us had we known either its true location or its peculiar history. What we would soon come to know would be simple enough: we were near Krems in Austria, on the north side of the Danube not far from Vienna. We could see neither Krems nor the river—now both on the other side of the hill we had just climbed. Nor, looking north toward Czechoslovakia, could we see more than a few miles to a green hillside beyond the valley.

In ragged columns of four, we straggled down the other side of the hill and stepped a little more lively when we saw prisoners running to the wires to watch our approach. The prison camp was clearly over-crowded. There were barbed wire enclosures on either side of the street that bisected the compounds. We passed thousands of scarecrows, a haunted gallery of mostly Slavic faces, silent witness to malnutrition and suffering. They watched us with doll's eyes sunk into their skintight skulls; some mouthed words we could not understand while others stood in blood- and sweat-stained garments and stared. Our own anxiety ensured that we barely acknowledged them as we continued our march toward the far end of the camp.

We came to an enormous outer gate that slowly swung open. I was too busy looking around to realize that I was entering prison and did not properly appreciate the gravity of my situation. I did not wonder how long I would be there or whether I would ever walk free from this place again, questions others admitted later had crossed their minds. They would remember hesitating and collecting themselves before marching into the camp. There were still others, and none of us could know then who they were, whose passing through the gate would be the end of something, a snapping of the cord that tied them to their remembered life. Incarceration, the complete and utter loss of their freedom, would come at them without warning and overwhelm them. Their identities, stamina and, all too soon, their will would fall away, and they would slide into a kind of stupor. We would all soon learn that the world we had known was to shrink. Gone the air armadas and camaraderie of crews, vanished the sense of belonging. Our field of vision was narrowing moment by moment, and soon enough, all that would matter to many of us within these wires would be survival, day by day. Men whose lives had encompassed the whole world would have to learn that the only things of importance now would be rogue bits of carrot or potato, a pack of cigarettes or a D-bar, the haven of sleep if you could find it. Even the strongest among us would be slipping their skins with no idea what that new skin would look like.

As we walked through a second set of gates toward the far end of the camp, along what appeared to be the main road, we were met by the sound of hundreds of American prisoners applauding in the next compound. They called out cheerfully through the fence, "Welcome home, fellas! The new kriegies!"

"What the hell is a kriegie?" I asked the guy in front of me.

"Beats me," he answered. "Maybe it's just a nickname for a poor sonofabitch whose war is over."

Many of the American prisoners seemed to be looking carefully at each of us, as if to recognize familiar faces, like an anxious crowd greeting passengers from a long overdue train.

"Hey you! Come over here," some called. "What's the news from home?"

"Welcome to the shithole, boys," hollered others. "Make yourselves comfortable."

"When is the war going to be over?" they shouted, and we all shouted back, "Soon!" and they cheered. Despite our fatigue, we were heartened. We were shuttled to a kind of warehouse where each of us was photographed and given a number. Mine was 105407, though I paid it little mind. The Germans insisted that we should consider the number our new identity. They were determined to establish their authority right away and intimidate us. They barked at us and at each other, and their manner struck me as both ominous and absurd, like something out of *Alice in Wonderland* or some silly fantasy. Dogs in uniform.

Without any time for comment or reflection, we were pushed on to another building where we were forced to take off our clothes, herded into showers, and deloused, and then our heads were shaved. We were taken to another shed to wait for our personal effects. It was an odd moment, all those naked bodies with odd-shaped heads, like so many bewildered cranes, stepping around one another. Men you had moments before joked and talked with, whose personalities seemed large and immediate, now moved about awkwardly, reluctant to speak to one another. I stared hard at them and they at me. *Who are you?* we all thought. Then someone said in a kind of stage whisper: "Jesus, and I thought you were ugly when you *had* hair!" It had an immediate effect. The sound of laughter, so unfamiliar to each of us, caught and spread like fire. Mockery turned to laughter, then outright hilarity (*"Is* that you? If I look half as bad as you do, hell, shoot me now!"). The guards, surprised and annoyed, first tried shouting over the sound of our laughter and then moved among us threatening and butting us with their rifles, trying to stamp out a fast-forming camaraderie. It was too late. We had suffered over these many days, and though we had not noticed it, we had begun to divide ourselves into smaller and smaller cliques. Out of necessity and habit we had, during the long journey to Stalag 17, begun to fashion new alliances among each other and identify new adversaries. Shared circumstance and immediate survival demanded you keep close to your own. Those you didn't know were strangers. The shaved heads and spontaneous mockery momentarily scuttled all of those initial alliances and granted us all the permission to clean the slate without explanation. Some who may have been at odds summarily forgave and forgot, while others who had been preoccupied or indifferent to the ones closest to them broke out in spontaneous celebrations of friendship. The Nazis, with their practiced instinct to humiliate, had looked to cripple our self-confidence and had, for the briefest of moments, succeeded. Some of us noticed that our guards were not so much angry as alarmed, as if they recognized that standing out there in the shed, shorn of our identities and ego, we had begun to do something supremely dangerous to them: we had began to resist.

Our stuff was handed back to us and we were told to dress. I was surprised to find that the guards had returned my dog tags and even the watch my mother had given me. I had assumed that anything of value would be taken from me as effortlessly as they had taken my freedom, but such was not the case. Again I did not know what to make of it.

Down the dirt boulevard we were marched into the new compound to which we had been "assigned." The large, uneasy crowd of shaved prisoners, each clutching a threadbare blanket, a small bowl and a spoon and a pair of wooden clogs, stumbled toward a spread of one-story barracks made of wood and tar paper. The buildings were rough and inhospitable, but as we arrived at each one, men moved up the steps to claim them as home. Names were shouted out as if sides were being chosen in a pickup game.

"Handy!" It was Thompson. He was standing with Dailey, Saccomanno (who we called "Sac") and a couple of other guys. I was relieved to see them smiling and slightly surprised by the animated way he waved me over. He was talking with a tall, athletic man who looked much older to me. With a square chin and a hawk's eyes, he seemed utterly self-possessed, more mature. Thompson introduced him with gusto.

"This is Gene Meese, Handy, and I've known him since boot camp. We were best buddies and I'd lost track of him until they were shuffling me out of the interrogation center in Frankfurt. They took me out into this long hall and who comes striding down the center of it like he owns the place but Meese!" Thompson seemed so relieved to find a familiar friend. Another man, standing off to the side, stepped forward and introduced himself.

"My name is Wilkens," he drawled with a good-natured grin, "Fred Wilkens. Covington, Kentucky." I was struck by the roughness and strength of his huge hand.

"Handy," I said, looking down in wonder at the ropes of his fingers. "Ned Handy." Thompson turned and introduced yet another smaller, strongly built fellow named Kozikowski. I was amazed at how Thompson had gotten so friendly with them all so fast, but I was glad he had. Meese was looking past the group and he said, as if a boat were leaving without us, "We had better get inside and stake ourselves a claim or we'll be sleeping on the floor." Men around us were pushing into the barracks. We climbed the steps to #32A as the guards shouted at us, one poking me from behind with his rifle.

Once inside, it took me a moment to get used to the dusky lighting. The barracks had a center aisle about eight feet wide that went right straight through from the front to the back. The camp had been built on a reasonably steep hillside that sloped down from the front end of the barracks. The entrance to our barracks might have been a foot to a foot and a half off the ground, but if you walked all the way through 32A, past the cement tubs in the connecting washroom, and then on through the full length of 32B, you would find that the back of the barracks was four to five feet off the ground. There were steep steps at the back.

The barracks had been built with used lumber, and the floor was a patchwork of unpainted, chewed-up boards of various lengths. Every ten feet or so on either side of the main aisle were bays about fourteen feet deep with triple-decker pine bunks on either side of a narrower aisle. At the end of the bay were rude wooden windows with blackout shutters. Each bunk held two men, so with four triple-decker bunks, each bay could support up to twenty-four people, but because we had been told to leave the lowest bunk empty, each bay held sixteen men. Barracks 32A had five bays on each side of the center aisle. We worked our way down to the back—the washroom end—and took the far bay on the right, falling on bunks like boys at camp. I took the upper "forward" bunk on the right side walking into our bay; it gave me a good view down the center aisle. Before we climbed into our bunks, we had to arrange the slats, three or four to a bunk, that needed to be properly spaced so that you would not fall through. On top was a burlap sack that was to be our mattress. It was filled with straw, sawdust and bits of cardboard, and if it offered a hint of comfort in the first moment you lay on it, it quickly flattened into unforgiving stiffness.

I remembered the last time I had seen such lonely bedding. On the night before my first combat mission into Nazi Germany, the Army Air

Corps informed me with a ruthless efficiency that I had already been shot down. They had stripped my bed to a skinny cot and taken all my gear. The 466th Bomber Group, to which I belonged, had just received a directive from Eighth Air Force HQ that belongings of crewmen lost in combat were to be immediately taken from the barracks and processed: personal items to be sent to the man's home, Air Corps equipment stored for future use. I knew of only two other Handys during the war, and I learned that one of them, Grover Handy, had been shot down earlier the same day on our group's first mission, a long one to Berlin. It was late into the night before I was able to convince authorities I was still present and ready for action. In the end, I thought as I arranged my slats, HQ got to strip my bed again, this time once and for all.

Men looked bewildered as they tried to make these small spaces habitable, stretching out awkwardly on their bunks. Dailey and Thompson whispered and laughed with each other. In spite of their strong California connections, Thompson had chosen to bunk with Meese rather than Dailey. Dailey, in turn, bunked with Sac, though it seemed that Sac was anxiously hoping to see his younger brother. Despite the fact that Dailey and Thompson were my crewmates and that we respected each other, I had little in common with them. They were both from California, both a little aloof to those they did not know well. Thompson, with all-American looks and a trim, athletic physique, was a man certain of his opinions and a continual critic of his circumstances. He was capable of a quick humor and his physical gifts lent him an unmistakable charisma, but he had little in common with the rest of us. Dailey was a tall, brooding man with heavy eyelashes and big ears. I knew very little about him. He spoke freely with his fellow Californians (Don Brown, our navigator, had also hailed from California), and together, during training, they had made it clear that while they played cards and ate together, theirs was not a table you joined unasked. Once, Dailey had surprised me while we were flying across West Texas. On a moonless night at about ten thousand feet, the stars outside seemed so large, bright and close that you felt you could sweep them in with your hand. The crew fell into a kind of trance, watching the stars pass and vibrating to the hypnotic thrum of the plane. And then, in a voice that I had never heard before and was never to hear again—a warm, almost friendly whisper—Dailey said he had found some great music on the shortwave coming from a radio station he knew in Canada, and he piped it through the intercom. For some minutes we had sped along to a haunting melody, a bunch of boys caught up in a wordless longing.

Dailey and Thompson fell into an easy conversation with one another. Their talk was relaxed, inclusive. I had a moment of concern—this was going to be a very good place to have a trusted friend, and while I liked my crewmates well enough, I wasn't sure I'd have one. I was a good listener and a diligent worker, but I had never fit in easily with a group. I wasn't one for trading stories or teasing. In this moment of settling in, with all its banter and jocularity, I felt awkward. I saw Meese also sitting quietly amid all the commotion. There was something cool and forbidding about him; he had the aspect of a leader and I knew I wanted to get to know him better.

A number of others quietly went about securing their bunks in our bay. I noticed a short man, barely five feet but powerfully built, hoisting himself onto the top bunk across from me. With a round face and eyes that were almost Asian, he drew around him a measure of space, a buffer of silence. He spoke to no one and no one spoke to him. Dailey told me later that his name was Pierre Joseph and he was an American Indian. Being an Indian lent him a certain defiance in my imagination, though his expressionless face showed an utter disinterest. Scrambling below Joseph onto one of the middle bunks was an energetic kid who talked all the time and to everyone, and already guys were beginning to ignore him. Across in the next bay the blond boy from the boxcar lay on his bunk. His wound was crusted and black and he seemed comatose, speaking to no one and staring at the ceiling.

Kozikowski, a shy, watchful type, sat on his bunk and swung his legs like a little boy. Amid the bustle of men introducing themselves, laughing and mastering their own fears, Kozikowski watched with a curious interest. He was from Moline, Illinois, had a kind of good-natured smile, but said little. The bay was already forming itself into a world of talkers and listeners.

"Hey, Handy," said Sac, "this guy here is from Boston. Hey, Sanford, aren't you from Massachusetts?" And the fellow to whom Sac spoke nodded. "Yep," Sanford said, "Auburndale."

"Well, this guy here is from Boston, too," said Sac.

"Cape Cod," I said to Sanford. He nodded. I nodded back. Disappointed that his enthusiastic introductions yielded so little, Sac shrugged. "Yeah, well, there's nothin' in Massachusetts to speak of except the Red Sox and they aren't worth a damn anyway."

"You're from Boston?" said the kid, butting in.

"Cape Cod," I repeated.

"I'm from Massachusetts, too," he said eagerly, looking between Sanford and me. "Buzzards Bay. The most beautiful sailing in the whole world. I had a baseball with Jimmie Foxx's name on it, but the Krauts got it now," he added with a frown.

"How the hell did they get it?" asked Sanford, not certain he really wanted to know, since the boy had already demonstrated he could talk your ear off.

His face fell. "They took it off me after we got shot down. I always carried it with me. It was," he added ruefully, "my good luck charm."

"Lotta good that good luck charm did you," snorted Sanford.

"Well, actually it did bring me a lot of luck, fellas. Really. Once when I was . . ."

"Man, you talk too damn much," growled a guy in the aisle. "You're like an itch that can't get scratched."

"Yeah, Itchy, put a lid on it for a while," someone else chimed in. The boy, grateful to be acknowledged, grinned. I smiled back. A friend of my father's had once told me to ignore the boys who were the first to act friendly; they were the neediest and never made good friends. It was advice I never followed: from boyhood I'd had an instinct to support the underdog. This kid was already becoming a big one; I wasn't going to make it any harder for him.

I noticed Wilkens had laid out his few things with a kind of meticulous order that was all the more surprising given the mayhem and roughhousing that went on around him. Someone teased him about his fastidiousness and he straightened up and spoke without humor or defensiveness. "Fellas," he drawled, "I aim to keep one thing squarely in my sights and I aim to keep it there every day, every hour, every minute in this hellhole: I am goin' home. That's all that matters. And if keeping my stuff here like the way I do at home reminds me that I won't be here forever, well, so be it." Smiles faded and a certain sobriety descended. Only Meese smiled, wide as a Cheshire cat.

"Well, that don't mean you got to act like an old lady," said Sac in such a good-natured way that everyone laughed. Even Wilkens nodded his approval. Another man, tall, sober-looking with great raccoon shadows about deeply set eyes, seemed utterly apart from everyone. He neither smiled nor showed the slightest interest in the chatter. I thought of talking with him but decided there would be time enough for that.

There was a burst of short sharp shouts as the German guards came into the barracks. They slapped bunks and shouted, *"Raus! Raus! Aufstehen! Raus! Schnell!"* Men dropped out of bunks and took to the center aisle. There was a drumming of the wooden clogs on the floorboards as the kriegies of 32A headed for the doorway, confused, worried and resistant all at once. The clogs had wooden soles about an inch thick and a strip of roughly cut canvas cloth across the front that acted as a slipper. We had immediately recognized their value would be for walking through a muddy compound to roll call or the latrines. We would need to limit the wear and tear on our leather army boots. The chaos agitated the guards, whose noisy insistence was punctuated by whistles and threatening gestures. It was mayhem.

At work pulling the splinters out of my bunk boards, I decided to take my time. If I hurried, I was likely to have to wait, and I hated waiting. My father had encouraged me to look at time as a gift to be used fully, and I took that advice to the extreme. In school I had always been the last student to get to his seat. Often I would swing into my desk under the annoyed glance of a teacher who had already begun the lesson. So now I continued pruning my bunk until I sensed the last guys were going out the door. Once out in the compound, I saw hundreds of men stumbling around driven by guards. In other compounds the same drill was under way, except the prisoners seemed to be moving more slowly and haphazardly. Some were in long johns or were still pulling on shirts and coats as they walked slowly out to the center of their compounds. Our crowd was not certain how to behave: move and obey, stall and resist? They were trying to form themselves into lines. Some jostled each other and laughed, others, frightened and confused, simply wanted to do what they were supposed to do. It was chaotic. Many of the guards standing on the perimeter seemed bored and indifferent, but several were aggressive, imperious. Always an overefficiency, always the shouting.

I joined the lines, and soon enough, we were made to count off in fives. And then we waited. It was warm and the midday sun was bright and there was a good deal of grumbling, coughing and occasional nervous laughter. Our first roll call had an anxiety about it, a sense of uncertain expectation. The waiting went on.

Before long, a German officer came into the compound, his black leather boots sporting an ostentatious shine, his clean blue tunic rising to the prow of his chin. He wore a peaked cap. (Later, when winter came, he would drape his coat across his shoulders and carry his leather gloves like a riding crop.) He had a slight limp and was followed by several junior officers. They seemed to parrot his gestures and movements, and when they drew up behind him clicking their heels with a kind of vaudeville gusto, it sounded like balloons popping at a child's party. Kriegies up and down the line poked one another in amusement and snickered. The guards sounded off the numbers and confirmed that we were all present and accounted for. He surveyed us like a composer before a lackluster orchestra and then, in a loud, clear voice, addressed us all:

"Gentlemen. I welcome you to your new home. By now you all understand, I'm sure, that for all of you, the war is over. I look forward to your spending the rest of the war here with us at Stalag 17. We will treat you as fellow airmen and see to your needs as best as the fortunes of war will allow us. You will be treated with respect and we will expect the same in return. There may be some among you who have ideas of getting home before Germany wins the war. I caution you, escape from Stalag 17 is not an option. Try, and you will be caught. When caught, you will be shot." It was quiet. Many guards had now fanned out along our perimeter, their gun muzzles like so many pinholes.

"You will note the warning wire that runs three meters inside the camp fences. Cross it for any reason and you will be shot. Look around you, gentlemen. This is your new home. Make the best of it." Someone whispered, "Fuck you," but the rest of us were realizing with full force that we were now prisoners of war.

After the dismissal, men drifted about, uncertain, confused. I decided to stretch my legs and case our compound a bit. Walking around it close up to the fences, I figured its size as about a hundred yards wide and two hundred deep—big enough to hold the four big two-barracks buildings and the large latrine while still giving us a lot of open space running downhill to the north outer fence. Across the west fence—like the north one, a double fence with a narrow path inside it paced by guards—was a compound in the other part of Stalag 17. Inside, hollow-eyed men stood like melting statues, and someone said they were Russians. All along the west and north fences was a single strand of wire—some ten feet inside the fences, running about a foot off the ground. Clearly, this was the warning wire the German officer had talked about. Partway along the outer (north) fence I came across a crude sign that said in English: THEY THAT TOUCH OR CROSS THE WARNING WIRE WILL BE SHOT WITHOUT WARNING. Beyond the adjacent compound, I could see a grove of trees outside the outer fence. I was glad to see those trees so near us. There was to be little of Mother Nature in our lives save for the farmlands and hills across the valley to the north.

Back in the barracks men milled around their bays. The conversation was subdued; no one was sure of the routine. Occasional jocularity was greeted with bemusement, but men, even crewmates, moved uneasily around one another. Someone grumbled about food, another about the growing smell of too many nervous men. Finally a tall prisoner came down the center aisle and called everyone around. He had a pleasant southern lilt to his voice and an occasional stammer that made his eyes close when he stumbled over certain words.

"I'm sure I'll get to know you all before too long. I work with Shattuck, who is the barracks chief for 32A. He's getting some things sorted out and asked me to come and welcome y'all. There's not much to tell you. Roll calls are the only thang the Krauts really care about. Twice a day. They want to know that y'all are in camp and accounted for, so they pull 'em in the morning and in the afternoon. Sometimes they do a spot check, sometimes an ID and dog tag search. Those ones take lots of time and are a bitch, but it don't happen near so often as it used to. Some of you are hungry and suppa is on its way, but t'ain't much to plan on. There's only one meal a day, so get used to it. It ain't like home cookin'. It's soup mostly, though the Germans like to call it stew. An' don' be askin' no one what's in it. Just figure that they growed some of it, they shot some of it and, likely as not, they found some of it." Behind him came two men carrying our first meal at Stalag 17, which came in a huge tub hanging from a pole shouldered by two prisoners. The tub, or kebo as it was called, was brought in and set down. We all lined up with our bowls and dinner was ladled out. The water was lukewarm; there was a flavor of potato about that first meal. Swirling my spoon through the murk, I found bits floating about that might have been potato skins and small, chunky bits of something else I could not identify that had gathered at the bottom of the bowl. It tasted awful and it occurred to me that the powdered eggs I had wolfed down before our last mission seemed a veritable feast compared to this slop. My teeth ground as I chewed, so there must have been sand or dirt in it. The blond boy set his bowl aside and I heard the soft cajoling voices of guys trying to encourage him to eat. He acted as if he did not hear them.

"Cut 'em six to a loaf. The cutter gets the smallest slice, so he'll sure as hell make it all even," said a guy tossing out rounded heavy loaves of black bread. "You'll get some oleomargarine when the Red Cross parcels come and you'll have to make it last. Spread it as thin as you can and still taste it. Sometimes you'll even get a little jam that'll help make the sawdust go down easier. They mix the sawdust in to thicken it and get more bread out of the baking. Chew the bread carefully, boys," he added. "Occasionally there's a splinter that didn't get ground up and it can cause you a lot of trouble." I thought he was teasing, but just to be sure, I chewed carefully. The bread was hard, tasteless and quickly dried out my mouth.

"Now eat up, boys," said one of the guys who had delivered the kebo, "and if some of you are lucky enough to have some weevils in your soup, don't worry none. They make good eating. The Weevil Stuffer always mixes 'em in for protein. You can't depend on the Krauts for nothing, though they will throw in a little rat or dog or horse, if some farmer got unlucky, but we never know what we're gonna find. On good days we'll get some barley soup. Very tasty but don't count on it. We'll get potatoes for sure, cabbage and rutabaga turnips, lots of turnips. The turnips can be mighty fine, but the centers are stringy, and no matter how hard you chew them, they won't give in. Chew everything you can until it turns to mush and then swallow it. We'll get carrots, too, later. When dinner is over, you'll want to use this water to wash your clothes. Waste not, want not," he added in a falsetto voice. I decided right then that I would eat whatever was in that bowl; if it had form, I assumed it had some remote chance of being nutritional. It was going to be hard to get by on what they fed us, so we were going to have to get by on whatever came along. I was thankful for having been brought up to eat potato skins and whatever else might be provided.

Kozikowski came over to me. "They say the Red Cross parcels will start coming soon and that there will be some better stuff to eat." He seemed nervous and lowered his voice.

"Hey, Handy, lemme ask you something. I was on the boxcar with this kid Itchy and he's telling everybody that I'm his friend. I don't know him from a plug and I wonder about him. There ain't no one to vouch for him. Guys say I should tell somebody," he said.

"Well, if he were a spy, he'd be the strangest one I ever saw," I said.

"Well, just how many spies have you seen?" asked Kozikowski, and I guessed he had a point. I looked at the witless boy standing at the edge of a crowd sipping from his bowl, eager to join in. He was already a complete outsider. Weren't spies supposed to be cool and trusted?

There was a kind of stirring at the other end of the barracks, as if a wind had blown open a door. I could see guys craning their necks, poking one another, gawking. Soon enough, the furrow of men rolled back into their bays to reveal the approach of two bedraggled characters walking down the center of the aisle. They said nothing; they did not smile. Their clothes were stained by sweat and dirt, their hair was matted and they looked like a pair of bearded Robinson Crusoes. Despite their appearance, they had a kind of authority about them, and they reviewed each bay they passed with a purposeful intensity.

"Spooky sons of bitches," Sac whispered as we watched them come down the aisle.

"They look old. Like they've been here for years," said Thompson, a little awed. As they passed us—I sat on my bunk watching them—they abruptly stopped. One of them walked forward and, to my astonishment, said in a gruff voice: "You're Ned Handy."

Everybody else looked up at me, too, as if they had never seen me before, as if they had never even heard my name. How had this Rip Van Winkle, who seemed to have dropped from the sky, known my name? Taking a second look, I recognized him.

"You're Alex Heyburn," I said, and for the briefest moment, he grinned. He had been a class behind me at Milton Academy. From a

leading family in Louisville, Kentucky, he had been a popular guy at
school. His older brother and mine had been classmates and friends. I
had last seen him standing on the school green with his friends, the picture of health and careless joy. But he was no boy now: his face was
gaunt, streaked with fatigue, and his demeanor quickly hardened when
he saw my shock at his appearance.

"It's been a long time since I saw you last. You graduated in 1940,
right?" he said.

"Yeah, 1940, that's right," I said, still thinking to myself, *What the
hell happened to you?*

"A long four years, that's for sure."

"How'd you get here?" I asked.

Heyburn seemed not to hear me. He looked about at the guys in
the bay and said, "You know all these guys?"

"Some of them," I said. "And the guys I don't know seem to know
the guys I do know."

Heyburn then spoke in a louder voice, addressing us as a group.
"I'd welcome you all, but there isn't much to welcome you to. You guys
are the new kriegies, short for a German word that translated just
means you aren't worth a shit. You'll learn the drill soon enough. Keep
an eye out for each other, but in these first days keep an eye on each
other. Make sure you talk only to those guys you know. If you don't
know a guy, no matter what he tells you about your hometown or his
favorite baseball team, don't talk to him until someone you trust can
vouch for him. We have some guys in here who may not be who they
are supposed to be." Then he looked slowly around at all of us, and
soon enough, we were all looking slowly around at each other. Itchy was
looking from face to face, a boy lost in a crowd.

"Anyway, fellas, you'll get sorted out over here. You can bet you've
got it a good deal easier than we had it when we first came. We were
shuttled up here from a worse hellhole than this place and they didn't
have anything ready for us except Russian lice and German bedbugs.
And those goddamned German bedbugs have sharp teeth." We all

chuckled but he spoke seriously. His sidekick said nothing. "When they dumped us in here, they'd scraped the Russians off the floors a few hours before. It was grim. We didn't even have palliasses, not that they are worth a damn anyway. We had to break down every bunk in the place, scrub them with lye soap and rebuild them. I see you still have some wood left in your windows; most of ours has been used for fuel. Keep your Red Cross cartons. They make great windbreaks. It can blow hard down this little valley and it gets cold, though you won't have to worry about that for a few months. Maybe by Thanksgiving we'll all be out on the town in Paris."

"Or Brooklyn," said Sac. "Brooklyn beats Paris every time."

"Jesus, what would you know about Paris, Sac?" someone teased. "First place you ever saw outside Bensonhurst was Krems, for Christ's sake." Someone asked about the Russians and Heyburn shook his head.

"When we first got here, our barracks were right next to the Russians. We knew right away those poor sons of bitches were in trouble. The Nazis hate 'em. Russia didn't sign the Geneva Convention, but the Jerries wouldn't have given a damn even if they had. We used to throw supplies back and forth over the fence when we first got here. We'd toss them cigarettes and D-bars and they'd throw back some of the potatoes and onions they'd collect on their work details. Sometimes something would land in the death zone, the ground beyond the warning wire, which all of you should stay out of, by the way. Well, when we would step over the wire to get the stuff, the guards would shout and stare us down with their guns, but when the Russians went to get their stuff, they got shot dead as soon as they stepped over the line. Believe me, guys, when you start feeling sorry for yourself, go stand by the fence and look at the Russians. You'll be glad your momma was an American." He looked at us all and we stared back dumbly. "So that's it. Good luck to you all. We don't have much to give you. We're trying to keep our boys going, too. You're welcome to come see us any time, but there isn't much to see." Then he turned to me.

"Can you come over and talk with me about some things tomorrow in my barracks?" he said very quietly. I didn't know why he was in such a hurry, but I wasn't about to argue. It was a good start to find an acquaintance among these old hands at the camp, and I was eager to respond to his request. It seemed exciting, almost mysterious.

"Come see me in the morning if you can. You can come any time, except be careful if it's in the evening. Curfew's at nine and they take it seriously around here, so come over no later than seven." And then he gave me directions. After they left, guys crowded around me as if I had just won a raffle. Who the hell was that guy, they asked with incredulity. I thought of young Alfredo Orlando, our missing tail gunner, and how, some months earlier, he and I had decided to walk to the PX from our overnight barracks at the Valley Airfield in Wales. We had landed only a few hours earlier after a long hard flight from Morocco and had been warned that it was a long walk, but we were determined to see the local sights. A passing jeep stopped and offered us a ride. In the front seat was a first lieutenant—I could see his bars—and I listened to him as he talked to his driver. I knew the voice, and just as I leaned forward to get a better look at him, he turned around and looked at me. "Hey there, Handy," said a classmate of my brother Jack's casually, as if we had met at a neighborhood bar. I turned to introduce him to a surprised Orlando, who saluted him, muttering, "Now that's the damnedest thing." Orlando would have thought I knew everyone in the world if he could have seen me now talking to yet another schoolmate in a German prison camp in Austria. I thought of the big-hearted Italian and his excited description of the dogfight in the skies around us. Where was he now?

The next morning after roll call, I found my way from our compound into the old kriegie camp. Men with beards and heads of matted hair milled about. My shiny, bald head made me quite a novelty, and I could see them watching me out of the corners of their eyes as I passed. Talk fell off and most everyone looked at me like an intruder. I followed Heyburn's directions to his barracks until completely lost. I stopped and asked a tall, thin kriegie, leaning against a barracks wall and smoking, if he knew Heyburn. He said nothing, drawing languorously on his cigarette. Could he at least tell me who might know where to find him?

"If you don't know who to ask, Jack," he said, turning away and staring straight ahead, "then, sure as shit, go on back to wherever you came from."

I walked on. It was more down at the heel than our compound, and the men looked considerably older. How old were they? I was barely twenty-one, and most of the guys in our barracks were the same. These men looked older, though I had already learned that anyone north of twenty-five was an ancient. Their barracks windows were rough-edged, and patches of cardboard covered the occasional hole. There was enough laughter and easy argument to identify it as an American compound, but the voices were wearier over here. Most of the men walked around in clogs that seemed thicker and bigger than ours. Finally finding the right barracks and a bay at the far end, I saw Heyburn sitting on his bunk. He rose to meet me and pulled up a chair for me as if he were welcoming me to a business meeting.

"I had a hard time getting to you," I said with a trace of accusation. "Guys over here don't seem very friendly. And they weren't in any hurry to help me find you." Heyburn nodded.

"They know you're a new kriegie, but they don't know who you are."

"What's wrong with a new kriegie? We're Americans in a bad spot, just like them. What the hell did we do to them?"

"It's a matter of degree," Heyburn said. "Most of the guys here have had it rough for a while. Many of them flew the Schweinfurt raids last August and October, and you know how that was." I did. Those raids were already legendary. Schweinfurt was home to Nazi Germany's principal ball-bearing factories, and they were heavily defended by anti-aircraft and the Luftwaffe. The Army Air Corps was tasked with demolishing those plants, whatever the cost. It was bad. Schweinfurt was well out of range of the fighter escorts, so the bombers went in alone. So many crews and planes were lost that the target's name became synonymous with doom. The American factories were turning out plenty of B-17s and B-24s, but raids like Schweinfurt were fast thinning out the crews qualified to fly them.

"Forget about it," Heyburn continued. "They're just sore that they've been here this long. They think they had a different war than you guys did. Longer, tougher. You came in looking tired but fresh and strong. Most of us came in here battered and beat all to hell. Last winter was so damn cold men cried. They figure that most of you were still stateside, bunking in warm barracks and going out on Saturdays with pretty girls. But don't worry. Their bark's got no bite. Come with me," he said in a burst of cheery goodwill. "I've got a little surprise for you. You hungry?"

"Sure, who isn't?" I said, following him out the back of the barracks. He led me into the compound to a small group of men sitting in front of a scarecrow, an old kriegie unlike anyone I had yet seen. Grease spots up and down his pants, a torn shirt and the mangiest tangle of hair I'd ever seen. He was tall and thin as a flagpole. One side of his mouth seemed almost caved in, a broad gap between ruined teeth.

"Boys, this is my friend Handy. He's a new kriegie, so I thought I'd have him come for Axel Jack's breakfast. Handy, this is Axel Jack of Fort Wayne, Indiana, the greatest griddle man the Army Air Corps has ever known."

"Pleased to meetcha," said the flagpole, his long arm rising to meet my grip.

"OK, OK, let's get on with it," said an annoyed fellow sitting cross-legged at the flagpole's feet. "I am hungry as hell."

"Easy, boys," said Axel Jack. "We are gonna have ourselves a feast, and you can't enjoy yourselves none if you's grouchy. So now, you know the drill. Let's just close our eyes and set right up to my griddle. She's good and hot. Ready as she can be for this morning's special. An omelet, boys, a big, beautiful, fluffy omelet."

"Hot damn," said one of the men, his eyes shut tight, his mouth wide with pleasure.

"Now there's a trick to making an omelet fluffy and tasty. First thing I am gonna do is separate the yolks and the whites. You got to be real careful. You got to beat each of 'em real well." He moved his hands in the air, despite the closed eyes of his audience. "Now you can add milk to the yolks, as many tablespoons as you have eggs." "Yeah, Axel, add the milk," said someone eagerly. "OK, OK, don't rush me. Then you get some salt and mix it all. Now it is always best to use a heavy pan, like your mama's iron skillet. I got myself one that I like just fine. I made Joe Louis a full breakfast in it once. We're gonna use my skillet, and first thing is to put the pan to heat while you are beating your eggs. Then you melt enough butter just to cover the bottom of the pan. Now, pay attention, boys, don't let that butter brown—you'll kill the flavor and we won't get ourselves the perfect omelet if that butter cooks too much. Now. Let's just pour it all right into the pan." He spoke now in a slow, drawn-out manner. "You want it to be an inch deep or so, no more. Now, boys, here's the secret to the perfect omelet, and if you listen carefully, I am going to teach you one of Axel's greatest secrets, one of the things that will guarantee that Axel will always have a job somewhere in America as a griddle king. Cook it real slow. Low heat. Even heat. Pour it all in slowly and cook real slow." All of them sat with their eyes closed, even Axel Jack, the griddle man. He lightly lifted his hands in a kind of slow twitch.

"See, the air can expand and raise the omelet before the egg and milk set. Everything will set nice and easy if you cook slow; the omelet cooks through and nothing gets too tough. Use a spatula to lift the edges of the omelet so you know that the omelet is light brown on the bottom. Let's take a look. Can you see that?"

"Perfect," said one of the listeners dreamily.

"Goddamned perfect," said Axel Jack. "Now be gentle. You can cook the top of the omelet with steam by covering it over, or some folks will broil it just to be sure. Either way is fine, but be gentle. Smell that beauty. Now let's crease it through the center, fold it over and turn it out onto a warm plate and you got it. The perfect omelet, boys." They sat very still, eyes closed. Everyone was quiet.

"Thanks, Chef. Best goddamned omelet I ever ate," said one of them.

"Pleasure, boys."

They all opened their eyes and began to poke one another good-naturedly and stretch. Axel acted like a man gathering his things, though there was nothing much to gather. Then he set about taking off his boot and rubbing his blistered foot with great care.

"What was that all about?" I asked Heyburn gingerly, still astonished.

Heyburn smiled. "Just a little breakfast treat."

"Everyone imagining a breakfast that they can't have?"

"You think because they can't eat it, they can't have it?"

"Look, it's not my place to say a thing, you guys have been here long enough to know what you're doing, but it seems a tough thing to do to yourselves, driving yourselves crazy with dreams of food. It doesn't seem practical."

"How hungry are you?" he asked me, looking bemused.

"Plenty hungry," I answered, "but not hungry enough to start eating dreams."

"Not yet, anyway," said Heyburn softly. He looked at the men walking away. "Do they look crazy to you, Handy?" The men were ambling away, laughing and talking to one another. One of them came back and cuffed Axel Jack lightly on his head, leaned down, and as the scarecrow rubbed his feet, whispered something in his ear. They both laughed. "Not by a long shot," said Axel Jack, looking up at his companion with his lopsided, gap-toothed grin.

"Was that my surprise?" I asked, still troubled by a scene that made me wonder about what could happen if you stayed in a place like this for too long.

"No, that's coming. But you know, Handy, that omelet's more

important than you think. You aren't hungry enough yet to know how to eat like that, but you will be. You see, we do what we have to do to get by here. Here's some advice that you may or may not want to take, but I've learned it the hard way. Use everything you have. Remembering who you were is the way you stay alive. The Jerries want you to forget. They want you to think that who you were doesn't matter. You're a kriegie now and you do what they tell you to do. But they can't get at your own ability to remember, to dream. Dreams are fine if you know why you have them, if they help you remember what it is you love best. If a dream reminds you of the face of the woman you love, well, that's a whole sight better than walking around every day losing the memory of that face bit by bit." Heyburn's tone was melancholy. I wondered if he was losing the face of someone that he loved. No wonder these old kriegies thought we had it easy.

We walked the compound's perimeter and talked a bit about Milton and mutual friends, but the conversation was polite, almost forced. We both knew there was something else on his mind and the sooner we got to it the better.

"Here's what I want to show you," he said, taking out a piece of paper. It was an ink drawing that at first glance seemed simply a strange series of diagonal lines with numbers on either end.

"Do you know what this is?" he said, looking at me carefully.

"Not a clue," I said, wondering if this was some kind of test.

"It's a map, and it's going to get me and you and some others out of here." I had not been here long enough to even consider the idea of escape, but looking at these odd diagonals, suddenly nothing else mattered.

"Where did you get it?" I asked.

He continued as if he hadn't heard me. "Running diagonally past the uphill, right-hand corner of your barracks, maybe ten feet beyond it, is an abandoned storm sewer. It's barely big enough to crawl through. It runs downhill under your compound, out under the north fence and out into the fields. You probably haven't had much time to look around. East from your barracks, two compounds over, is another fence and then a hundred yards beyond that is a little wooded area where they bury the poor sons of bitches from the Russian compounds. There's even one of ours out there—he tried to escape and they shot him dead last winter. Anyway, this abandoned storm sewer goes out to those fields under the north fence, not the east fence that faces that grove of trees. Do you follow me?"

"Yeah, I think so." I hoped I did.

"I've put in a lot of time here as a prisoner of war and I gotta get out."

"When were you shot down?"

"Late '42. We got ambushed on the way home. Listen. I've known about this sewer pipe for some time but couldn't do anything about it, because until you guys came, your barracks was full of Russians. Would you be willing to try to find it, get together a tunnel-digging team and see if you can find that sewer pipe and break into it? Then we can all get a move on and head home."

I had no idea how to do what he was asking but quickly warmed to the idea of escaping and of digging to find that sewer pipe.

"Sure," I said enthusiastically. "Great." And that was it. He did not give me the paper; he just made sure I looked very carefully at it and then he folded it up again and put it in his pocket.

"Don't tell anyone about this plan except those guys who are working with you on the project. Don't ever use the word 'tunnel.' Ever. Talk around here can get you killed. I don't need any updates, and though I'd be glad to help in any way I can, there's not likely much I can do for you from over here. Anyway, Handy, I'm glad you're on this." We fell into small talk, both oddly heartened. The day was almost gone when we got back to his barracks. I returned to 32A in the cool of the early spring night.

That night sleep came slowly. At first I had watched the swinging of the weak little lightbulb and listened to the dozens of conversations that bubbled across the bunks. At 9 P.M. exactly, the lights went out.

Curfew. And in the subsequent hours, men dropped off to sleep. Now, somewhere in the middle of the night, my thoughts were still racing. Around me men were stirring, groaning, talking to one another in whispers, talking to their dreams. The camp searchlights periodically washed over the blackout shutters, turning the cracks in the wood, for a moment, into veins of light. I had no ready knowledge about how we might build the tunnel, and though I was not one to think too far ahead, I wasn't entirely sure now how to start. We would obviously need to get a go-ahead from Shattuck, our barracks chief. Also, it occurred to me that I could talk to Meese. He seemed sensible, reliable. Working together, we might come up with some good ideas. I decided to talk with him soon, and that eased my mind.

Listening to the unhappy noises of men accommodating themselves to a most unhappy place, I began to consider how it was that I was going to survive this place. The straw under me was prickly and the wood hard on my bones. It was late April, but the night air was cold. I'd put both my blanket and my heavy coat over me. I had nothing for a pillow but didn't mind that. It reminded me of nights lying flat out on the beach, looking up at a vast crowd of stars that seemed to be saying something to me. That had been years ago, when each summer I joined three other boys on an overnight hike in a wilderness of beach and dunes. It was good to remember, but the relentless demands of this war were making such memories ever fainter, like lights on a fading shore. Now there was more to think about than the beauty of those long-ago stars and what their message might have been. It was two years since I'd said good-bye to my mother and boarded a train to the skies over Germany and to defeat by the Luftwaffe fighter planes. The major at Dulag Luft had said, "For you the war is over," and had shipped me off to this prison. A disaster. Or was it? Though a mystery why, I'd been spared. I was alive. "Make the most of it" was the message of that cold night air; "survive if you can, but more important, keep fighting. For you the war is *not* over."

Heyburn. I pictured him as the boy I'd last seen on a long-lost lawn, the promise of summer in his laughter. I lay on my palliasse, elbow under my head, feeling the slats under me. What had happened to him here? War making men of boys—that's what the old men liked to say—but at what cost? Heyburn seemed drained of light and vitality. His face was hard and there was suffering in his eyes. Would I look like that? Though it was all strange and new, I can't say I felt real fear, but I could sense hard going ahead. *I've put in a lot of time here and I gotta get out.* Heyburn bore a message all of us new kriegies were going to learn soon enough. The sound of the German guards banging the bunks and shouting "*Raus, raus!*" for the morning roll call had reminded me that a brutal routine was already closing in like bad weather. It was going to be quite different from anything I had known before. The Army Air Corps offered its own suffocating routine, but you tolerated it because you knew you were preparing for a greater endeavor. We were learning to be fliers, warriors. No one had taught us anything about how to survive imprisonment. At a briefing, we had been advised that we could try to escape on the ground provided we harmed no civilians in the process. If captured and interrogated, all you needed to give was your name, rank and serial number. Should we end up in a prison camp (no doubt many of us by this time were looking at our watches and wondering if the mess hall was still serving lunch), we could attempt to escape provided we harmed no other prisoners or civilians in the process. I had paid no attention, planning to be neither shot down nor captured.

The night moved on and still no sleep. My last sleepless night was my very first in the military. I had arrived in an army barracks late at night along with a bunch of other recruits. Big coffee mugs were brought in and handed to each of us, part of an effort to make us feel welcome. I'd never tasted coffee in my life, but at nineteen I wasn't going to say a word to anyone about it. I joined the others in downing what seemed like hot mud. Later that night I lay on my cot with eyes wide open. It was a short night because we were routed out and by sunrise were taking our entry tests. The war was on; the military needed live bodies and fast. Though a desk sergeant had assured me he'd go with my request for the Field Artillery, he sent me on an Air Corps troop train headed south to mechanics school. So much for honoring promises to volunteers. The Air Corps needed a thousand warm bodies that day, and I was one of them. I thought again of Heyburn. Life in this pen was going to demand useful work from all of us, or we would grow weaker by the day. I was grateful that mine had already surfaced. It occurred to me that my life in Stalag 17 could quickly fall into a long and deadly process of waiting for the war to end, and that thought scared the hell out of me. I had had the good fortune to live my life out in the open—in woods, in fields, on oceans and beaches—and now I was locked away in a muddy square mile wrapped in barbed wire. I didn't want to learn to wait here and, it would seem, neither did Heyburn and probably many others. If escape was the plan, the sooner we began it the better.

"I CAN HELP, BUT YOU'RE RIGHT, you'd better go and see Shattuck before we do anything at all. There are probably procedures we need to follow. We should know what they are," said Meese quietly as we stood together in the compound. There was still a good deal of confusion as the guards hustled us into lines for roll call. "I like the idea of getting out of here," he added, as we watched a guard in the tower, his helmet low over his face, menacingly repositioning his machine gun. "But if we're going to do this, Handy, we've got to do it right. It's not a game, and somebody could get killed if we don't mind every step. Talk to Shattuck and then let's meet this afternoon in the bay."

After roll call I went to see Shattuck. The camp leaders had reorganized a front bay in each barracks so that the barracks chief could have a desk and room for the people who assisted him with the task of managing his affairs. There were a number of guys waiting outside his "office" to talk to him. Many of them were nervous, as if they were going in to see a superior officer. Someone said we were to vote for barracks and compound chiefs, but I hadn't heard anything about a vote or how Shattuck had gotten the job. I asked the guy in front of me.

"Oh, no, there was no vote yesterday," he said. "Shattuck was named by Kurtenbach, our head guy. The Germans call him the Man of Confidence. He knows how to talk to those Jerries. One of the kriegies told me he's a cool customer." The guy was a radioman who wanted to get his crewmate into his bay from another barracks. He was a real talker, and while we waited he told me everything he had learned in the last twenty-four hours about the camp, whether I wanted to know it or not.

"Shattuck's a smart guy, too," he rattled on, "and he knows a lot of people in the other barracks. They say he could be a compound chief if he wants." I wanted to remind him that Shattuck drew the same monthly pay as we did. I marveled at how, despite the fact that we were all sergeants, a hierarchy was already formed, and I wasn't sure I liked it at all, though I understood the need. Nothing could be worse, I thought, than a sergeant who thought he was a colonel. In my experience in the Army Air Corps I'd seen my share of superiors who acted that way. I remembered landing in Trinidad on the way to Brazil because of a gas leak in one of our wing tanks—the small ones at the far upper ends of a B-24's wings. (We later learned that a large number of Liberator B-24 bombers built at the Willow Run plant in Ann Arbor had this problem. Given how hard it was to work in the cramped space approaching the wing tips, there may have been a wing tank installation team that shoved one of our wing tanks into its far crevice and accidentally punctured it.) It was a serious problem—gas dripping into the bomb bay could blow a plane apart if touched by a spark. At least we didn't have to fly long before we had used up the gas in those wing tip tanks. The remaining gas was at a level below the punctures. When we landed I had reported the leak right away and a colonel, who must have been the base operations officer, came out and challenged my report. He didn't ask me to clarify or explain, he just spoke to me in a loud and theatrical voice, as if he were making a public example out of me. He said that there were already dozens of Liberators in and around the hangar area with mysterious problems, and he was beginning to wonder if the problems lay with the bombers or with some of the men who flew them. That comment enraged me—he didn't know us or have any reason to believe we might be fabricating a story. He was using his rank as cover to say something one man would never say to another unless he knew that man was a slacker. So in front of our crew I told him to stay right there, bring out the gasoline trucks, fill up the tanks to the top (so as to include the wing tanks) and we would all watch the gas run down into the bomb bay. It wasn't the way that flight engineers were supposed to talk to their superiors. He was clearly incensed but cornered. Likely he felt he now had to stay the course of his own challenge. When the ground crew finally got the gasoline up to the level of the wing tanks and a minute or two had gone by, the heavy dripping began again from the ceiling of the bomb bay. The colonel turned beet red, swung around and left without a word. I was still angry at him for what seemed like an insult to our crew, but was well satisfied that he had been proven wrong in a dramatic, visible manner.

Later, Lieutenant Tedrowe called me over to a table where he, our copilot, bombardier and navigator were eating supper. "Sergeant Handy," he said softly, "I just got an earful from the colonel. He thinks that my men aren't as mindful of rank as they should be. He said either you think you are a colonel or you think he is a technical sergeant. And either way, he is sure that I am not doing my job as an officer because I did not reprimand you for the way you spoke to him." Tedrowe paused and looked at me without expression. "He may have a point, you know." I felt bad and understood that I had put Tedrowe in a pretty tough spot. "So in the future, can you hide your pleasure a bit more when you are so damned right?" he said, and they all laughed. They knew, as I had, that the colonel's self-importance was a joke, but Tedrowe was also telling me something about myself and the Army Air Corps as he saw it. Order depended upon deference to rank, and not necessarily on common sense or personal integrity. One could not afford to make for oneself the determination that one man's orders were worth following while another's were not. I believed in the deference of rank—I had always been shocked by Dailey's and Thompson's constant reference to Lieutenant Brown, their superior officer, as "Brownie," even in front of the rest of us. My problem, and Tedrowe understood this about me and was warning me of it, was that I deferred to superiors only as long as they returned the respect due a man of lower rank—and as long as their orders made sense. Tedrowe always spoke to his men with respect, as one man to another. His decisions were anchored in common sense and clear to the rest of us, and he never used his rank in an irrational way. He wanted me to learn that if there were officers in the Army Air Corps who I saw as wrong or insulting or both, I had no license to challenge them. It was a lesson I was never to fully learn. As I waited to talk with Shattuck, I was uneasy about what he might say to a new prisoner with a skimpy plan to start digging a tunnel out of Stalag 17 on his third day in camp.

SHATTUCK ROSE TO MEET ME. HE seemed much older than I was; tall and affable, he carried himself with great self-confidence. He had a broad, open face, very Irish. I had already learned in the Army that a man who had a few years on you could seem almost like an uncle. You had the feeling that you could never be as old as they already were. Shattuck's grip was firm, his smile genuine. My uneasiness fell away in an instant.

"Where are you from, Handy?" he asked.

"Massachusetts," I answered, not certain what to call him.

"Well, now you're talking," he said with a laugh. "So am I. Greenfield. You anywhere near there?"

"No," I countered. "Other end of the state. Barnstable, on Cape Cod."

"Well," he nodded approvingly, "you can bet I know where Cape Cod is." We stood for a moment and I still did not know what to say. I was poor at small talk and it was painfully obvious.

"Well, I suppose we could swap stories of home," he said, graciously ending my embarrassment, "but you have other things on your mind. What do you need?" His aspect was immediately different. Sober, almost stern.

I explained my trip to the old compound to visit Heyburn. Shattuck listened carefully, interrupting me only once when he asked me about Heyburn and how I knew him. My praise of Heyburn made no impression on him, but when I spoke of his family in Louisville, he seemed more relaxed. Maybe he liked Kentuckians; he didn't explain. When I finished, he was quiet. He put his hands together in the aspect of praying, though his hard stare was anything but prayerful. After a moment, he spoke:

"Go to it. Put together a team and do what you have to do."

"That's it?" I had expected more questions.

"That's it. Pick your team carefully," he added.

"I thought the guys from my bay would make a good team. I know most all of them."

"Good. I don't need to know too much about your team, but you do. And remember, before long you are going to need a lot more help, in the end, maybe even most of the barracks."

"We have some capable fellows in our bay. We should be able to do what we have to do without too many other people," I assured him.

Shattuck looked at me and then gazed out into the compound.

"Well, if you aim to hit the pipe you're looking for, you're gonna want to start as close as you can to that pipe, right? So you're likely to need to start your dig at my end of the barracks. That means a tunnel entrance in someone else's bay."

I nodded, beginning to understand.

"Don't talk to anyone who is not directly involved in the tunnel or the escape. Even if they're buddies of yours. And don't talk about the tunnel progress among yourselves. Tell people only what they need to know and nothing more. Loose talk will get folks killed, that's certain. Give me updates if you want, but no details. Understood?"

"Yes. Can I ask you a stupid question?"

He laughed. "It's the answers that are usually stupid."

"How do we start? What do we do?" I asked.

"My grandmother always told me it's best to start right from where you are. Make do with whatever you can find." As he walked to the window and looked out, his voice became oddly philosophical. "It's a strange thing, but you'll get more help than you can imagine. Men here don't yet know what they're capable of, how willing they'll be to do what's needed. They're going to see another side to their natures in the months ahead . . ." Then he snapped awake and turned to me as if I'd been eavesdropping on a private conversation. "Get used to the drill. Ask for what you need and then wait. If what you need can be gotten, someone on your team or someone else'll get it or make it for you. The hows or whys don't matter. Sometimes you'll have to get something for someone else. It's that simple. No one gets to know the whole story. It's safer that way. So let us know when you're ready and we'll make certain the White House is informed."

"The White House?"

"The barracks chiefs all report to their respective compound chiefs, who in turn report to Barracks 16, the one painted white. They call it the White House. They got it going last fall when the old kriegies were dumped here. It's where all the decisions get made, all the plans are coordinated—it's the camp's central nervous system. Sergeant Kurtenbach is our camp leader. He speaks German, knows the rules of the Geneva Convention and isn't afraid to challenge Peg Leg—the top Luftwaffe officer in the camp—on proper procedures. Kurt knows how to deal with the Luftwaffe and he's as stubborn as a mule when he needs to be. We caught a break having the Luftwaffe run the American compounds, that's for sure. They insisted on it because they see and respect us as their equals. He'll know nothing of your plans. But the White House has a security team. I'll be in touch with them when the time is right."

I was impressed with all this organization and surprised the Germans allowed it. As I had barely figured out where my bay was and who my bunkmates were, it was comforting to know that I was part of something so well made, so orderly. He wished me luck. On the way out, I passed a line of men, many of whom might have had plans similar to my own. Shattuck's immediate acceptance of the tunnel was inspiring, as if an escape attempt were more than a possibility; it was a duty.

WE MET IN OUR BAY, MEESE, Wilkens, Sac, Kozikowski, Thompson, Sanford and a few of the others, to map things out. Meese understood that we had to prioritize our problems. Shattuck was right: the first challenge was the tunnel's entrance. To get as close as possible to that sewer pipe, it was going to have to be, as Shattuck had observed, in the bay opposite his "office," on the front left (southwest) corner of our barracks.

"Shattuck warned us that the more people that know about this, the more risks there are," I pointed out, "but we're going to have to get the guys in that bay on the team."

"We've got no choice," said Meese. "Let's be alert and careful, but we need their help. We can't do everything ourselves." Someone volunteered to scope out the right person to talk to in that front bay. Talk of how we would get the material and tools we would need to dig the tunnel made everyone somber. None of us knew the procedure for trading with the guards, and we couldn't exactly go ask for a pick and shovel. Wilkens, who had been listening with a good-natured smile while whittling on a piece of wood, leaned forward, his elbows on his knees.

"I'm pretty good with tools, fellas. In fact, I can make whatever tools we need, and if I can't make it, you ain't likely to need it." Everyone's spirits rose with his casual confidence. Someone asked about what we would do once outside the wire, and Meese turned toward him like a teacher.

"Listen. Whenever you begin something like this, there is a whole lot to do and lots of problems to sort out. You have to take things one at a time or you'll get yourself in trouble. You'll make a mistake on the task at hand or waste energy worrying about things that may never happen." Men were quiet. "That isn't to say we aren't going to get out of here. I just mean we'll need to figure out what to do beyond the wire when we're ready to worry about it. Right now, let's focus on getting this tunnel started."

He nodded at a small, wiry fellow whose upper lip promised a mustache that would never come. "This is Skinny. I asked him to take a walk around the barracks while you met with Shattuck," he said, winking at me. "He's had a close look and has some observations. Skinny?"

Skinny rose and started speaking in a fast and nervous voice. "As you guys probably saw, the Jerries built these barracks into the hill. The front is held up by these wooden posts. The floor at the downhill end is about four feet off the ground. The clearance at the uphill end is about fourteen inches. I don't know when they built this camp, but they sure collected enough used lumber to do us a big favor. See," and now he began to talk faster, more excitedly, "they put sheathing on *both* sides of the posts and right down to the *ground*. I guess they felt they had to do it to cut down heating costs because they built the sheathing around the posts—which have a diameter of maybe six inches—and the posts are sunk well into the ground. See, they could just as well have made the siding on the outside of the posts so you could see the posts from the inside, underneath the barracks—or they could have had the siding just go down to the level of the floor. That's the way we would have done it back home. If they'd done that, they would always have been able to see everything there was to see under the barracks. But they didn't. Don't know why. Without that, fellas, we would be in a fix, so God bless the Nazis on this one." Skinny was sounding like a kid planning the smashing of pumpkins on mischief night. "See, because the siding went right down the posts to the ground and the barracks is built on the side of a hill, the siding has to get longer and longer as the hill slopes down. And that means as the distance from the floor to the ground grows longer, they lengthened the siding as needed to get it down to the ground." Skinny grinned at all of us, sure that what he had said would make us all as happy as it made him. "What the hell are you talking about, Skinny?" someone cracked. Meese nudged him. "Tell them what all this means, Skinny."

"It means," he said, immediately sullen, "that we'll always be protected from the view of passing guards by that sheathing going right down to the ground. Now at the north end," and here he spoke to us as dunces, "that's the downhill end for those who ain't following me, we'll have about four feet, maybe even five, from the floor to the ground. The Germans will have the ferrets in there—the guards who look for tunnels and spy on us when they can. An old kriegie told me they have very powerful searchlights and they check under the barracks all the time." *When did all these guys learn all these things?* I thought again. "But," Skinny said, recovering his excitement, "they ain't gonna crawl the whole length of the barracks to go up to our far end where the space between the floor and the ground is more like twelve to fourteen inches. No guard or ferret would ever crawl up there, and even a dog won't fit too well. They'll just use a searchlight from farther back and look around, going no more than halfway at most from the far end up to our end. So if we can be sure that they don't find the tunnel inside the barracks, we won't have to worry too much that they'll find it from the outside." Then he sat down so abruptly and with such relief, that we all realized how nervous he had been.

"Thanks, Skinny," said Meese. "So we build a hatch in the floor and then a shaft down into the ground. We'll need another hatch to cover the shaft. Everybody got it? A floor hatch—let's call it a trapdoor—and a hatch over the tunnel. We'll also have to make sure that when we put the earth back over the tunnel hatch, we sort of smooth it out so that a torch won't pick up any irregularities in the dirt. We have to try to make our packed-in earth over the shaft look very much like it hasn't been touched for years. I'll wager the Germans don't go in and rake up or tidy under the barracks."

After a moment, Kozikowski said, "The dirt. What are we going to do with the dirt?"

"That's a tough one. We can't just carry it out and tip it in the compound. There's going to be a lot of it," Thompson volunteered.

"Mix it in with our soup. It'll remind all the bugs in there of home," said Wilkens. Everybody laughed.

"If you can't drink dirt soup, pour it down a drain," said Joseph from his perch. Everyone looked up in surprise. He had not said a word to anyone before. Now we all knew he was listening, and carefully.

"Well, now. There's an idea," said Sac. "Mix it in with water. That ain't half bad. We can get rid of it in the washroom during the hours we have water."

"Just wash it down the drains," repeated Wilkens slowly, as if he were tasting the idea. "Just wash it down the drains. It's a right sweet little idea."

Then Beast, the large man I had first met in the boxcar, spoke up. "We got to watch that little guy Itchy. I don't trust him, and we still can't find no one in the barracks to vouch for him."

"Somebody's talked to Shattuck and they're asking around," said another.

"Well, if we can't find anyone to stand for him," Beast said, "I say we break his arms and dump him in the middle of the compound, a nice message to the Jerries."

"Beast, I don't know about this kid Itchy, but you've reminded me. We'll have to be very careful about security. Can you think about how to keep a lookout while we get rid of the dirt in the washroom?" asked Meese. Sanford spoke up immediately in his distinctly New England accent.

"You get the dirt out of here. We'll see to it that there's no trouble from the Jerries. Just save some of those bugs for our soup."

"That suit you, Handy?" said Meese.

"You bet," I said. Though the men were listening carefully whenever Meese spoke, he never failed to reinforce my position as team leader. These men were posing problems I had not yet considered and offering solutions I might never have imagined, yet there was never a discussion as to whether or not I was the best one for the job. It wasn't that leadership was in big demand—this was clearly going to be a team effort—but there was a kind of unspoken acceptance of my role on major decisions. It was as if, should any key matter about that tunnel be debated, I had the right of final say. In some sense, it was a microcosm of the entire camp. Hierarchy was required in order to manage, and given that we were all sergeants, rank offered no natural solution. (Though there were three levels among the sergeants imprisoned at Stalag 17, we paid no attention to the distinction.) Other factors would have to establish the order of things: expertise, humor, calm, all the natural characteristics that establish one man's credentials as momentarily superior to another's. Kurtenbach happened to be the lowest level of sergeant, but no one inquired or cared about that. He was elected—and then reelected every six months—because he had matchless capabilities for the job. In my case, rank had been conferred upon me by Alex Heyburn and his mysterious map. I was mindful that working with others in a rankless hierarchy meant that authority had always to be earned. It was in no way a right.

SHATTUCK CALLED A BARRACKS MEETING, THE first we had had since arriving. It was for 32A only, half the building the Germans called 32. Separated by a cement-lined washroom, 32B was another world, and one we knew or cared little about. Efficient, almost formal, Shattuck explained that he wanted to make a few things clear about our barracks.

"We have to keep this place clean, fellas. The Russians are dying by the pallet full next door, and you can bet that one of the things killing them is disease. Disease travels and rats are the cruise ship of choice. Flies, too. They love the latrines and will make a damned nuisance of themselves."

"What the hell do we have over here that any rat would want?" growled Beast.

"Well, what we have we've got to keep clean. You won't get sick as much and you won't be as miserable if you stay on top of the place and yourselves. When you get the chance to get clean, get clean. My father always said that if you were unemployed, the worst thing you could do is wake up and not shave. Now shaving here isn't the point, but doing everything you can to make yourself feel better—that's it, guys. You aren't keeping it up for the Army or the regimen of it. The Army's got nothing to say about it in this place. You're keeping it clean because it gives us our best chance of surviving and getting the hell out of here."

"And maybe smell better. Got it, Beast?" jibed a voice.

"Who said that?" Beast asked, looking around in annoyance.

"A clean house is a happy house, my mother always said," cracked a handsome, wry fellow in a southern drawl.

"Well now, Pappy, that says it just about right. Boys, we're going to keep our house like the Barksdales of South Carolina," said Shattuck.

"You any relation to the Mississippi Barksdale who got himself killed at Gettysburg?" asked another man.

"Sure I am," said Barksdale, straightening up and losing his jaunty grin. "But he didn't get himself killed, it took half the Union army to do it." Everyone laughed, though Barksdale did not.

"Yeah, well, it's going to take the whole barracks to keep 32A clean, so let's get a system going," said Shattuck with a wink at Pappy Barksdale. He laid out plans for sweeping the center aisle and bays to manage dirt; he talked of the tricks for conserving water so that what we did not use for washing ourselves we could use to clean our clothes and later the barracks.

"We don't waste the water from the kitchen 'cause it's warm—if there is any left (and most times there is), we use it for washing and shaving." He made it clear that the washroom had to be regularly scrubbed, and the "one-holer" just inside the barracks kept as clean as possible. He explained that the burlap palliasses, the Germans' crude excuse for mattresses stuffed with straw and wood chips, were to be taken outside and shaken in the fresh air.

"Sure, it'll buy us a few hours while all the fleas and bedbugs march right back to our barracks," somebody cracked. The Red Cross parcels should be carefully but steadily consumed. ("What you save might be taken away by the Germans, where it will do you no good at all.") He explained that the White House had at least some limited activities to help keep the prisoners occupied. On a small scale, there was a school, a tiny library, an off-and-on camp newsletter, and occasional movies and camp productions on the kriegie-built stage they called the Cardboard Theater. "We're not trying to make it like home, guys," warned Shattuck. "It's just a way to keep busy. Most of the time life is likely to be pretty boring around here." He winked at the words "most of the time," and some of us smiled.

SOMETIME THE NEXT AFTERNOON, SAC'S LITTLE brother, Tony, walked into our bay and I was immediately struck by the resemblance. Like George, he conveyed enormous strength in his compact body, but right away you could see that where his brother was sensitive, prone to quiet, Tony possessed a confident swagger and carried about him the open, unapologetic energy of Brooklyn. Sac was dozing in his bunk. Catching sight of him there, Tony raised a finger to his lips and crept to his brother's side. He grabbed Sac's shoulder and shook it hard.

"Get up, ya lazy bastard, it's daytime and the whole world's workin'!" he shouted, turning for an instant to us with a broad smile. Sac woke and his eyes, typically a squint, opened wider than I'd ever seen before.

"Jeeeeesus Chrrrrist," he shouted. "Pee Wee! Where the hell ya been, ya bum? What the hell ya been doin? Waiting for me to come and get ya?" Bailing out of his bunk, he grabbed his brother with uncharacteristic warmth and hugged him. We were all moved by the reunion.

"I mean it," he said sternly, every bit now the older brother, "tell me where in God's name ya been. I told ya to stay home. Momma's gonna be pissed, I'll tell ya."

"Aw, we're not goin' through that one again. What would Pop say to see us in the hoosegow together, eh?"

"It ain't about Pop now. Where the hell have you been?"

"It's a long story, and there ain't enough time to tell it."

"That's about the only thing we got plenty of," said Meese. "We're hungry for a new story around here." We closed in on him, and a few men leaned out from their bunks. For a few moments there was silence. Tony had an audience and he knew it. He made eye contact with each of us, one by one, before he took a deep breath and spoke.

"Look, guys, we don't know one another, most of us don't anyhow, but this can be for all of you, not just for my lazy big brother. We all got our stories, and this is mine. I'm sure before too long, you all will tell me yours. And by the way, my brother can call me Pee Wee if it makes him feel better, but if anyone uses that name, I'll break his nose." He managed a little smile, but it did not last. Everyone knew this fireplug from Brooklyn meant it.

"I christen you Tony Sac," said Wilkens with a grin.

"Well, let's start at the beginning," said Tony Sac, relaxing. "I was on a B-17 out of England, skippered by Captain Clinton Firestone. Any of you guys know him? He's some guy, I'll tell ya. A grand-nephew of the guy who started the Firestone Tire and Rubber Company, but you'd never know it. He's experienced, smart as hell, but a regular Joe. We flew our last mission—it was to Tutow in northeastern Germany—on April eleventh."

"That's when we flew our last one, too," said Sac. "We were going to Brunswick."

"Yeah, the same damned day, George. Ain't that a mother's nightmare, both of us going down the same day?" said Tony with a shake of his head.

"If you'da done what I told ya, she'da been fine," said Sac grouchily to his younger brother.

Tony Sac ignored him. "Our flight path home was over the Baltic, and the Luftwaffe jumped us out there. The first pass was a turkey shoot and they riddled us. My waist gunner was shot through the neck and died looking at me. The third pass, they took us for done because they shot out all but one of the engines. After they left, Captain Firestone tried to get the plane over land on one engine. We were losing altitude fast. He called me to come forward to the cockpit. Our copilot was hurt bad.

" 'We got to get him out of this plane,' the skipper shouted. The copilot looked dead to me.

" 'He's gone,' I shouted.

" 'No, no,' the skipper said, 'not yet. But he is sure to be if we don't get him out of this plane. You too. And all the others.'

" 'What about you?' I asked him.

" 'First things first,' he said. 'Get going now.'

"I pulled the copilot out of his seat and carried him back to the bomb bay. I pulled his chute's ripcord and then fed him out into the sky." Tony Sac paused. Everyone looked away.

"By the time I got him out, the guys who were left were ready to go, too. We all went except Firestone, who couldn't bail. By the time we jumped, he was too low to get out. I couldn't see the plane but I heard it. It was flying low over the trees, and then I heard the crash. Two of our crew who bailed out died or were murdered when they landed because we never saw them again."

"How about your copilot?" asked Sac.

"Naw, he didn't make it neither. But Firestone did and he told us that he had taken that plane down and that he had hit the ground with a five-hundred-pounder still in the bay. It didn't blow when he hit the ground—it was a dud. Well, we were rounded up and taken to this interrogation center. There were a lot of guys there and they ordered a lot of us to line up. A German Luftwaffe officer walked along our line, and every once in awhile he would tap someone on the shoulder. When he came to me, he tapped me and said everyone not tapped on the shoulder should fall out and scram. There was four of us that was tapped. Now they took us alone into a building, and of course I was wondering what the hell was going on."

"There were no other members of your crew in that four?" Thompson asked.

"Just me and three other guys I didn't know. They were from the Eighth, like me, I guess. I saw my crewmates—Joe Sparacchio, my tail gunner, and Bojack, our top-turret gunner and cargolier—fall out and I thought, *Well, I won't see those guys again.* They probably thought that too. So now the guards put me in this tiny room with nothing in it, except that in the corner there was another guy."

Sac, who had been leaning on his bunk, now sat down in the only other chair in the bay and looked closely at his little brother.

"Did this room have a bath and sink?" he asked.

"Nothing."

"Whaddya mean, nothing."

"What are you, deaf? I said nothing. The room was empty."

"Well, they gave you a little bucket to piss in, right?"

"You got to forgive my big brother, fellas. He musta taken a knock on the head or something. What part of the word 'nothing' don't you get? Nothing is what was in there. No bed, no chair. Just a floor. And if ya gotta know, when it came time to piss, I had to knock on the door and the guard would take me out, and then he would bring me back. It was a dark room with nothing in it, and every day you'd hear them come around with food and pour food into some sort of bucket. They'd open the door and start bringing it in, and then some guy would holler and they'd slam the door shut—just to torment us. They didn't give us nothing. So we starved. This other fellow in the other corner was a sad sonofabitch. Every day they would pull him out, and after awhile he'd come back and they'd pull me out—and they'd do this twice a day. He was takin' it a lot worse than me. He was more beat up, too. So each day they took me to the same officer—a colonel—and he interviewed me. He would have this application, and every day was the same old story. Name, rank and serial number, which I gave him. And then, after that, there were all these questions.

What was your bomb group, what were you bombing, what kind of bombs were you carrying—this, that and the other thing. Then on the bottom we were supposed to sign it—and every day I would just fill in the name, rank and serial number part and hand it back to him."

"That's my little brother," said Sac with a grin. "He's so damned stubborn he wouldn't have signed that damn paper for nothin' in this world." Tony Sac ignored his brother and continued.

"That colonel would say to me each day, 'How long do you think this can go on?' And he used to tell me how he hated the Germans. He knew a lot about America. He told me he was a college man, said he went to the University of Pennsylvania. And I said to him, 'Well, how come you're here?' He said to me, 'That's a good question. I came to visit my mother and father, and Hitler wouldn't let me go back.' I said, 'Well, that makes a good story.'

"I sort of liked the guy until he told me he was a New York Yankee fan, and Joe DiMaggio was his idol. And I said, 'Oh yeah? Well, Joe DiMaggio is overrated and ain't got no heart. You want a fielder, take Joe Medwick.' Well, you shoulda seen the blank stare. I knew he was just a Kraut and knew nothin' about baseball. So then he offered me a cigarette, and I wouldn't take it because I knew if I took that cigarette I'd be flying. And he said, 'Sergeant, let's put an end to this. I'll tell you what. Just sign it and I'll fill it out.' I said, 'How are you going to fill it out?' 'Because I know everything,' he said. 'I just want you to verify it.' And I said, 'No, I'm not signing. Why don't you sign it?' He said, 'What good is my signing it?' And every day this went on, for eight days, twice a day, the same thing. Then he said to me on the eighth day—he got me into his office that morning—and he said, 'Are we going through this again, Sergeant? How long do you think you can last?' I said, 'I'm from Brooklyn. I can last as long as I have to.' "

"Were they feeding you anything?" asked Itchy.

"Nothing. Eight days with nothing."

"Just water?" Itchy pressed.

"Don't mind him," said Beast. "He talks too much. No water, no food, you little snitch. Go on back to wherever you came from before I smack you." Itchy slunk back to his bunk.

"Eight days without eating. Sounds like it was worse than this place," said Kozikowski from his upper rear bunk. He and Sanford were up there carefully listening.

"I kept saying this was against the Geneva Convention and he'd say, 'Really? Go tell the Geneva Convention. We'll bring them in tomorrow and *you* can tell them yourself, OK?' It was clear he couldn't care less about the Geneva Convention. One of those days while I was with the officer, he had asked me if I had a brother in the Air Force. And I said to him, 'I don't have any brothers.' 'Oh yes you do,' he said, like he knew something I didn't. 'You have a brother who's in the Air Force. His name is Florento.' I said, 'Well, my mother kept that a secret from me. I got no brothers.' He says, 'Well, I just want you to know we have him, too.' When I got back to my cell, I said to myself, 'It can't be. That lug is in the Pacific or laying about some California air base. They're just tryin' to break me,' I thought. Anyway, on the eighth day—I don't know how I made it from the cell to his office, I was so weak—he said, 'You're going to die, you know.' I said, 'Yeah, well, so will you and Joe D., too.' At that he called the guards and they took me back to my cell. I figured this was it. I was done. Then ten minutes later they opened up the door and a guard came in and got me and brought me outside and set me loose with the other prisoners. This American, I don't know what his job was, but he saw me wobbling around and he said, 'You haven't eaten.' I said, 'No, I haven't eaten.' He said—and others around us did, too—'Them sons of bitches.' So he took me in and said, 'Now don't rush it,' and he gave me some coffee, bread, and some kind of meat. Then he said again, 'Just take it easy.' And the next day we were shipped out. And then I had to come find my big brother, who wouldn't be able to find his way out of a closet without me to help him."

He cuffed his brother with affection. No one spoke. He looked around at all of us.

"Is this how you guys treat your guests? I'm still starved." He smiled for the first time, and there was an immediate scurrying around that soon produced a chunk of bread with some Red Cross margarine on it and—a little later—a cup of Red Cross instant coffee warmed on the barracks' little wood stove. We took his things and, for the moment, it was agreed that Tony Sac would bunk with me. Soon enough, the brothers' reunion was retold all over the camp. The Saccomanno brothers were local celebrities.

The next day, Sparacchio, Tony Sac's tail gunner, walked into our bay. The news about the Saccomanno brothers had filtered into 32B, where he was bunking. He came in and the two pounded each other and grabbed each other around the necks. Behind him trailed another prisoner, a modest-looking man who wore glasses and seemed so studious that he looked to me like a professor. While Tony Sac and Sparacchio were cackling and storing stuff in the bunk below mine, the Professor entered our bay and stood behind Itchy, who was watching some guys playing cards.

"Paul," he said softly. Itchy turned and his odd, earnest grin faded. It was as if he had seen a ghost, and his face paled. Rising slowly, he came to the Professor's side, almost nuzzling him as he awkwardly tried to shake the Professor's hand.

"I wondered where you were and was worried about you, pal." The Professor was soothing, talking carefully, as if to a frightened animal. "Why don't you get your things and thank these fellows for their hospitality." Itchy turned, and without looking at any of us, gathered his coat and things from his solitary bunk. The Professor looked at all of us and said quietly, "I appreciate you boys looking after him. He had a rough go of it. In the air and then on the ground. I am the only crewmate he's got left. Don't you all worry, he'll be fine with me." We all stood dumbly watching him. In a voice barely audible, Itchy thanked us all and they left.

"Well," someone said. "That's that."

"I guess so," said Beast, watching the young man leave.

· · ·

THOUGH I FELT A TWINGE OF SADNESS at no longer bunking with Tony Sac, who I had come to like, I was reminded of the top bunk's advantages. In particular, it gave me a fair amount of privacy to think things out. It also came with a good view of the bay and the activity in the aisle. Joseph was on the top bunk kitty-corner across the aisle—a spot he seldom moved from—and I could get a much better sense of him up there. A full-blooded American Indian, he was unusually interesting to all of us. He was like a wise old owl up in his bunk; he watched us quietly, rarely speaking but somehow conveying to us all a sense that he saw through each of us and was dismayed, even sometimes angered, by what he saw. When he spoke, however, he was always diplomatic, always expressive in a low-key, self-possessed way. We all liked and respected him. Mostly sitting with his back to the wall, he would sometimes turn his head and stare out the window. He was utterly still save for his eyes, which darted about as if he were watching a bird-filled sky. Guys took to calling his bunk "Joseph's Indian Heaven." In time, some of us would come to value the wisdom he dispensed from up there.

It was an hour before curfew. I had been walking the perimeter for exercise and on getting back to the bay ran into Meese. "I've been looking for you," he said. "Let's take a stroll. The guys in the bay where we need to put the hatch want to talk to us." He called to Wilkens, "Got a second?"

"For you, Meese? I got all the time in the world." We walked up 32A's center aisle to the front bays and stopped for a moment. Already my sense of our barracks' geography was beginning to shrink. That front end of the barracks, once as alien as the old kriegie camp, now seemed closer, though the faces were still unfamiliar. Surprised by our appearance, they looked at us suspiciously, as if to say *who are you and what are you doing here?* We went to the last bay on the right, closest to the sewer pipe we sought. The hatch would have to be somewhere near here in this bay. As we arrived, a tall, lanky man slid off his bunk and came forward. He stood close and whispered, as if aware that the conversation we were about to have was best had quietly.

"My name's Wolf. The guys asked me to talk for them."

Instinct said that it was now my job to talk for our team. It never occurred to me, though it should have, that Shattuck should've handled a request like the one I was about to make.

"My name's Handy," I started crudely. "You know what we want to do, right? We've got a problem. The entrance needs to be under that far bunk. It's closest to the sewer pipe we're trying to hit."

Wolf seemed tense and awkward, clearly an uncertain representative of the guys who lounged around the bay pretending not to listen. "Yeah, well, everyone here wants to be of help to you, and I hope you take no offense, but there will be no tunnel starting in this bay. If there is anything else we can do, we'd be happy to pitch in, but your tunnel can't start here."

Alarmed by his hard line, I figured he needed a little time. "We can understand your reluctance. Could you guys go over it again and talk with us tomorrow?"

"Absolutely not," he fired back.

None of us had expected an answer like that one. Meese and Wilkens stood slightly behind me. This was the moment to bring them into the discussion, but I barged ahead on my own.

"Sergeant Wolf," I said more forcefully, "we're asking you to talk about this again with the guys in your bay. We appreciate it's a lot to ask, but . . ."

"No, I don't think you do." He cut me off and his voice rose now, so that everyone could hear. "I don't think that for one moment you've tried to appreciate what you're asking. We all just got here and we don't know how things are going to go. What's your goddamned hurry? If you have to start tomorrow, start somewhere else. Like I said, we'll help in any way we can, but we're not going to have guys," he dropped his voice to a hoarse whisper, "digging a tunnel right here where we sleep."

"Look, Sergeant," I said, trying to be more reasonable than tough, "we all have a duty to try and escape, to cause the Nazis as much trouble as we can."

"I have a duty to the men in this bay. And we have a duty to stay alive."

"Of course, and we respect that. Tunnel diggers should just risk their own skins, but how does our tunnel risk yours? Lots of inconvenience, plenty of dirt. But if we're caught, you won't be the ones to face a firing squad. I'm asking you not to make us start somewhere else." Others in the bay, seven or eight men, watched us intently.

"I'm asking you," I added bluntly, "not to make us start somewhere else farther away from the sewer pipe. The tunnel is going to be long enough as it is, and we're going to have a hell of a time just getting that far."

"It's your tunnel. You made the decision to dig it. Don't blame us for the work you have to do. And don't ask us to put ourselves right smack in the crosshairs of trigger-happy goons who want to make a point early, as a warning to all the new kriegies. If they discover that there's tunneling going on, they aren't going to stop and ask whose tunnel it is. They're going to take the guys in this bay out and string 'em up on the wire."

I was getting nowhere. I was not one to compromise when I thought I was right and, it seemed, neither was he. Still, I came at it again.

"If your guys help us, they'll be part of the team that gets out of here. Right up front. You guys can be right up front and early out," I offered.

"Aw, for Chrissakes." Wolf's voice was nearly a shout now. "You don't have a clue. You don't know how to find that sewer, you aren't sure it's even there. You're going to risk the lives of these guys and the guys who are going to dig the damn thing because some pal of yours from nursery school promised you a way home? How the hell does he know what's out there? You don't know shit, mister. All you know is that you want to put a hatch in this bay that could easily get all these guys here smoked. The fact is we don't like the odds, and we're the ones who get to make that call. Like I said, thanks but no thanks."

"Well, if you're afraid . . ." I got no further before Wolf cut me off.

"Fuck you," he growled, moving toward me.

He eyed me for a moment and then spoke slowly, deliberately.

"You're one mouthful away from getting a lot more than you bargained for . . . You got some nerve coming into this bay and lecturing us about duty. I was bombing Germany when they were wet-nursing you. The guys in this bay have sacrificed plenty. Three guys who should be sleeping in this bay are dead and scattered so far and wide we wouldn't be able to find them if the whole goddamned American Army went looking for them. We don't owe you and your swashbuckling buddies a goddamn thing. And," he said, moving right up to me, "if you were any bigger, I'd bust your chops."

I felt Meese's hand on my arm and heard Wilkens say with a chuckle, "Well, Sergeant Wolf, you surely have made yourself mighty clear. Anything else on your mind?" The sound of Wilkens's easy drawl softened us both for an instant, and Wolf winced as if caught by bad manners. When he spoke again his voice was even, steady.

"We want to help you any way that we can, but the boys just don't want in on this one," he said, as if appealing now to Wilkens's more affable nature.

"Fair enough. C'mon, boys," Wilkens all but whispered to Meese and me. "There ain't much of this orange left to squeeze." And they sort of edged me along with them back toward our bay. I was now getting angry. These guys had a duty, just like the rest of us. They were soldiers. But mostly I was angry at myself. I had carelessly chosen a word that would put any man on the defensive.

"I thought you were going to get your nose broke, Handy." Wilkens laughed.

"I was only going to say that if he was afraid we'd botch the project, we could swap bays with him."

"Handy, my daddy always told me to stay away from sentences that when sawed in two would mean different things. Hell, you boys were starting to get at it. Anyway, let's sit tight. I got a feeling about old Wolf.

Maybe he had to speak for the others, but he didn't like it none. I bet it's going to eat at him a little. And some of the others, too. Let's just let it ride for a little bit." Then he laughed and poked me in the ribs.

THERE WAS A LIKABLE TEXAN IN our barracks named Gutierrez, who had been asked to start a Spanish class. The White House was trying to encourage men to keep busy with their minds as well as their bodies. He had agreed but was worried that not enough kriegies would show up. Meese, Sac and I, along with a few others, promised him we would come to "class." The first day, sitting cross-legged out in the compound, I was handed a small blue workbook and a pencil.

"For writing vocabulary words," said Gutierrez, as if to say "and not for anything else." I dutifully wrote the words he gave us in that first class—"*casa*" and "*caballo*" and others laid neatly on the front page, but I lasted only two or three classes before the demands of the tunnel project, still early but mounting, became too much. Gutierrez let me keep my workbook (you were supposed to give it back), as I thought it might be useful to me later. One evening, I opened it and on the back page wrote down a thought that had come to me earlier that day. The audacity of the letters, of seeing a thought written up for future use, filled me with a long lost joy. The day's best ideas need no longer slip away. In years past I'd found that getting those ideas on paper gave my life a missing dimension. It made concerns of the moment give way to the long view. What was really important—what I should really be trying to do—would come to the fore. But the little notebook had few pages and if written in every day would soon give out. So I had to settle on a once-a-month entry and chose the eleventh, the day we were shot down. Each eleventh now said to me, "You were given a gift; what are you doing about it?" The eleventh became my ritual day of retreat and reflection, a day for dusting off the diminutive blue notebook and writing in it with the ever-smaller stub of Gutierrez's pencil. It drew on shorthand daily notes now scratched on scraps of cardboard from our parcels. None of the notes, though—none of the entries—could risk being read by the Germans. There could be no talk of the tunnel, of Wilkens and his tools or the growing admiration I had for Meese and his work with our tunnel team.

IN KEEPING WITH SHATTUCK'S RULES, WE kept 32A pretty clean, and before long guys were bragging it was the cleanest barracks in the whole American camp. I had to sweep the floor in the bays and the center corridor with a twig broom, a bundle of little tree and bush branches tightly bound together by wire, and it reminded me of the broom made by Hansel and Gretel's father. It was an ingenious and effective little broom with a diameter of about four inches at the bound handle and a length of between four down to two feet, depending on how much use the broom had already been given. There was plenty to sweep each day. Springtime mud may have been thick, but summer dirt was relentless, a film of grit always gathering. After the passing storms, men would track in mud that layered on so quickly that when it dried, we would pry it up off the floor in chunks, "rearranging the turf," Sanford said. Somebody repeated the remark of a kriegie who had said that if they gave him "a goddamn Missouri mule and a plow," he'd grow turnips in the center aisle.

THE TALL MAN WITH THE RACCOON eyes was sitting on his bunk as if he were asleep. I decided to speak with him since we had not yet exchanged a word.

"Hey," I said. "My name's Handy."

"I'm Young," he answered warily. He didn't move.

"Where you from?"

A yell came up from the front end of the barracks. "Rat! Rat! Holy shit! Big as a house! Where the hell did he come from? Get him! Get him!" The large rat had appeared out of nowhere, and it perched for a moment right out in the middle of the corridor between the front two bays. It had probably come through the doorway left open on this warm spring day. We had no rats in 32A and liked to believe we were the only barracks in camp without them. But when I turned to see what all the fuss was about, I was staring at the biggest rat I'd ever seen. The thought struck me that it could have eaten Kitta, my grandmother's small Manx cat, for a midmorning snack.

Up front, the hue and cry rose to a crescendo: "Get your brooms! Kill the bastard! Move your ass!" The chase, the campaign to get the rat, was fast building up a head of steam. All the big guy had to do, figuratively, was to say "Oops, sorry," turn around and rocket out the door he had just come in. But in the pressure of the moment he came up with a different idea: make a run for the washroom door at the other end—nearly half a football field away. For us it was a great decision; he gave our hard-pressed men the time of their lives. Now he was one of Notre Dame's four horsemen making a last-minute broken-field run— a zigzag through the opposing team's defense entirely on his own. Our guys pulled together all their latent athletic abilities as they flailed at him with their twig brooms, rifled tin cans at him, even swung with chairs. But to the surprise of all of us, the rat proved a broken-field runner of unbelievable ability; he made it all the way down to the washroom door—weaving his way through those ranks of athletes—without taking a single hit. There were muffled cheers, including mine, as his tail disappeared into the washroom.

Barrackswide, it was a lark; we had been handed a rare lift by this encounter with the talented rat. It was the excitement, however brief, that he generated for us; it was the rest of the day opportunity he gave us to razz buddies about failed blows: "Hey, Johnson, are ya blind—ya missed him by a mile!" "Get yer eyes checked, Knight; ya damned near hit me, not the rat!" "Polanski, whad ya say yer position was on yer sister's hockey team?" The rat had handed us a great day—a carnival day; not until the next morning did we get back to the business of survival. As for Red Grange, we learned that he exited the washroom's back door into Barracks 32B, where—now well up to speed—he made a straight run down its corridor and out to freedom without a blow being swung at him.

Walking back to my bunk I saw Young still sitting there, his eyes hooded in shadows. He had not moved at all. I wondered about him. Later that night before curfew I walked with Meese along the edge of the compound.

"What do you know about Young?" I asked him.

"Not much, nothing really. He keeps to himself in a big way. The guys don't like him much. They don't trust him, either."

"Why? What did he do?"

"Young doesn't ask anything of anyone, and sometimes guys who stand back aren't very well liked."

"Well, a guy shouldn't be made to pay for minding his own business."

"In a place like this, Handy, guys who mind their own business so much they seem unfriendly always pay a steep price." It seemed wrong to me, and it occurred to me that my first instinct was to like him.

"That was some rat," I said, changing the subject quickly. The conversation felt particularly awkward for me. I had enough of the self-reliant loner in me to be wary.

Meese smiled. "Yes indeed. He did us all a power of good today."

And of course Meese was right. Had that rat been a good man imprisoned, by some magic curse, in the rodent's body—his humanity lost till he did some great good deed—he could hardly have chosen a better one.

While walking with Meese I caught sight of Wilkens and Wolf strolling along the warning wire. Wilkens was talking and Wolf's head was nodding thoughtfully. I could see the length of Wilkens's arms from a hundred yards, and his hands looked like flags. A shy man until he spoke, Wilkens had a voice that conveyed great goodwill and a kind of lightness. I was half a compound away, but I could imagine the sound of his soothing chuckle. I wondered what he was talking about. Later that night, I found out. He came to my bunk.

"Handy, good work. You got that kriegie thinking and talking with his crew. I think they're willing to let us dig the tunnel there."

I was dumbstruck and knew I didn't have a thing to do with his changing his mind. Wilkens saw my look of surprise.

"You know how it goes. Most folks want to help. They just need a little time to soak it all in. We'll go see them and hear what they have to say . . . And Handy," said Wilkens like a playful conspirator, "let's never mention that little debate again, right? You did well, but let's let 'em up real easy."

When we returned to the front bay, Wolf was leaning against the shuttered window. He never looked at me but spoke casually as if the project were entirely his own. "Ideally, you want the hatch to be as easy and accessible as possible, but the Jerries will be checking the floors like bloodhounds. So we looked at putting the hatch under the bunk. We knew that sliding these bunks was a nonstarter. They're heavy, and the Jerries might come around when the bunk was poking into the aisle or out of place. It can't be done. Then we realized we didn't have to move them at all. We'll just take up the slats from the lower bunk when you want to get in there to work. You'll have about four feet of clearance; that should be enough." He was quiet for a moment. "If we lay that hatch down there and bevel it like a dream and cover it with just enough dirt to make the cracks go away . . . "

Meese nodded thoughtfully. "We could do that. Wilkens?"

Wilkens pulled back the slats, climbed into the bunk and squatted over the floor. He brushed the dirt off the floorboards. It was a patchwork of boards, each a different length and color. "The lines of the hatch running north and south will be easy enough," he said, running his long finger the length of the boards. "It's the east-west lines that'll cause us the trouble." He crawled around for a moment like a blind man, his hands groping along the boards, and then sat up on his knees. "Here," he said, pointing to roughly a two-foot-square space. "Right here. There's a natural length we can cross without looking too obvious. They're not likely to notice, and if the dirt is dirty enough . . . ," he said, as if thinking aloud. "Yessir, this dog'll hunt. And Meese, you and your guys gotta bevel her so she's no wider than a hair!"

"We'll keep it dirty enough," said a kriegie I had never seen before.

"But not too dirty," said Wolf. "Let's not get too clever."

"Right," said the first one. Then Wolf paused and pushed the dirt about with his boot. He turned to me and said evenly, "You know what you're going to find under those boards?"

"Not yet," I said, remembering Meese's comments about worrying in advance. "We'll find out once we pry those boards up."

"Well, that's it then," said Wolf, as if bringing a meeting to an end. "I guess you boys are under way. Good luck." And with that, everyone dispersed.

That night I heard Wilkens talking to Meese.

"There's a barrel halfway down the fence side of the barracks. You get me the upper hoop that wraps around that barrel. It's iron and it'll make a pretty little saw."

"Won't the barrel split when we pull it off?"

"Naw, those barrels are old enough that they have swelled up. The barrel will hold just fine. You ought to be able to wriggle that top hoop right off. Be careful, though, don't let anybody bend it or break it. It may be old, but handled right, it'll do the trick."

"OK then, you'll get your iron," said Meese, as if taking an order from a customer.

"And you're gonna have to get the guys to give me every tin can they can get their hands on. Don't let anyone throw anything away. They don't need to know what I might do with it. They don't need to do my thinking for me, they just got to figure that if it's made of metal of any kind, it belongs to me. OK?"

"OK," answered Meese.

It was quiet. The breathing of men grew longer, slower. The lights passed over the shutters. I thought for a moment that I was the only one awake in the bay until I heard Wilkens's voice again, as if he were still in midconversation.

"I'm gonna need a file," Wilkens said. "A good one, though it doesn't have to be very big. How do we get that?"

Someone spoke up, an unfamiliar voice, maybe not even in our bay. "There's a guy in 32B who told me he knows an old kriegie who trades for all kinds of things. They say he gets incredible stuff from the Jerries with cigarettes and D-bars. You tell him what you need, he'll tell you what it costs and then he'll go and get it."

"Be careful," said Meese. "But see if you can get him to get us a file."

"You betcha," said the voice.

Several minutes later Wilkens spoke again. "Thanks, Gene," he said very quietly. It was the first time I had heard anyone use anyone's first name since we had been in the barracks. Meese didn't answer. Likely he was already fast asleep.

The next morning was overcast and drizzling. At roll call everyone came out with attitude. There were mock arguments, jostling, and we all moved so slowly that the guards grew impatient. They shouted and threatened the prisoners, who moved into lines laconically saying, "Yeah, yeah." It wasn't until one or the other of the guards showed a willingness to butt someone into line that we moved with any purpose. The plan after roll call was to use maybe a dozen guys and roughhouse our way over to where the barrel was standing. While we were messing around the barrel, someone on the inside of the group just wriggled the hoop right off it. Wilkens was right. The iron hoop came off without any effort. The wood had swelled tight. Later, Wilkens looked at the hoop like a chef regarding fresh produce: "Nice, fellas, nice. This'll do just fine." And then he walked away from us all, turning the hoop over and over in his large hands. As we watched him, it occurred to us all that our escape from Stalag 17 had really begun.

PART II

SUMMER

> *The poetry of Earth is never dead.*
> *When all the birds are faint with the hot sun . . .*
>
> —JOHN KEATS

WILKENS SAT ON the far-right bottom bunk. He had insisted that the lower bunk be set aside for his own use and had turned it into a compact workshop. Covered by cardboard, his workshop bunk was spread with bits of wire, odd-shaped scraps of metal, string of all lengths and pieces of wood. The barracks wall at the far end of his workspace acted as a table gone vertical where he could measure and cut. The level workspace in the double bunk began as just the slats to support a palliasse, but he had skillfully covered the slats with cardboard available from empty Red Cross parcels, tying the pieces together with tin binders he had designed and cut from flattened cans. Around him men kept watch and did whatever necessary to mask his work as it progressed. Sometimes they would sing; other times kriegies made noisy music while he beat the tin. They had a system when the Germans were coming of picking up the whole workspace in one swift move and neatly hiding it on the floor underneath. Wilkens was back in his workshop all the time. Soon after we had scored the hoop, I watched him fingering it carefully.

"How are you going to make what you need?" I asked.

He acted as if he had not heard me, as if he were still finishing a conversation begun long before I had arrived.

"Never make anything," he said absently, "until you can see it first. Then once you can see it, go back to the beginning and imagine every step needed to make it. If you can't see the tool and build it in your head from start to finish, you'll waste good material and valuable time." Rolling the hoop in his large hands he continued to speak softly, as if to himself.

"I don't need a long saw, but when I get that file I'll have to pay some attention to the teeth. It will have to be a crosscut. A ripsaw will make too much of a damned mess." He looked up and saw me, as if for the first time.

"Is your father still alive, Handy?"

"Yeah, he is."

"Well, you're lucky. Mine isn't. He died right before I enlisted."

"I'm sorry," I said.

"Yeah, me too." He held a coiled wire up and seemed to be measuring it with his eyes, his head cocked like a bird's. "My father was a big man. Strong. Smart, too. We used to go to my granddaddy's farm, a real spread with apple trees that rolled all the way to the horizon. We'd work all day picking apples, baskets of them. I'd say, 'Don't Granddaddy have folks to pick these apples?' and my father would say, 'Sure he does, but we are here first, picking the best ones for your momma.' She made the tastiest things from apples: jellies, jams, applesauce, apple butter. Anyway, one time I remember he found what looked like a pair of old rusted pliers in the grass, except these pliers had rounded balls on the ends. He asked me what they were and I said pliers, and he said, 'You ever seen pliers like these?' and I sure hadn't. He said, 'Look at it, boy. What are they for?' And for the longest time I couldn't figure it out. I kept guessing, and each guess made my old man laugh like I'd said the stupidest thing he had ever heard. 'Course, he never *said* it was stupid, I suppose he just laughed like that to keep me thinking. He said, 'Look at the balls on the ends. Why are those ends rounded? Every part of a tool's design is practical—no matter how fancy it might look to you and me—everything is made to help the fella using that tool.' He began opening and closing the pliers, and I watched those two rounded ends click together. Before long I was thinking about those rounded ends and where they might go and how somebody's life might be made easier by using them."

"What was the tool?" I asked.

A smile unfurled over his craggy face. "It was a pair of nose pliers. Those rounded balls fit into the ox's nose and you owned that poor sucker. I remember thinking that I could get my little brother to go wherever I wanted with those pliers. Damned if my daddy didn't get me thinking. I spent the rest of that day thinking about how tools could make my life easier. By the end of the day, when we had all these bushel baskets ready for the truck, I told my daddy about a conveyor belt we could build to haul those baskets for us. I told him where the engine would go and how you'd shape the baskets so they could be tipped into the bed of the truck. My daddy listened, asked a few questions and then said: 'From nose pliers to conveyor belts, you've come a long way, son.' I was pretty pleased until he added: 'But until you build that belt of yours, it's still up to us to haul these apples home.' We carried those apples until long after the stars had come out. But you know, I got so used to considering how things got made that I didn't never look at tools and machinery the same way again."

"Lucky for us," I said.

"Yeah, well, maybe so," he said, peering at the iron again. I knew our conversation was over. He was busy building his saw.

SPRING NEVER REALLY CAME INTO STALAG 17 with us. It stayed up on that hillside, leaving us to a hard, airless Austrian summer. On most hot mornings, men would fall out after roll call and spread over the compound, their thinning white bodies growing red too quickly. In the gathering swelter, we began to learn more about what surviving in Stalag 17 would require of us.

The first and understandable obsession of all prisoners was food. We thought about it all the time and talked about it almost as much. The lack of food was already taking a slow, relentless toll on our bodies. First, familiar to anyone who skips a few meals, was the onset of hunger pangs. These came early, while we were still on the shuttle from the fields in which we had landed to Stalag 17. Once in camp, however, when the adrenaline of getting there had worn off, the pangs turned to the kind of pain that made you want to sit or lie down. In time, our bodies began to understand that hunger was to be our ever-present companion. The meals, welcome though they were, offered little beyond a faintly comforting, watery warmth, so our bodies went to work, scaling back the needs, living off less. Though talking about, describing and dreaming of food was a passionate pastime, our morale was best served by learning how well we could do without it. I knew little about nutrition (few of us did) or my own physiology. I knew only a primitive instinct to seek whatever nutrition I could find, and quickly learned that as long as I could sift through my murky water to find a shard of potato or turnip, I could survive. The root vegetables would keep me alive, while the bread would give my teeth a needed workout. I lost weight, all of us did, but not to the degree that I ever thought I was going to starve to death.

The source of our health, even our very survival, was the Red Cross parcel. From the moment the first ones arrived, they became our single greatest source of food and nutrition. Those parcels (arriving first weekly, then monthly before stopping altogether by late fall) came in something like an oversized shoe box and were filled with scarce and prized items: Spam, powdered milk, oleomargarine, corned beef, coffee, D-bars, raisins (or prunes), salt and pepper, vitamins, liver pâté, salmon (sometimes), processed cheese, soap, biscuits, cigarettes, lump sugar and various kinds of jam.

The old kriegies had established a workable system of barter based on the contents of the Red Cross parcel, and it worked for us as well. The camp's economy was founded on three items: canned goods, D-bars and cigarettes. The greatest item of value, the veritable gold standard (so rare I never actually had one), was a sealed can of Spam or meat. The guards routinely stabbed all cans to ensure their immediate use. They did not want prisoners storing food for escapes. The occasional can of meat that escaped the bayonet commanded the most astonishing value and trumped every other item.

The base currency for trading among ourselves was the chocolate D-bar. This was something like the Baker's chocolate one would buy at the grocery, a sort of heavy-duty chocolate for cooking. Scored to be easily broken apart into six pieces, the D-bar could be priced down to the "sixth of a D-bar." Anything that could be bought or sold between us—from bars of soap, bread and bowls of soup to Red Cross items, handmade items, blankets and caps—was meticulously priced in whole or fractional D-bars. A bar of soap might cost a sixth of a D-bar, a pack of cigarettes a D-bar and a half, the day-to-day price dependent on supply and demand. I never actually saw anyone *eat* a D-bar, though I suppose there were some instances where it was done. The D-bar would grow white with age, but you hung on to it as carefully as you had cash, back in the life that seemed, with every passing day, more of a dream than a life.

As for the cigarettes—the Chesterfields, Camels and Old Golds— they were also of immense value, though given the love some had of smoking, a tempting currency to spend on oneself. I had resolved to quit smoking the occasional cigarette and use my allocation for trading. Poker games and outrageous wagers (the dangerous kind that only bored men can compose) depended mostly on cigarettes. Soon enough, men looking to avoid anything that would cost them cigarettes and offer no value in return took up games like canasta and bridge. The price of cigarettes in D-bar terms fluctuated according to the oldest principles of supply and demand. When we were no longer getting Red

Cross parcels by the end of the summer, the cost of a carton of cigarettes in terms of the D-bar shot up. When we first arrived, for example, a packet of cigarettes could be bought for a single D-bar. Throughout the year, the price rose to as many as fifteen D-bars.

We soon learned from the old kriegies that the most enthusiastic consumers of American tobacco were the German guards. They were often willing to trade items of significant value to us for a coveted pack of smokes. Their cigarettes were sweet-smelling and foul-tasting, possessing very little tobacco. I was always surprised to see those guards, guns slung over their shoulders, bending over to scavenge discarded American butts like hobos. In the first weeks after the Red Cross parcels arrived and cigarettes were common, guards would pace the outside of the barracks in the dark waiting for the tossed cigarette out the window. It amazed me that for the few months that we had Red Cross parcels shipped to us, they would let pass into the camp the very items they themselves would so desperately trade for later. I never had the savvy to trade with the guards, nor did anyone in our barracks that I knew of, but many of the old kriegies did a booming business.

The other passionate activity was washing yourself and your clothes. It was ritualistic and a matter of the most personal routine. If you had Lux or Ivory from the Red Cross parcel, you kept it carefully. The Germans sometimes gave us yellow chunks of German soap, but its quality was poor. Some men washed as they went, keeping their washings small and immediate. Others, like me, often let enough time go by that everything we had needed to be washed. The cold water generally ran in the washrooms about four hours a day, and in the summer men would hang their clothes outside the bay window or even on the fence that ran between us and the compound to our east. When winter came, the older kriegies told us, there would be almost no washing of bodies or clothes. It would be too cold and there would be no warmth for drying. If something was washed out of necessity, it hung over the side of a bunk toward the center aisle. In the dead of winter, they said, the barracks looked like Brooklyn on a summer day.

· · ·

SEVERAL DAYS LATER WILKENS CAME INTO the bay twirling a file in his hands like a knife blade. In his other hand he held a saw. "Teeth as sharp and eager as a shark's," he said with a grin. He was right. It had a wooden handle with a blade wired to it and was small enough to work in a tight space. He tossed it to Meese. "Don't say I never did nothing for you," he chuckled. Meese nodded and rolled the saw over in his hands. I was beginning to understand what Shattuck had meant. All these men, these new kriegies, were bringing their talents one after the other, just as he had predicted.

Meese and his carpentry team were going to design and build the barracks floor hatch and the second one to cap the tunnel shaft. He and Tony Sac and a few others thought it through right there at the daily bay meeting. We took our cue from Meese's no-nonsense approach. The carpentry plan settled on, we got the go-ahead from Wolf and the men in his bay to start work on the tunnel's entrance in their bay. Like all barracks floors, this piece under the bunk was a mixture of long and short boards, all secondhand, weathered lumber. Meese then went to work with Wilkens's saw and made two beveled-edge cuts that were masterpieces. He carefully nailed cross braces to the back of the two boards, using some wood we'd traded for in 32B with nails pulled from the barracks sheathing. Meanwhile, Wolf and his team protected us by standing around the outer bay and carrying on a lively conversation. Later they swept enough dry mud under the bunk to make the hairline bevel cuts invisible.

The next morning at the daily meeting, we congratulated Meese and Wilkens on their floor hatch. Each of us had stopped to look at it. We were amazed at the hairline saw cuts and how the lightly spread layer of dirt made the hatch invisible. The men in Wolf's bay pointed with pride to the knothole we could use to pull up the hatch. The next step was building the cover and underlying frame for the tunnel's seven-foot vertical shaft. We wanted to have the depth as shallow as possible so as to cut to the bone the amount of earth we'd have to dig up each time we went down to the shaft cover. We thought six inches would be a safe depth, but Tony Sac argued convincingly that Gestapo dogs might very well detect so shallow a cover. He suggested twelve inches, and we knew he was right. Every one of us was eager to be part of that first crew to start the dig and get the tunnel under way, but after talking it over we decided that the crew would consist of Tony Sac, Kozikowski and me. Our medium builds figured into the decision.

We were to start the next morning, but when I went that afternoon to check our plan with Wolf's bay, I found Thompson working on the underside of the hatch. It was upside down in the middle of the bay. I asked him what he was doing. He said that Meese had told him to add a third cross brace. Taking a look at the back of the hatch, I thought that two were enough; the more braces, the more chance the hatch might be spotted from below by a guard hunting for tunnels. I asked him to stop, put the hatch back in place, and said I would talk to Meese. Moments later, Meese caught up to me in our bay and said, "I need to talk with you, let's go outside." He sounded stern, upset. A light rain was falling. Once outside, he looked me in the eye and said, "Handy, I didn't want to say this in the barracks, but you're a very inexperienced manager. Let me tell you something I see you don't know. When you're in charge of something and you give someone a job to do, don't take it away from him. *Do not take it away from him.* You've given me this carpentry job; let me do it. OK?"

"OK," I said, stung. He turned and walked away. That night after the hanging bulb winked out, I lay in the darkness and thought about the clash with Meese. Still smarting, I wondered whether I should have said at least something in my defense. Of course I knew that overall he was right. But if I was overzealous, wasn't it in the best interest of the project? Couldn't interference be justified if the interference had merit? I considered the times I'd left jobs in the care of others who, as it turned out, did not take the work as seriously as I had. I remembered the day we were shot down. After our briefing, we'd gone out into the gray drizzle to our bomber. It was not the B-24 we had first been given back in Herrington, Kansas, a beauty that we were certain would last us the rest of the war. Making use of the thirty-day layover in Trinidad, we had made many improvements to that plane, customizing it in little ways to our own particular preferences. Before we arrived in England, however, the Eighth Air Force changed procedures for newly arrived bomb groups: crews were to fly whatever plane was available on the morning of the mission. Aircrew deaths and crashed planes had taught headquarters to make bombers and crews interchangeable.

The plane we were sent to in the gray drizzle of that morning was a disaster. Other than for loading the bombs for that day's mission, it had not been touched at all since its return from combat the day before. I knew something about the crew chief responsible for its maintenance. He had a great opinion of his abilities and fancied himself something of a cowboy (with boots and swagger to match). Although an experienced ground mechanic, he took every opportunity to fly in the place of any crewman unable to fly on a given day. Later, often at the poker table, he would claim he'd shot down an unbelievable number of German planes. Perhaps he had, but his real job was to get these planes ready to fly. A ground crewman on an adjacent plane saw our plight and told me that our crew chief had played cards all night and perhaps was still at it. We were to take off in about twenty minutes. I could see that the plane hadn't been refueled, its guns hadn't been checked, the spent fifty-caliber shells from its last mission were still scattered all over the interior. I wondered for an instant how much more might be wrong with this plane—damage that could only be picked up in the standard overnight inspection that hadn't happened. I talked with Tedrowe. We had grounds to have the crew chief court-martialed and refuse to accept the plane, but this was war, and anyway the cowboy was now walking toward us across the tarmac. We'd go forward, regardless. I told him what I wanted done. Later he reported to me that all the jobs were completed and I took his word for it; engines firing, we had to pull out right then to get in line for takeoff. Once in flight, I learned otherwise. Guns jammed, equipment was not where it belonged, our fuel gauges had not been drained—an order I'd given him with special emphasis. I lay there and steamed awhile over that memory before circling back to Meese. He was right. Getting things *done* right was only as solid as one's ability to delegate to another who was reliable and competent. Meese was competent; the crew chief back in England wasn't. Obviously I wasn't as good as I should be about telling the difference. Only then did I consider that he had ripped me in a voice no one else could hear, as if his advice were for me and me alone. Hurt as I was by the sharpness of his words, I appreciated the way he delivered his management lesson. There would be plenty of time to use what he had just taught me, and I was determined to learn from it.

The next morning, Tony Sac, Kozikowski and I were in our bay getting ready for the tunnel shaft dig. I'd taken them both up to Wolf's bay earlier to show them the hatch, or what could be seen of it.

"Man," said Tony Sac, catching Meese's eye as he came in, "your hatch is aces. We got ourselves a tunnel."

"Not by a long shot," laughed Meese. "But we sure as hell have a floor hatch, and that's a start."

We went back to our preparations and were talking about ideas for digging when Wilkens came in with something in his hand. He wore that expectant grin on his face we had all come to depend on. Men were beginning to look at him with smiles of their own, as if saying to themselves: what have you got for us now?

"Well, now, fellas," he said giddily. "I made you some shovels, hot off the line." He held a pair of Klim cans, the tins of powdered milk that came in Red Cross parcels. These cans, slightly oversized, were wide-mouthed and strong. He had sharpened their edges with his file. Perfect for digging.

We opened the floor hatch, screened from view by our new teammates in Wolf's bay. The headroom under the far bunk was tight, but it worked for us. We surveyed the dirt below. It was about a foot below the floorboards and looked forbidding. Could it be too claylike, too full of stones? Without ceremony or pause, we went to work. I went down to be the mole below while Tony Sac and Koz dug down from above. We wanted the shaft big enough to handle heavyset diggers and had settled on a twenty-inch square. That gave us twenty-eight inches on the diagonal; even the heftiest of diggers could squeeze in. With a rough-hewn ruler Wilkens had made for us, I measured the square on the ground below the hatch and marked it out with my fingernails.

From up above Tony Sac dug in with the "Wilkens shovel." It sunk cleanly into the earth and he brought up a Klim can full of light-bodied, stoneless dirt. What a *gift*. We were under way. Working inside the square, the two diggers took turns and reached farther and farther down through the floor hatch as their excavation deepened. We got to our planned twelve-inch depth far sooner than we'd believed possible. About four cubic feet of earth had been pulled up by them and heaped by me in piles that left room for Meese and Wilkens to later work below the floor, their bellies on the ground, to build a square wood frame and set it into the earth at the proper depth. After that they built a wood cover to cap the frame and hold the surface earth that was dug out each time the shaft was opened. The ground below our floor hatch would always have to be level and look normal when the shaft was shut down.

We had to keep Wolf's bay as clear of our guys as possible, so after digging the first foot of the shaft, Tony Sac, Koz and I went back to our bay and cleaned up. The team had already figured that any signs of dirt on a crew member's body that could catch a guard's eye would prove disastrous. (Clothes weren't a problem—we had quickly learned to dig in our shorts.) Meanwhile Meese and several of the carpentry team went up to Wolf's bay and began building the frame for the shaft cover. Later, Meese came back into our bay and slumped down next to me on the lower bunk. I was digging dirt out from under my nails.

"I'll let these guys work out the details. They know what they're doing," he said with a sigh. He was tired.

"Where did they get the wood for the shaft frame?" I asked.

"I asked Joseph to climb up into the attic space under the barracks' gabled roof," replied Meese with satisfied pleasure. "He confirmed that there was excess bracing. He took along Sanford and some of Wilkens's tools. He said there was more wood up there than the roof needed. When winter comes," he chuckled, "we may learn that the Nazis are better architects than we thought. Anyway, we're going to need more wood for tunnel bracing—once we get down the shaft and head for the sewer pipe—so I got some kriegies from other bays to hunt down wood in every possible place. They've already come up with several useful-looking pieces."

"Where are they storing the wood?"

"Around. I'm not sure. Likely under their bottom bunks and perhaps . . ."

Someone shouted "Jerries coming!" Everybody scrambled into action. Meese put a hand on my knee. "Don't move." Men grabbed brooms, leapt into bunks, stuffed hand tools into the middle of the palliasses. In seconds it was a casual scene. Meese and I stayed sitting on the bunks. Two Wehrmacht guards came in followed by an unusually tall, slender officer with a stiff right leg. He was Luftwaffe, impressively dressed in his crisp blue tunic. He had an intelligent confidence, a sculptured head and unusually blue penetrating eyes. He surveyed everything around him with a king's ease. As yet I'd seen no officers or guards who possessed such a dignity. Perhaps, I thought, this is the best that Germany has to offer. So what is he doing limping along in Stalag 17?

"As you were," he said to us in impeccable English, though we had barely acknowledged his arrival. "So," he said, casually surveying Dailey, who leaned against the bunk where, an instant before, he had thrust Wilkens's saw under the palliasse. "Another lazy day in camp, yes?" The Wehrmacht guard behind him, a short, stocky man with a massive, square head, saw Meese and me sitting against the wall. He gestured to us to get up and shouted, *"Raus!"* Meese got up slowly and I even slower. I couldn't resist a mocking smile. The guard moved toward me in anger, but as he came forward, the elegant officer shifted ever so slightly to block his path.

"You men are not so used to obedience, I think," he said in a voice almost kind. "You have not learned what makes an army successful. Perhaps you will learn such things while you are with us in Stalag 17. You will have time to learn many things here. It is never too late to learn."

"We ain't doin' no learning in this place except how to try and stay alive," said Beast in a voice perched between observation and defiance. The square-headed guard again tried to push his way forward, growing more agitated, and the Luftwaffe officer again blocked his path, more forcibly this time. He looked at Beast and smiled.

"We are both airmen. I was a pilot and paid for the honor with my leg. You pay as prisoners, but we are both alive. Many of our comrades are not. So we must both learn how to live on the ground." No one spoke. It was the first time I had heard a German speak of himself. It may have been the first time in my war that I'd seen a German soldier as more human being than enemy. I liked him immediately, and that somewhat bothered me.

"I am looking for Shattuck," he said after watching us all for a moment.

"Here I am," said Shattuck, strolling down the center aisle of the barracks. "Welcome to Barracks 32A. Why don't you come this way to my office?" Shattuck's posture was erect but informal, and I almost expected him to offer to shake hands. The respectful but unmilitary bearing was not lost on the Luftwaffe pilot, who understood the nuance of the attitude and its theater. His eyes narrowed but he said nothing, and they walked to Shattuck's bay.

"That Shattuck's the greatest," whispered somebody as we all began to disperse.

"That Luftwaffe guy, he doesn't seem half bad really," someone added.

"He's a pilot, give him that," answered another.

"Hey, Handy," whispered Kozikowski in my ear as we walked down the aisle. "Ol' Max has his eye on you." I looked back and the guard with the square head was glaring at me. *Careful,* I thought. *He could be trouble.*

SOON ENOUGH, MEESE AND HIS CARPENTRY team had done the job. The shaft frame was in, complete with a snug cover that set over it so that we could seal the tunnel entrance and cover it over with earth that we'd dug up at the outset. That dirt was important. You had to fill the hole and rough out the dirt so that the guards who looked in under the barracks with their torchlights would see only leveled earth. We knew from the start that the key to success would be getting out of the tunnel fast, dropping the cover, spreading the earth around, closing the hatch and looking utterly bored.

We started to dig down, and it took a lot of time. There were many days when you couldn't dig at all for one reason or another. The guards might have been hanging around, the ferrets could have been on the loose. (I never saw the ferrets myself, though guys talked of them like goblins and bogeymen, never seen but always lurking nearby.) There were also activities that prevented us from being able to dig at the right time or to dispose of the earth. We were starting to dig large quantities of earth. If we had once been able to get rid of the earth as quickly as diggers sent it up, that was no longer the case. We dug during the hours that the water was available so that we could get that earth immediately out of there, but after the water began to be shut off at night, there was a limit to how often the tubs could be used. With unplanned roll calls keeping us occupied, the guards would case the barracks, so we could ill afford to leave any trace of dirt beyond the normal floor layer the guards had come to expect from us.

We got our shaft down about seven feet deep—enough to allow us to consider starting the tunnel along its horizontal path. We had planned to have a three-foot ceiling that left a full four feet of ground above us. Meese went down into the shaft and was gone for a while. We all waited in the bay above, expectant. It was very quiet. Then up his head came. He climbed out and smiled at us. Handing me a Klim can he said, "Go west, young man," and everybody whooped. I went down and started digging west toward the sewer line and, hopefully, toward freedom.

I NOTICED THAT EACH MORNING AFTER roll call, the blond kid with the neck wound would not return to his bunk. He stayed in that bunk most days and nights but never after the morning roll call. One morning I followed him as he wandered between the barracks, across the compound and around behind the latrines. Coming around the corner, I saw him sitting cross-legged in the dirt. He stayed there for some time before walking back to 32A. After I was certain he was gone, I found the source of his pilgrimage: a small tuft of grass. I was startled; it was the only grass I had seen in the compound. The blades were tough and sparse, but they were long enough to catch the wind and shimmer green. An insect might have found a momentary home there, an oasis in this vast flat of mud. Squatting down, I could smell the tang of summer in that grass. I decided to keep his secret, and soon enough, I was to make visits of my own.

THE DIGGING BEGAN IN EARNEST, AND though we didn't have a timetable or deadline, we worked as often as was practical. Days passed. June gave way to July. The Fourth brought some cheerless talk of hot dogs and barbecues among the kriegies, but not much else. It was hot outside and the tunnel was a welcome cool for me. The practical issues were increasing. We were bringing up an immense amount of dirt that in the beginning was easy enough to pass up in cartons. Soon, however, it required another solution because the digging was going more smoothly than anticipated.

"You're going to need a rope and a bucket," said Wilkens. "The bucket is easy as pie, but the rope is gonna take a bit more time." We were gathered around him one evening.

"Here's what we're going to do. I want you to scour the camp for every little thing you can find. Don't crawl around on your hands and knees and make a big production out of it, but when you're walking, always look down at the ground. There's not much else to look at, so it's not costing you anything. I want everything you can find. Just bring it back to me. Any damn thing, no matter how small or useless, you bring it back to me. You let me decide if it's got any value. OK?"

In the following days we learned that the ground was filled with those little treasures: pieces of wood and metal, bits of string, scraps of paper, foil and cloth. We walked the compound with determination and focus. I developed a sixth sense and made a game out of predicting where I was likely to find stray items. Everyone had their favorite haunts, but mine was along the main road that passed through the American compound. Along its treasure-strewn banks, I found a thimble, a coil of copper ("Oh, now, Handy, that's a thing of beauty," said Wilkens), two buttons, several pieces of ceramic, a few coins, a strip of metal, a good deal of wire and twine. I never found anything as notable as the guy who came to Wilkens with his hands behind his back, a look of great satisfaction on his face.

"Want to see what I found by the warning wire?" he said proudly, opening his hand to show four rusty, but straight, sixteen-penny nails. Everybody gathered round like admirers of a hard-won trophy. We envied him like boys who had placed second.

Wilkens received everything we could find with surprise and enormous pleasure, as if each item were precisely what he had been looking for, but it was the tin cans he sought with a greedy enthusiasm. He gathered them up and assessed them like a seasoned buyer at a flea market. We weren't exactly certain what it was in these cans he was looking for, but we brought them to him all the same. One afternoon, a kriegie came to Wilkens with an item that caught the eyes of everyone on the tunnel project.

"I got something for you," said the kriegie. "They say you're the guy who can use stuff like this." He held up a broken hoe. The metal was bent but intact, the handle long enough to still use. It was a real prize. I looked at Wilkens with big eyes.

Wilkens looked at the hoe and then at him. "What would I do with that?"

"I'm from 32B. A guy in my bay told me to come over here and show it to you."

"Well," said Wilkens, still not taking the hoe from the man's hand. "It sure would be a beauty for gardening."

"Yeah, well, I found it by the showers. It's yours for five D-bars."

Wilkens's smile faded and he looked at the man blankly. He was not one for anger or ill feeling, but I recognized the shadow that passed across his face.

"You're from 32B, are you?" he asked coldly.

"Like I said. They call me Boxer. You want the hoe or not?"

"Well, Boxer, maybe you should take up gardening and feed your friends in the bay. That's a mighty nice hoe." Wilkens looked away.

"Call it three D-bars," said the kriegie, looking bewildered. "And we're even."

"Go dig your garden," answered Wilkens softly.

"Fuck you," said Boxer, tossing the hoe onto Wilkens's palliasse and walking away. Wilkens grinned.

"Dang, boys, this will come in handy," he said, winking at me.

AT NIGHT, AFTER THE ELECTRICITY TO the lightbulb was cut off, casual conversation would continue between bunkmates. Before long, a theme might emerge that would draw in the whole bay at one time or another and a discussion would ensue. Men lying in the dark quickly become boys trading stories. The etiquette of storytelling was simple: each man had his moment to say (or remember) what he wanted to with neither interruption nor censure. Humorous editorializing was accepted and enjoyed, but not at such expense to the speaker that he either stopped or was permanently interrupted. He could continue until finished and was always afforded the respectful custom of silence when he was done. Talk became a vital connection between men who, though they sweated and stank around one another for months on end, were still relative strangers.

Early in the conversation, when most guys were awake, talk of home or food was a favorite. Men loved to describe their place of origin, the city or town they had left behind, the streets they knew best, the places they could get a hot meal or meet a pretty girl. Later, after some men had drifted off to sleep, the subject matter would grow more somber, more personal, more revealing. Conversation often moved from idle chat to assertion and boast right down to the bone of memory. One night, the subject was what we were going to do when we got home. There were meals to be eaten and girlfriends to be visited and, as always, the return to doing precisely what we wanted to do.

"I'm telling you, the first thing I'm gonna do is get myself a bottle and sit on my daddy's porch and drink until I pass out," someone was saying. "When I wake up, I am going to stretch, take a hot shower, shave, change my clothes and go back to that porch with a new bottle and start all over again."

Someone else then turned to the harvests of summer: sweet corn, the tang of fresh peaches, the burst of melons and ripe tomatoes. Wilkens told us of his grandfather's apple cider and how the old men would come and test it before anyone else was allowed to drink. They would wipe their mouths on dirty sleeves and, smiling their approval, call for the jugs to be opened and passed around. Tony Sac described the fruit vendors on the streets of Brooklyn, how they sang as they rolled their fruit-laden wagons through narrow streets.

"Tomatoes big as softballs, melons fat as babies. We'd trail after them guys hoping for a dropped apple or an orange tossed to us as a treat. Aw, fellas," he said in a heartfelt voice, "it was the fuckin' life to be a little boy in Brooklyn." Meese, his own voice soft with memory, described his family's great watermelon hunts and how, as they gathered around the fattest, juiciest catch, his father's knife would part the skin to reveal gleaming red pulp and black seed.

"The juice," he said, "would spill down our chins. We'd spit the seeds at the dogs sleeping on the porch. It was a distance, say from the barracks door to the washroom. Those dogs would jump to their feet like they'd been stung by a bee." After each speaker, the bay would grow quieter. Listeners gave in to their own memories or fell asleep. I said nothing, but I did think about the last time I had seen fruit. We were hopscotching our way to war from America to Trinidad, then Brazil and on to North Africa and England. We had put in at Waller Field in Trinidad for replacement of the punctured wing tanks that had led to my run-in with the heavy-handed colonel. On the last day before flying south to Brazil, we were given the afternoon off. Mintz, experienced traveler that he was, convinced a few of us to come with him to see the local sights. He had commandeered a jeep and drove us high up into the mountains. We found a cold mountain stream that ran through a grapefruit orchard long gone to seed. I had never seen anything like it—plump, wild grapefruits hanging off the trees or ripening in the grass. Mintz said it had probably once been a working grapefruit farm. Those grapefruits were tart but as good as any fruit I'd ever tasted in my life. We picked as many as we could carry, carted them back to the airfield and stored them in our bomb bay.

"They'll go nice with a little rum, that's for damn sure," said Mintz. Later he and a few others went down into the nearby village and bought a dozen bottles of rum for a few dollars. We had no idea when or where we would drink the stuff, but we were going to war, so some use would surely come of it. Days later, as we approached England, we were looking for the small airfield they called Valley, a staging area in Wales for American bombers to refuel after their long runs over North Africa and the coast of Europe. After Valley came the many airfields that lay along England's southern and eastern coasts.

Flying up from Morocco, low over the Atlantic and in heavy cloud cover, it looked as if we might have a hard time finding the little Valley field, but our navigator brought us in without a hitch. ("Nice work, Brown," said Tedrowe over the intercom in that cool voice of praise that all of us sought. "Very nice work.") It had a small runway and we landed with great care. A large crowd of civilians came right onto the field to greet us when we came to a stop. They explained that they hoped that the American crews might have some scarce goods they might be able to buy. We told them all we had was grapefruits and rum and they pressed forward, excited. They offered us the equivalent of five dollars for each grapefruit. Mintz looked at us with wide eyes and then thought better of it:

"Tempting though it may be to you bums, let's do the right thing," and he began to lob those grapefruits out the door and into the crowd. The people cheered, shouted encouragement and thanked us until we felt like kings. Only later, an old hand at the airfield told us that we had given our grapefruit to traders who resold the items in town for outrageous prices. Mintz was crestfallen. "I shoulda known better," he said. "They suckered us with all that cheering. It's a damn good thing we didn't give them the rum," he added. I never knew what happened to that rum. I wondered if any of it might be buried somewhere in a burned-out bomber, along with the good man who had acquired it.

Mintz. I could see him clearly. I had met him eighteen months before on the way to aerial gunnery school at Wendover, Utah, in the mountains overlooking the massive salt flats near Salt Lake City. In his mid-thirties, he seemed old enough to be our grandfather. He was, by his own candid admission, afraid of flying, but he was determined to be an airman. He liked the idea of flying, he said, because war on the ground didn't suit him one bit. ("I like to see where I'm going and not have to mind some poor sonofabitch who keeps telling me to 'walk on,'" he would say.)

When we ended up in the same barracks at aerial gunnery school and found that we were both from Massachusetts—he from Dorchester and I from Barnstable Village on Cape Cod—he took an interest in teaming up with me. Easygoing, with a great sense of humor and a genuine humility, he nevertheless lived hard. He had a real taste for gambling and racetracks. Once he and Sac took me with them to Elko, Nevada, where gambling was legal, to see my first big craps game. I had seen it played around the barracks, though I had never known how it worked. Mintz, a canny gambler, had me bet with a cook from our unit who was on a giddy winning streak. The cook kept rolling the dice and I kept winning until Mintz quietly took my money off the table. Barely two rolls later, the poor cook's dice cooled off, leaving him nothing and me with several hundred silver dollars. "There's only two tricks to craps, Handy. Knowing when to jump in and when to climb the fuck out. The rest is just making money." Later, in our final test of aerial gunnery, where we were shooting at moving targets towed by planes, I racked up the highest score for the day and Mintz pounded my back and wrapped his arm around my neck. "I want to be on your crew, Handy." As it turned out, we were then both assigned to the same bomb group, squadron and crew, and with that he had always expected me to look after him. I never thought it odd that I was to keep watch over him, though I was the much younger man. It just seemed right. Had he come to Stalag 17 I might have watched over him as Tony Sac did his older brother. But he had not come to this camp. I wondered if I had done everything for him that I could have done. There was always the chance that he and poor Orlando had somehow survived, but for the first time, I really began to know that they were dead. Their names tolled in my head, a mournful chiming, long into the night.

THE KRIEGIES PLAYED A GAME AT roll call that drove the Germans crazy. Procedure for roll call was always the same: kriegies were lined in rows five men deep. We were to count out by fives. On lazy days, when there was nothing better to do, the fifth guy would scoot down, run around behind the others, and stand at the far end. He would be counted twice. It drove the guards crazy. Many kriegies thought it was hilarious, though it often seemed to me, and to most of us in 32A, a colossal waste of time. If it was kept up for too long, the guards would threaten us with a dog tag search, a process that took many hours to complete, often in the long hot glare of the sun.

Periodically we would get news from the outside, because some enterprising radioman had built a wireless set. Though I never saw it or knew who made it, the wireless was our link to the world. Made of wire, tin cans and something that served as a crystal, this homemade device provided us with updates on the different theaters of the war, life at home and odd tidbits from around the world, courtesy of shortwave technology. It was all the more important because the Germans had their own propaganda that they loved to pass along. Guards would tell us of strikes in our cities, food shortages and civil unrest. Even if they knew it to be nonsense, some guys were unsettled by the rumors. The designated kriegie operator would listen to the wireless and then whisper the news to a reader, who would go out and spread it to the barracks. Our newsreader came in and stood on the stool, calling out his customary signal, "At ease, at ease!" He was a small guy with a sharply pitched voice and his arrival sent guys scurrying to the windows to watch for guards while the rest gathered around. I was never much for the news once the war's developments had been covered. A lot of it was material chosen to assure us that all was well and going strong at home—down to the details of Betty Grable's latest movie—and in the big picture it *was* important material, but I wasn't big enough to understand that. My thoughts would wander back to projects and concerns close at hand. Tonight would be another matter altogether. Looking at a few, like me, who were lounging in the back, the reader called out, "You fellas are gonna want to hear what I have to say." My interest piqued, I swung down from my bunk and walked over to the group.

"The Americans, British and Canadians have landed at Normandy and are fighting their way inland." There was a wild whoop caught in midthroat as all of us tried to suppress the joy. The invasion had begun.

"It's about goddamn time," said someone.

"Man oh man," said another, "the cavalry is comin'!" There were backslaps and quiet laughter, and then everyone turned their attention again to the newsreader. He described the Channel crossing as the BBC had done, calling it the greatest assembling of men, ships and machinery the world had ever seen. Fierce fighting had taken a heavy toll, but the Allies were onshore and driving into France. The time we had left in the stalag might well be a great deal shorter than it had been only a moment before. I had lost track of the days and had heard almost no talk of the invasion since that first morning when we marched in over a month ago and the old kriegies were asking when it was going to come. I had never once considered the invasion during the long hours of digging, nor now, hearing this news, did I think much beyond the simple promise it offered that all of this could soon come to an end. Exultant, I was also cautious, sensing as we all did that it would likely take the Allies a long time to fight their way across Europe. At our next day's tunnel meeting, we agreed that we would continue digging.

WILKENS'S INSATIABLE APPETITE FOR TIN CANS finally became clear one morning. He proudly unveiled a two-gallon bucket. We all passed it around like curators at a museum. The cans had been hammered to a smooth flat surface and the edges carefully crimped so that one can could fit neatly into the next. Two smoothly fashioned pieces of wood were tightly bound by wire so the bucket had a sturdy handle.

"Like I said," Wilkens continued as the bucket moved from hand to admiring hand, "I always knew how we'd get ourselves the bucket. Tin is easy. It's the rope that's the challenge. All that stuff you brought back to me when I asked you to comb the compound was good, but we still don't have the makings of a rope. We can't just go trading for it. The guards will trade for a lot of things, but rope just might get one of them shot. So we're going to have to keep trying to make our own. Go out there again with eyes to the ground. String, twine, thread, I want everything you fellas can find, no matter how small." So we went back to it. Scouring the camp, guys would pass by Wilkens's bunk and say, "Can you use this?" and toss him thread, pieces of rope, wire, twine, even long pieces of cloth. "Oh, nice, real nice. Much obliged," he would say. Before long, to our amazement, he had tied all those items together with tiny knots, lengthened them into strands and then braided the strands carefully into one strong stretch of rope. We were in business.

The night he displayed that rope, I wondered about what Wilkens and Meese had accomplished. The work was so simple, so ingenious. How had they managed to make a bucket, rope and a beveled hatch that lay invisible on the floor? How many men with talents and resourcefulness were in this camp? There were radiomen, machinists, carpenters, teachers, artists, electricians, and farmers anywhere from eighteen to twenty-five years old. We knew about Normandy because some enterprising guy learned home electronics as a kid. The radio was kept in a wash bucket that had been fitted with a false bottom they could lay over it and fill with dirty water and a mop. We had a complex and workable economy because the camp was filled with young, practical men who had grown up on farms and had learned to barter and trade as a way of life. I lay on my palliasse amazed at the huge and endless energy of it all. On one of my first missions, just after we hit the coast of France, we had begun to get fairly heavy flak. We were well hidden from the anti-aircraft batteries by the cloud cover, but you could tell they were zeroing in on us with radar-equipped guns. You could see the bursts closing in. Tedrowe asked me to work with the crew to ready the "chaff" to be thrown out of the rear hatch in the waist. I had never known much about the stuff, had never even seen it. I was skeptical of those little stars of aluminum foil that promised to confuse enemy radar. The flak was scattering along the walls of the plane, first like pebbles at a window but soon like heavy rocks, getting heavier. They were finding their range. Thompson and I opened the B-24's rear-waist hatch, just ahead of the tail turret, and fed the chaff out like metal confetti. It was like magic to see how quickly the flak bursts followed that chaff down.

"That's textbook," said Thompson, watching the flak burst below. "Those gunners are blind, and radar'll chase anything metal that moves. Beautiful." By the time they readjusted their sights, we were long gone. I was amazed at how simple and effective chaff was compared to the sophisticated technology of radar-controlled artillery. Who had thought of such a device? Little pieces of aluminum had saved our lives, guiding death away from us. So many bits of ingenuity from so many people. I felt a twinge, wondering whether I'd ever think of anything so remotely useful. For the moment, all I could contribute was sweat and doggedness. Did that rate?

MANY HANDS HAD MADE THE DIGGING of the shaft go quickly, but once the tunnel itself was under way, matters got a little more complicated. First there was simply the issue of size. We needed men who could fit into the confined space of the tunnel. "We got enough ball and tail turret gunners to make it easy," joked Pappy about the medium to small stature of most guys who flew the turrets. Someone like Beast or Meese, men who were more than six feet, with great big wide shoulders to match, were at a disadvantage in the tunnel. So the digging fell more and more to the smaller men who fit first into the shaft and later, the tunnel. At five feet eight and 140 pounds—I had yet to be hit by the big weight loss—I was just about right for the job. So was Tony Sac. Meese, despite his great height and build, also remained one of our best diggers.

The other issue was that many men had an understandable reluctance toward very small spaces. I found myself more and more in the role of the digger. I was shaped for it and probably had the right temperament. If you were claustrophobic in any way, the tunnel quickly became more of a mental than physical challenge. Kozikowski was open about it—"It's not for me, Handy. There's a lot of things I can do, but crawling around in the dark down there is just not for me." Koz was intelligent and far more mature than I. With no real grasp of the danger, I took to tunnel digging in an animal, almost childlike way. I looked forward to getting down there and going at it; we were doing something worthwhile, and being a part of it was easy to feel good about. I was to soon learn a few things about my own anxiety down there, but initially it was a great way to spend my time.

We got ourselves into an efficient rhythm. We usually dug, time permitting, in two shifts per day, each with a three-man tunnel crew backed up by kriegies to move the earth and keep a lookout for guards. The digger and his teammate, the man at the bottom of the shaft, would go down into the tunnel, stripped to their shorts. The first one down, the digger, had to get into knee position at the bottom of the shaft and then knee-walk into the tunnel, carrying his Klim can with him. At the far end of the tunnel, facing its far wall (he couldn't turn around), he would go to work scraping loose the hard-packed earth. After dumping about a dozen Klim cans' worth between his knees, using his legs and feet he would push that little pile of earth back to his teammate kneeling at the bottom of the shaft. The shaft worker now loaded the new earth into the Wilkens bucket, which then was hauled up through the floor hatch by the third crewmember—the teammate at the top of the shaft—using the Wilkens rope. From there the disposal crew took over. Soon enough, though, as the tunnel moved forward into the earth ahead of it, we came to see that the digger could push a Red Cross box ahead of him as he crawled forward and, with the box between his knees, empty as many Klim cans of freshly dug earth into it as the box would hold. This worked for a while, but as the tunnel lengthened, the digger's legs became less and less able to push the heavy box back far enough. The shaft man had to crawl into the tunnel himself to pull it out, and this wasn't practical.

Wilkens again took to the problem. From his flattened-out can resources he designed and built a metal-bottomed sled that moved easily over the tunnel's dirt floor. Meese and his carpentry team finished it with wood sides so that it could carry a fair amount of earth. We attached some of Wilkens's rope to both ends of the sled so that it could be pulled back and forth over the length of the tunnel. Instead of having to deal with the Red Cross box, the digger could now pull the sled behind him—or push it ahead—to the far reach of the tunnel, put it between his knees and fill it as he dug, then pull hard on the sled's back-end rope running to his teammate at the bottom of the shaft.

Getting that signal, the shaft man would haul the sled back, dragging it slowly as it was chock full. (Diggers tried not to overfill the sled and risk breaking the rope or bringing about spillage that could make a quick exit tricky.) Once back at the shaft bottom, the sled earth was emptied into the bucket and the rope up to the floor-hatch tugged as a signal to pull the bucket up. The man at the hatch mouth—the third member of what became the three-man digging team—had his own helpers working to get rid of the earth and keep a careful lookout.

Control over how the tunnel was shaped more or less fell to me because I spent so much time down there. Clearly, it had to be high enough to allow your head several inches clearance while working on your knees, and it had to be wide enough for your hips and shoulders. You had to be able to move around in your tunnel—though, of course, not to the extent that you could turn around. You simply had to have enough room to do your work down there without bumping into the ceiling or walls, because you had to have a sense of not being hemmed in. Engineering those clearances soon made the tunnel's shape something of a Roman arch, and—as I learned only years later—this afforded us great protection against cave-ins.

The diggers' overriding concern was the earth underground. How would it hold for digging? Could it sustain a tunnel? Tony Sac had brought up the first Klim can full of dirt, and its consistency was encouraging. It was excellent earth and seemed ideal—neither too soft (like sand) nor too hard (like clay), just solid, homogeneous brown earth. There weren't even any rocks or pebbles in the soil—great conditions for those of us who dug. I never considered the dangers down there. What would happen if, while we were at work, the Germans drove a heavy maintenance truck across the ground above? Or if a collapse occurred where the shaft and tunnel ceiling came together? Or at the front of the tunnel in the dark? The list of risks was endless, I suppose, but we never spoke of them. The only concerns that mattered were the ferrets and the guards poking around, and there were others to worry about that. I had only to dig. In that tunnel, I felt more like a soldier doing his job, devising my own war plans and executing them in the face of the enemy. It was deeply satisfying. I liked the directness of the tunnel, the measured success, yard by yard. Since early boyhood, measurable action had always been important in my limited scheme of things. I loved the sensible organization of time and energy. As our crew's first engineer I'd come to see that responsibility for our plane's mechanical and overall condition—its flightworthiness—meant setting up a sequence of carefully thought-out monitoring functions. Before long I'd put together pre-flight, in-flight, and after-landing checklists for my own use and had expanded these as experience added greater knowledge of the B-24's complexities and fine points. (Tedrowe once asked to see those checklists, saying that he thought the group commander might want to have them standardized for all first engineers, but the war moved too fast for that.) No written checklists were needed for tunnel digging, of course, but a set of procedures did evolve in my mind and—like those for keeping our B-24 flying—grew as the tunneling went forward. I liked that part of the work—probably each of the other diggers developed their own procedures that they liked, too—and far from being lonely down there, I found the working out of procedures a kind of companion and the solitude a kind of sanctuary. While digging, one's mind locked into the routine of sweat and progress and made possible going at it for hours at a time.

The deeper we dug the tunnel, the darker it got, and darkness brought on a new set of challenges. Diggers dropped out, reluctant to work in the close, dark space. Soon there were only a few of us who would go all the way to the tunnel's front to continue the digging. The farther in, inevitably the narrower the tunnel became, as you couldn't see well enough to frame it out evenly. It became more and more difficult to keep a bit of space between one's upper body and the walls of our Roman arch. Bumping around down there was not good for the tunnel or one's own confidence. At first, it had been easy enough. You just waited until your eyes could accommodate themselves to pick up the dim light from the shaft. When you had a sense of how to go about your work without bumping head and shoulders against those close-in walls, you began to dig. But now, with that light all but nonexistent, came further difficulties. Although our earth arch had evolved to a size workable for men like Gene Meese, the clearance for my head was still no more than four inches and even less for my shoulders. As long as I worked within that clearance—free of contact with the walls—I had no sense of confinement. Without my being aware of it, the shaft's dim light had helped me maintain that key relationship between the walls and me.

On my first day of total darkness, that relationship fell apart. Reaching forward and up with the digging can at the far wall, I bumped my head hard against the tunnel's earth ceiling. A little shower of dirt fell and surprised me. It was no more than a cup's worth of dirt—not a cave-in—but I reacted with a jerk that slammed my left shoulder hard against the invisible earth wall. It was a terrible moment, one that bordered on panic. I had a feeling of being buried alive, though of course the tunnel had not given way at all. My breath shortened, my heart raced and I felt a whirling dizziness. With no word to my teammate at the shaft end of the tunnel, I pushed the sled away with my feet and lay down on my back and began to breathe. He heard me stop.

"You OK?" he called.

"Fine," I said. "Fine."

The sense of confinement—the terror—was soon gone. I rolled over, got back into digging position and went to work. Could it happen again? I hoped not. I vowed to guard against it by being alert to any suggestion of crumbling dirt and moving with greater deliberation near the walls and ceiling.

I spoke to no one about that moment in the tunnel until several nights later, after "lights out." Instead of sacking in like the rest of our bay, I was sitting up in my bunk thinking about the day now ended—a habit I had begun since coming to the stalag. At first, it was as if I were storing up thoughts for my journal, but soon it became a kind of daily meditation on the events of the day. I sensed someone else in the dark. Across the bay I could see a darker shadow within the shadows.

"I was dreaming," Joseph said in a whisper. He seemed to be speaking to no one, but I knew he was speaking to me. He sat on his bunk against the wall, still as an animal. Staring out the window, his profile came up in sharp relief only when a searchlight passed.

"You were down there, under the ground, among large roots. Do you see roots down under that ground?" he asked, turning toward me.

"Not so far," I said. "But we're likely to hit some soon. Before the Nazis built this resort, there must have been lots of trees around here."

He was quiet for a while and then asked, "It is not dark down there for you?" Somewhere out in the night a truck backfired, the engine revved and someone shouted. It seemed very far away.

"No," I answered, "it's not dark down there for me," wondering what Joseph was getting at.

"So you're not frightened down there?" he whispered.

"No," I said.

"You are brave. I could not go down there."

"I'm not brave," I said, uncertain what "brave" really meant. "And sure you could. It's not as bad as you think."

"Oh, but it is," he said, his face growing more and more visible in the dark. "It is exactly that. A man in a tunnel has only his thoughts, and what you think is what you are. What do you think about down there?"

The question surprised me. I had not really considered what I thought about. I typically took a lot of interest in the dirt itself, the texture of it, the satisfaction of making progress, marking it foot by foot. I felt like an animal, a mole or a woodchuck. I told Joseph that I did not think much of anything at all.

"You do not have so great an imagination, perhaps?" he said, with a trace of humor.

"I suppose not."

"So you never feel worried about being buried alive?"

I remembered the dizziness, and I was reluctant to tell him that I had had just such a moment. He was quiet and waited for me to answer.

"Sometimes, once maybe, a few days ago. I felt . . . kind of trapped. I moved my arms around and felt how little space I had, I bumped my head against the top and I started to feel kind of clammy. It wasn't a big deal. In fact it was kind of stupid." I was unaccustomed to something that felt like a confession. I wondered how he might take it.

"No, not stupid at all," he said thoughtfully. "What did you do?"

"I tried not to think about it. I told myself that I was OK, that there was nothing to worry about. I told myself that the tunnel was strong and I would be OK."

"So you were afraid?"

"Well, I don't know. Sort of. Maybe."

Joseph said nothing for a long while. "There is nothing wrong with being afraid. I am afraid to go into that tunnel and I am not ashamed of it. What shame is there in not going where a man is not meant to be?"

"Well, under the circumstances," I countered too quickly, "I'm one of the guys meant to be down there."

I heard him laugh. "Of course. You got us into this in the first place." His voice grew more solemn. "You are good to dig as you do. All of you are." He stopped and was quiet so long that I began to listen to the snoring and the breathing of the other men all around us. Then he began again in a whisper.

"When I was young, we had a game that we played. A boy would have a sack put over his head and he would be spun round and round until he fell from dizziness. And then he would have to stand up and run a gauntlet of boys for about a hundred feet. Your hands were free so you could strike back, and you had to run fast and be strong to make it through the gauntlet. My brothers made me play this game once when I was very small. I did not mind the gauntlet. I was small and fast and knew I would be hard to hit, but the sack was different. I didn't like the idea of a sack over my head. When it came time and they pulled it over me, I began to shout. I ripped off the sack and refused to play. The boys teased me and said I was a coward. My brothers were very angry.

"Later that night, my oldest brother came and sat with me in the dark. He knew I was angry and ashamed. He asked me why I was afraid of the sack, and I couldn't tell him because I didn't know. He asked me what I thought when the sack went over me, and I said that I thought I was going to be smothered to death. Who would do such a thing? he asked me. That is what it feels like to me, I told him. Then he said with great seriousness: Do you know who smothers you? You do. You smother yourself with that sack. Then he told me how the mind and the heart were often at odds. Jealous of the heart's greater power, the mind was strongest only when it could cripple the heart. Why does the heart let this happen, I asked him, if indeed the heart is the greater of the two? Because, and here my brother leaned so close to me that his breath was hot on my ear, the heart is tender and merciful and grateful to the mind for its protection. And the strongest power is always the most gentle. Then he told me what to do. Before the sack is put on your head, he said, look at everything around you: the trees, rocks, people and sky. When the sack goes over your head, become very still. Do not move at all. Try and remember the world around you. See it in your mind—the clouds and the sky and the laughing faces of your friends. Remind yourself that the bag is as thin as your own eyelids. And all that you know and love is right there around you and only your eyes are closed. You will feel your heart slow down, he said, and you will realize that though your mind is a trickster, your heart knows better."

"I will try that," I said. "Thanks." He was quiet again. The snoring around us was now thunderous, as if we were talking in a storm.

"There's a difference, you know," I added after thinking on it for a moment. "When you shut your eyes, you were surrounded by everyone you loved, your brothers, your friends. When I shut my eyes, I'm still in a camp surrounded by wires and guards who want to kill me."

"Think on it again," he said kindly. "The tunnel is not the sack." I wasn't sure what he meant.

"Shut up, for Christ's sake. You two have been chattering all night," someone shouted. We both stopped for a moment and then began again, barely audible.

"Did you ever put the sack on and run the gauntlet?" I whispered, not wanting the conversation to end.

"Yes, I did."

"How did it work?"

"Well, I did as my brother told me, and I wore the sack on my head. I did not shout and I felt calm. But he had told me nothing about the gauntlet, and I ran in circles being slapped by the boys until I passed out."

"Your brother can't teach you everything," I offered.

"That is true," he said. "Good night."

"Good night."

When I returned to the tunnel the next day, I thought about Joseph's roots, swelling with rain and ready to burst the ground. He would be disappointed that there was no sign of anything remotely like a root, so I decided I would never tell him.

IT WAS SEVERAL NIGHTS LATER, SOMETIME after midnight, that I thought of the talk with Joseph once again. I had gotten up for a night trip to the latrine. Every barracks in Stalag 17 had a small indoor "one-holer" reachable from the entryway, but it was foul-smelling and could be bypassed by walking through the dark to the outdoor latrine. The main latrine was a large building centered behind the compound's four barracks and built with dozens of "holes" for the 1,200 men of the compound. Every so often the horse-drawn "honey wagon" would come around and empty the contents of that latrine into the wagon's big tank. You could go there after curfew if you made sure the guards could see you and where you were going. If they thought you were out there for any other reason, or you strayed from what they considered "the path," it had been made clear they would kill you. From our door, the walk was a long one, a kind of zigzag around Barracks 31 and across open ground to the latrine.

I liked going outdoors at night. The air was fresh and clean and the searchlights, like octopus arms reaching and contracting, made the walk something of an adventure. I could challenge my own fear, and each outing to the latrines became a test and subsequent triumph over my confinement, over the menace of the guards themselves. It wasn't bravery—I was no more or less brave than anyone else—but I never thought too much about what could happen in dangerous straits. I had an animal's ignorance of my own annihilation. Breaking the rules of safety where they seemed irrational was something I instinctively liked to do. That particular night's trip began without incident. I stood at the doorway waiting for the guard to "find" me, then walked down the narrow corridor between the barracks and crossed the open space. The guard's searchlight stalked me in a dazzle of light, as if daring me to make a sudden movement. I walked with deliberate slowness, as if to say: no problems here. At last his beam moved on, leaving me in a sudden and absolute dark. I stopped. It was as black as the tunnel, only here there were no walls. Above me, as if surfacing from an inky deep, came a hundred lights, growing brighter every moment. Stars. They winked and flickered and swam in close, tiny circles. I knew them; I recognized the constellations I had seen as a boy on Cape Cod and on my training flights through the night skies over Kansas and West Texas. I had seen these diamonds spilled across the darkness over North Africa. I located the Big Dipper and remembered how my mother always sought out that constellation first. I moved on to the latrine filled with a sense of vast time, of space and distance. The star-drenched sky made this camp suddenly small and insignificant. I thought of Joseph's story about the sack; let it be put over you, he said, but remember the world you love. He was right; the tunnel was not the sack, or even this camp. I vowed to remember those stars that, whether I saw them or not, were always there.

In the tunnel the next afternoon it happened again. Another careless butt of the head and spilling of dirt over my shoulders and head. The spasm of fear made me push against an unforgiving wall of dirt to my left. More dirt fell. Joseph's brother. The sack. I lay very still on the tunnel floor, stretched out. I first began to breathe. It was all right up there. All those stars, all that wind, right above me. I reminded myself what Joseph had tried to tell me: my fear was the burlap sack. I tried not to move any part of my body, tried not to touch the wall or the ceiling. I saw the stars bright in the dark above me, and before long they crowded the tunnel's ceiling. Soon I saw other things, too: beaches and long flat stretches of meadow and ocean vistas. I began to realize I had the freedom to move if I wanted to. If I wanted to stretch my arm straight out, I could. If I wanted to stand, I could do that, too. And so I got up. I began to run the dunes of Cape Cod and hike the fields behind my grandmother's house. I sat in the warm September sun of her wilderness garden. I started to laugh. Even Joseph was now somewhere above me, maybe walking the compound over the tunnel. I wanted to tunnel up to the surface and burst the ground to tell him in triumph that I did have an imagination and that it worked. As quickly as the anxiety had come, it was gone. Before long, I started to breathe easily and felt relaxed. I returned to the tunneling, fist over fist, moving through the dirt like a gopher.

"JERRIES. MOVE IT!" I WAS ALONE at the tunnel's far end with a half-filled sled between my legs. I scrambled backward using my hands and knees like flippers pushing off one to the other, and I could make pretty good speed. We always had enough time to get out when the call came, because the scouts kept an eye on every barracks' approach. At the base of the shaft they were hissing, "C'mon, c'mon!" Many hands lifted me out and the hatch went down, the dirt was spread and men immediately lounged about as if it were still another shiftless afternoon. I lay on a bunk on my stomach pretending to rest. The guards came in from the washroom end and passed quickly into Shattuck's bay, led by the tall Luftwaffe pilot with the wooden leg. We could hear the muffle of voices, but mostly the clipped formal voice of the Pilot. After a moment, they came out and stormed off through the front of the barracks. Moments later Shattuck came down to our bay. "The Jerries have noticed the storm sewer is running brown. Very brown. Some guard was out in the long grass down the hill where the water spills out and he saw the color. My Luftwaffe colleague paid me a visit to assure me that if the source of that earth in the storm sewer were coming from some unnatural means, everyone responsible would be in serious trouble. He was very brief about it and quite agitated." We were all silent.

"Duly noted," said Meese, leaning against a bunk.

So we had to find new places for the dirt. When not in the tunnel, the diggers sometimes joined the earth-disposal team, but for Meese and me it went further. In our bay's daily get-togethers about the tunnel, we were learning that getting rid of the earth was already a greater challenge than we'd imagined. Washing the dirt down into the field was now out. The men in the bay met to talk the problem through and decided that for now the dirt should be stored. Maybe down the road we could use the washtubs again, but for now the best place proved to be above us in the ceiling of the barracks where we had already stolen a good deal of wood. I climbed up there to take a look. It was not an attic as such, more like a space that had been enclosed when the structure had a ceiling put in. Given that the ceiling boards were old beat-up boards and probably not very securely fastened to the rafters, there were plenty of cracks for dirt to tumble down. Later some of the team built themselves little walkways to carry them from joist to joist across the ceiling area. They had to be able to cover a considerable distance so that they could spread the earth out and not leave too much weight in any one area. It was carefully managed so that there was never more than four to six inches of earth piled up in any one place. In those summer months we were still getting Red Cross parcels, so there was a lot of useful cardboard that could be flattened out and put up there to keep the dirt from coming down through the cracks in the ceiling. There was plenty of room up there and the digging went faster after that.

Diggers were warned about elbow and knee stains because the Germans were always looking for signs of digging. They had had enough experience with prisoners by 1944 to know that tunnels were the medium of choice. When we came out of the tunnel, someone was always there to help us clean away the dirt as best we could.

We had plenty of close calls. We were sitting once at midday talking about the greatest meals we had ever eaten when some guards came through. Their appearance in the barracks was rare enough, and you always felt uneasy, as if their arrival portended danger. They seemed to be bored and passed by the bay like idlers. Every kriegie had his own attitude toward the guards. Some saw them as potential allies who could be terrifically valuable if you needed them. I understood that—you don't want to feel threatened or think that every soldier with a gun wants to use it against you. Others made acquaintances of these guards, like fellow travelers. Many of the guards had been wounded or used up by war. The young ones were harder, more insecure, but most of them were neither abusive nor particularly harsh to us. Occasionally, and Max was certainly one of these, there was a lurking cruelty in a few of them and you had to be careful. If I paid them no mind, it was because I could not see them as anything but the enemy.

On this particular day, the guards stopped to listen to our conversation. I had not seen them before and they acted almost curious about us. They were young and twitchy and I always worried about guards like that. As I watched them, I felt Tony Sac poke me in the side. He looked quickly at the ceiling above the guard and there, plainly visible, was a gap in the wood where you could see dirt. At the guard's feet was a pile of it that had already shaken down. I looked away immediately. The guards were shifting about, and their boots stood on that dirt.

"Hey, Handy!" Tony Sac now said, standing so abruptly the guards drew back, alarmed. "I'm going to do my laundry while the water's running." And then he headed off toward the washroom. I followed, breaking up what might have become a moment's pause with the guards and the members of our bay. The Germans shrugged and sauntered on out after us. Later one of the crew went up and located the "seam" and moved the cardboard to close it.

Not long after, a far more serious event nearly cost me. After a morning in the tunnel, I had gone out to walk the perimeter, our chief form of exercise. It felt good to breathe the air, because even though it was pleasantly cool in the tunnel, it was close. A guard angled across the compound, calling out to two kriegies who were pacing the wire ahead of me. He handed his rifle to another guard and demanded to see the kriegies' hands. He looked closely at their palms, like a psychic. It was a strange, almost amusing sight, until I realized that though my hands and elbows were clean, I had not cleaned my fingernails, and they were full of tunnel dirt. I decided to walk on as casually as a stroller, but the guard called out to me in a short sharp voice. He came toward me and I began to run through all the options at once. Should I take off? Should I fall and get an excuse for dirty hands? The ground was dry and offered no help. At that instant, two officers strolled across the compound. The guard turned away and hurried toward his superiors. I walked on, making myself scarce in the nearest barracks. It was too damned close.

The days passed without any further security problems. As soon as any guard approached, there were the customary coded warning messages passed along and the digging-team member at the top of the shaft would quickly get the word to the guys below, step out from under the midlevel bunk, and put the slats back in place—all the time screened by the fast-reacting men of Wolf's bay. The warning gave about three minutes for digger and shaft man to climb out, install the below-ground tunnel cover and pull the loose dirt over it, exit the floor hatch and, with the team above ground, close it and put the bunk slats above in place. Not much time at all.

ONE AFTERNOON IN LATE JULY A newsreader announced that the Russians had swept into Poland and there were many Germans trapped in the Ukraine. The war was turning, and fast. The light was lengthening again and I decided to walk to the grass. I could touch nature in that grass; I could smell her. I got down on my knees to do this and some moments later started at a shadow that fell over me.

"It's beautiful, isn't it?" The blond kid stood there. I stood up, awkward and a little uneasy that he had found me there.

"Yeah. Really great."

"I found it the first day I was walking around. It kind of shook me up. I don't know why." He seemed so vacant, as if I were talking to someone who wasn't there at all. I found myself speaking softly to him, like the guys in his bay who were always trying to get him to eat.

"You don't have to know why. It's just grass and it's great to see. Reminds me of home. That's probably why you like it."

"No," he said.

"Then why?"

"It reminds me, all right, of something. But it's not home. I just don't know what it is. Sometimes I come here and try to remember what it is, but I can't. I just can't . . ." he said, his voice trailing off.

"Where are you from?" I asked.

Over his shoulder I saw three guards coming. They came bearing down on us like birds of prey. One of them was Max. He shoved us both out of the way, looked hard at me and then smiled. Handing off his rifle, he walked around the building and soon returned, carrying a shovel. He grunted at the blond kid and thrust the shovel at him.

"Dig!" he shouted. The blond kid looked dumbly at him and then at me. His face was without expression. Max began shouting louder and the other guard began butting the kid with his rifle.

"I can't," said the kid without any emotion at all. "I don't know how." Max moved toward him. We were behind that building. No one could see us. It was a dangerous situation. I grabbed the shovel from him and in three quick strokes had dug the grass up. Max watched and then shuffled through the clods, spreading the sparse grass into the dirt with the front of his boot. There was now just a brown patch of freshly turned earth where the grass had been. As they left, the third guard poked the blond kid in the ribs with his rifle and laughed. The kid wandered away.

Walking back to the barracks, I took a turn along the downhill fence of the east compound. I could see two disheveled men carrying between them a sagging paper sack. A bony blue foot sprung from it and bounced along as they walked. With a German guard trailing them, they hauled the sack beyond the east fence near the grove of trees. A third man, clearly a prisoner, trailed them, dragging a shovel behind him like a tired child. Several old kriegies standing by the wire stiffened and saluted the passing detail. They told me these were Russians and the dead one was a prisoner. The Russian prisoners dug for some minutes and then tipped the body out, a flash of white and gray. That same foot caught the paper and pulled it into the hole and the guard shouted. One of the prisoners wearily climbed down and retrieved the sack, held it stupidly for an instant, and then, on another command from the guard, tossed it back into the hole again. It was a pathetic scene, though the tableau of the three standing against the long afternoon light seemed strangely compelling. Far beyond them, across the valley, I could see the farms and the houses with their red-tiled roofs. Someone had told me that farther, much farther on, was Czechoslovakia, but that was like saying that farther on was China or Kansas. The fact was that I couldn't see beyond the high hill, almost a small mountain, that enclosed our valley. I thought about the dead prisoner out there. He was free from having to gnaw on bugs and drink the smear of greasy water that served for breakfast and washing. On nights when you stood just inside the door of the latrine and there was no shouting or air raids, you could hear the hissing of the wind in those trees. Dead as he was, he was free of the mud and the hunger and, most important to me, he was outside the wire. I walked back to my barracks and sat in the hot afternoon sun. I tried to remember again how I had stepped so totally out of the life I had known.

Like many others, I might have said that World War II had begun for me on December 7, 1941. But I found myself thinking back to an overcast afternoon in June, eighteen months before the Japanese attacked Pearl Harbor. It was the day after Nazi tanks had rolled into Paris; I was graduating from Milton Academy. Our keynote speaker was Robert Sherwood, the writer who had already won two Pulitzer Prizes by the age of forty-three (he was yet to win two more, including one the following year). Remembering the trenches of World War I, the struggle, horror and utter waste, he seemed history-haunted, heavy with events. The relentless march of history was coming straight at us, he warned, whether we were ready or not. We were a solemn audience, and if we were all wondering what the future held, I had particular reason to be uncertain. College was not an option for me that fall. Some years before, my father had had a terrible riding accident and, after steadily deteriorating health, was unable to work at all. We lived mostly on the money sent to us by my mother's father. Whatever meager funds that could be found for education went to my brother, already in a nightmarish struggle to pay his college bills. Sherwood's graduation address suggested that the war would make the issue of college moot. From that day on, I began to consider the war as central to my future. I did not wish for it—war to me was a most insane and tragic way to settle differences between nations—but opposing Hitler was a clear and vital exception. I knew war was coming and that I needed to be a part of it.

Several weeks after Pearl Harbor, I was living with my family in Stamford, Connecticut, where my mother was the librarian at a small private school (she could educate my four sisters for free) and my father, testing his fragile health, had begun working again. I was working at Yale Locks in Stamford under the watchful eye of a supervisor who wore green eyeshades and sat on a raised platform in the middle of a vast warehouse-like office. One afternoon I overheard a colleague announce that he had just gotten a deferment. He was of draft age and said that he could, with the help of his doctor, arrange a draft deferment for seventy-five dollars. I was incensed at what he'd said and joined another colleague in telling him so. Wasn't his country at war?

How could he skip when his time came to serve? We pressed these questions and fumed. He laughed at us.

"Well, if you two guys are such heroes, what are you doing here?" That comment stopped us. We had both turned nineteen (still below the draft age), and looking long and hard at each other, we realized he had a point. Whatever our age, wasn't it time to enlist? After work we met outside and decided now was the time to do it.

If you were under twenty-one, you needed parental consent to enlist. My parents did not want me to go to war. Over the course of several evenings we argued, my father and I each becoming more set in our positions as the discussions continued. My mother wrung her hands and used convincing, touching arguments. As if to finally settle things, my father announced his own intention to enlist in my place. He marched around the living room and said, "I was a soldier in World War I and I'm going to go back and join the Reserves now—but you aren't going." Although he'd been a well-regarded Field Artillery captain, it was too late for him. He was too old to enlist; I was too old to plead for permission. They both signed the paper.

The next morning, I was ready. My friend had already cleared the parent hurdle and told me he'd decided to enlist in the Navy. That struck me as a sound idea; I had grown up around the sea and felt it in my blood. That weekend, we went to the Navy's recruiting station in downtown Stamford, where he was immediately accepted and I, to my sharp disappointment, was not. I was nine pounds below the minimum weight of 125 pounds, and the Navy recruiter waved me away. "You want to join," he said, "go eat your momma's pies for a few weeks and come back." Undeterred, I went to the Army recruiting center in Stamford, where they seemed more interested in recruiting than in enforcing minimum weight requirements. I volunteered for the Field Artillery because my father's gripping World War I stories had drawn me to it. Also, I knew he would be pleased with my choice.

·   ·   ·

WE WERE MAKING GOOD PROGRESS ON the tunnel. It was high summer and I was continuing to have a solid sense of being part of something big and secret and successful. It seemed as if all 143 men in our barracks understood the task and took their part without hesitation. Dirt was moved, hidden, tools were fashioned, bartered for, needs were met. Everyone was a part of the whole and no one spoke a single word about it.

Tony Sac and I went to see Shattuck to give him an update. We had said nothing to him since that first meeting and he had left it up to us to decide when to tell him of our progress. Shattuck was in his bay when we came in and on his lap was a drawing pad. He was drawing the profile of a man by the wire, though no one else was in his bay. We stood awkwardly watching him for a moment until he turned in surprise.

"Hey, fellas. I didn't hear you."

"That's some kind of drawing you do," said Tony Sac admiringly. "Where'd you learn to do that?"

"Oh, the same place you learned to do what you like to do," said Shattuck modestly. He rose and I was reminded how big and powerful he was. We filled him in and he listened without comment.

"Well, it sounds like you know what you're doing. Just let me know when you think you're getting close enough to make it pay. We'll go up to the White House then, not before."

We were getting ready to leave when Tony Sac turned back and said, "Hey, can I see some of your other drawings?"

Shattuck smiled. "Suit yourself." Tony Sac took the sheaf of drawings in his hand and started to flip through them. One caught his eye, an action shot of a bomber burning with an ME-109 on its tail. It was so real and accurate it made us both wince.

"That's my plane," Shattuck said quietly. "You guys know the tall officer who comes in here from time to time with the wooden leg?"

"Sure, the Pilot," said Tony Sac. "He's not a bad guy. I've talked to him. He was a fighter pilot before he got shot down."

"Well, that picture is for him. One afternoon he was in my bay and when we finished on camp business, we talked flying and air combat. He told me that he kept a record of all the planes he shot down and he pulled out a piece of paper and read the numbers off. One of them was our bomber."

We were flabbergasted. "That can't be," I said dumbly. "I mean, he must be tricking you to get information or something."

"Handy, it's good to be suspicious in a place like this, but you know how it is; two men talking when they don't think anyone else is listening will tell each other only the truth. He described everything exactly as it happened, and when I told him it was me he had shot down, he was as shocked as you were. He said he was sorry and seemed pained. I teased him that he was not as sorry as I was, and that if it had been me, I'd have done the same thing to him. He got shot down himself only a few days later. But it sure does go to show . . . ," said Shattuck, his voice trailing off.

"Do you think I could have one of these pictures?" Tony Sac asked.

"Take what you like."

Tony Sac boyishly thumbed them and then pulled out a stark line drawing of one of the guard towers. The wire lay along the base of the picture and it made the tower look as they did, tall, forbidding and deadly. "This one OK?"

"You bet." Shattuck, as was his custom, was preoccupied and he had no further interest in conversation.

"You know," said Tony Sac, bold now with the exchange, "you might think about drawing or painting stuff on some of the guys' bunks. They'd love to see something that reminded them of home."

"That's not a bad idea," said Shattuck. "Maybe I'll get around to that sometime. Meanwhile, good luck with the tunnel. By the way, you can tell the fellas that I heard at a barracks chiefs meeting they tried to kill Hitler. A bomb. It failed. He's alive and he's pissed."

The news moved through the camp like any good piece of gossip, though none of the guards would speak to any of us about it. If a kriegie teased them about it, they walked away. There was a lot of fear around these days. That night, lying on my bunk, I began to think about escape, about what it might mean and the excitement of being free and out on the German countryside headed for England and the 466th. I knew that if we got out I was going to make it. I was sure of it—however blind that confidence may have been. Stalag 17 life had been far from healthy, but I felt fit all the same, and my years of exposure to long-distance hiking and jogging would likely help. Also, my speaking French might be useful: we'd been told French prisoners worked the farms without being under guard because they weren't of a mind to escape. The tunnel had to be nearly to the storm sewer, and if the danger of it all seemed very far away, the possibilities seemed imminent. Then there was a sudden noise, and we all sat up at once because of the distinctly ominous sound.

"That was a machine gun," said Thompson, a man who knew his guns. There was another burst and still a third.

"Shit. Somebody's in trouble." And we all jumped from our bunks and crowded the shuttered windows.

"What's going on? What do you see?" We all called to the guys closest to the window. They peered out and one of them said, "Can't see nothing except there's one hell of a commotion." And sure enough, whistles were blowing, dogs were barking. Soon guards came barreling through the barracks, clearing the aisles and scattering everyone back to their bunks. They seemed angry, even a bit scared, and they shouted and looked all about each bay as if searching for something amiss. Men were quiet, and after the guards had poured through and everyone huddled in the dark, speculation was rampant about escapes gone bad, executions.

The next morning we had the answer to the gunfire. Lying across the wire like a Raggedy Ann doll was a nearly naked American prisoner, his underwear soiled and ragged. One hand reached through the wire and lay palm up. His legs were in an unnatural tangle, his body so thin and white that we wanted to cover him with a blanket. The Germans left him there.

"They did it to two old kriegies before we got here," Meese said angrily. "I heard that these two poor guys were trying to escape and got caught. Instead of taking them back, they just shot them both in a ditch in the snow. One of them survived but the other was shot a whole bunch of times. Like an execution."

Wild stories circulated. Throughout the day the recounting of the kriegie's death was endlessly speculated. He was killed because of what he knew; he was a high-level spy; he had overheard the guards talking in the infirmary about how the Nazis were going to kill us all before the war's end. The truth, as always, was the simplest one. He had been in the infirmary and something snapped. A nervous breakdown. He had bolted and made for the wire, screaming. The guards made no attempt to stop him. They simply shot him dead. He was a soldier like all of us who had tried to keep himself together and couldn't. If he knew what he was doing, it was a kind of suicide. If he didn't, it was a terrible tragedy. Either way, the stories and speculations soon subsided into quiet acknowledgment of what we all knew: he could bear it no more.

The day he was buried broke cloudless and still. All day men in the American compounds seemed quiet, as if waiting for something. Guys spoke to one another in whispers. By late afternoon, long shadows fell across the camp. The sky was still a canopy of matchless blue, and light still lit the hills and silvered the barbed wires, but it was fast fading. Prisoners gathered at the east fence, though no announcement had been made, and before long many of us were looking out toward the little grove of trees, near the burying ground for the Russians and Slavs who seemed to die so readily. Those trees were bushy with summer, the foliage at their base abundant and green. More and more men were gathering at the wire. Everyone was still. The leaves rustled, stirred by an occasional breeze. Muddy, disheveled, hungry prisoners stood so motionless that it was as if no one wanted to be part of disturbing the silence. Flies crawled over faces unswatted, there were no coughs,

Before all the lessons of war and Stalag 17.

Aerial Gunnery School, summer of 1943. I'm in the second row by myself. Mintz, who doesn't look awake yet, is standing right behind me.

Most of these photographs were taken with a Nazi camera and film smuggled into Stalag 17 under dangerous conditions. Miraculously, the prisoner-of-war scenes captured for posterity were safeguarded by kriegies Ben Phelper and Bernie Resnicoff and survived the rigors of the 1945 forced march west to the American lines, though with much deterioration. They were privately published by Ben Phelper in 1946.

Taken at the Wendover, Utah, aerial gunnery school in August 1943. Within a month our combat crew was put together at the Clovis, New Mexico, air base for first-phase training.

Our crew in flying gear. From left to right, top row: S/Sgt. Irvin Mintz—Left Waist Gunner; 1st Lt. Thaddeus Tedrowe—Pilot; T/Sgt. Ed Dailey—Radio Operator; 2nd Lt. Don Brown—Navigator; 2nd Lt. Jerry Leve—Copilot. Bottom Row: S/Sgt. Alfredo Orlando—Tail Gunner; T/Sgt. Ned Handy— Flight Engineer/Top Turret Gunner; S/Sgt. Florento George Saccomanno— Nose Turret Gunner; S/Sgt. Keith Thompson—Armorer/Right Waist Gunner; 2nd Lt. William Levins—Bombardier.

The Stalag Kriegie

The towers loomed over us and the guards who leaned against their guns seemed indifferent and dangerous. You did not want to be in the wrong place at the wrong time.

Barracks 32-A. A grim home for my year of five seasons.

Taken by the Stalag guards in the fall of 1944. My hair had already begun to grow back from the singe-cut that had made me look like a Chicago gangster to the German grandmother.

The barbed wire double fences that surrounded Stalag 17 and also separated the Americans from the rest of the prisoners of war. Note the piles of tin cans at the base of the inside fence. The Germans put them there to alert their guards to kriegies inside the warning wire. Often, in the dead of night, it was the hungry rats that made noise.

A kriegie airing out his palliasse. Hard to sleep on, filled with fleas, these sacks still offered some relief against the hard wooden bunks. Chet Shattuck, our barracks chief, made the kriegies of 32-A shake out their palliasses every week or so.

Tony Saccomanno in 1943 before his crew took wing for its combat base in England. Today, sixty years down the road, he serves as our Stalag 17 Association's elected CEO.

Gene Meese after getting back from the rugged March 23, 1944, Brunswick mission. His bomb group took heavy losses, including the other crew in his hut.

Carrying the kebo. In the morning, it brought us hot water for mixing with Red Cross coffee (if you had any). The leftover water was used to wash our clothes and shave. Later in the day a second kebo brought a thin soup thought to have everything in it from horseflesh to rat meat. They looked inside a tub like this on the manhunt for Frank Grey.

The latrine in Stalag 17 where I got the lime to mix into the earth over our tunnel hatch cover.

The Honey-Wagon. Pulled along by British prisoners, this wagon was used to clean out the latrines.

The main roadway that ran through Stalag 17 end to end was heavily gated at the point where the American flyers' compounds began. Shown here are kriegies carrying their Red Cross parcels to their barracks. These parcels didn't last long. During our final eight months, we received only one week's worth.

A funeral procession of kriegies to the grove of trees where prisoners were either buried (American or British) or dumped in a paper sack into a mass grave (Russians). This procession was from the winter of 1943 for an American murdered by the Stalag guards.

The double-gate that separated the American flyers from the other thousand Stalag 17 prisoners. This is the gate Frank Grey and I targeted for escape the night of the great snowstorm.

Frank Grey, home from Yugoslavia and WWII in 1946. Known as "The Grey Ghost," for his seven dramatic escapes from the Nazis, he was the only American who got out of Stalag 17 and was never recaptured.

Bill Clarke a few days before going down over Germany. A year later, despite the deprivations of Stalag 17 and the long "march," he swam the icy Inn River to keep American troops on the other side from shelling us.

Ed McKenzie, December 1943, before his flight to the 92nd Heavy Bomb Group base in England. He was just eighteen years old.

Watching from our trenches as the American bombers raid nearby Krems. We cheered these raids until we were reminded that our enthusiasm might not be well received by armed guards with families in town.

On the march. Loaded down with whatever we could carry, we hit the road. Robust as these kriegies seem, many quickly wore down on this march, sick with fatigue and malnutrition. Before long kriegies carried one another as we were herded west by German guards terrified of the fast-closing Russian army.

We wasted no time cutting down trees to make ourselves shelters. Thousands of determined kriegies (with only six or seven axes) were able to cut what wood they needed from the vast forest.

In the forest, ingenious kriegies, skilled at making do with little, built shelters from the rain. This one squats in front of his cozy new home.

His water bag filled with rainwater (or water from the nearby Inn River), this proud kriegie seems to have everything he needs.

These kriegies came from Barracks 37-B. By the end of the war, the kriegies were resourceful, tough, and formidable. Note the make-shift pocket on the kriegie in front with the leather jacket.

One of my two military dogtags and the crucifix Sgt. Young cast for me from a toothpaste tube melted over our kriegie stove. My other Army dogtag, along with the Stalag 17 #105407 prisoner-of-war tag given me on arrival, went back to New Zealand with Ray Bernie. He had become "me" after my going underground as "Frank Grey."

A– Double-gate that separated the 4,300 Americans from the 1,000 prisoners of other nationalities. Frank Grey got through it during the great snowstorm.

B– International part of Stalag 17, with barbed-wire double-fence to left.

C– Center road through the international compounds, running west to Stalag 17's entrance gate.

D– Warning wires, about ten feet inside the double-fence. To cross a warning wire meant getting shot at by the machine-gun-equipped tower guards.

E– Guard tower. (Other guard towers are shown with same symbol.)

F– Four of the twenty "Old Kriegie" barracks. Each building in Stalag 17 was divided into two barracks with a shared washroom separating them.

G– Alley between Barracks 32-A and fence where the guard caught me, now "underground," during March 1 roll call.

H– Our 14-man bay was in this left rear corner of Barracks 32-A. The tunnel hatch was at the other end, in the right front corner.

I– Gate to the "New Kriegie" compound (buildings 29, 30, 31, and 32).

J– Underground path of tunnel that hid Frank Grey and the three Russians.

K– Where Frank talked with me over the fence for 30 days while we waited for another heavy snowstorm.

L– Corner of Barracks 29-A where tunnel was started to get Frank over to the international part of Stalag 17.

M– This building was known by us as "The Russian Chapel"—one of the buildings in the Russian compound across the double-fence separating the American and international parts of Stalag 17.

N– American chapel where Gene Meese took me for Father Kane's Christmas Eve service.

O– Where 32-A roll call count was made first thing each morning by the guards.

P– The "New Kriegie" compound's 40-holer latrine. The supply of lime for throwing down the holes often ran out, but by good luck there was enough the night the tunnel needed it for dealing with the Gestapo dogs.

Q– The jagged air-raid trenches were about two feet wide and four feet deep. They got increasing use as American and British air raids intensified.

R– Approximate line of the rope put in by the guards to keep our compound's 1,200 men backed up to the north fence during the Gestapo's three all-day searches for Frank Grey.

S– Where we sweated it out during the three all-day searches. The covered wooden soup tub the Gestapo looked in for Frank Grey was down here.

T– Warning wire keeping us back from Stalag 17's north fence.

U– The north double-fence, eight feet high with an inside path about six feet wide between the two fences. Guards with rifles patrolled the inside path.

V– The wild-grass field beyond the north fence. We were on a hillside sloping down to the north fence.

AREA-OF-DETAIL WITHIN STALAG 17

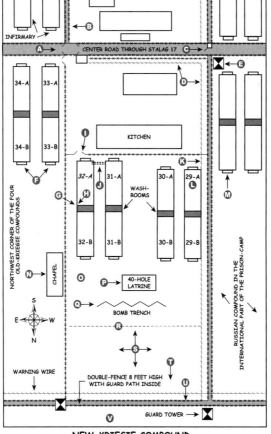

THE 5 AMERICAN COMPOUNDS

THE INTERNATIONAL PART OF STALAG 17

AREA OF DETAIL

INFIRMARY

A→ CENTER ROAD THROUGH STALAG 17 ←C

B→

E→

D→

34-A 33-A

34-B 33-B

I

KITCHEN

NORTHWEST CORNER OF THE FOUR OLD-KRIEGIE COMPOUNDS

F

32-A 31-A

G

H J

WASH-ROOMS

K

30-A 29-A

L

M

32-B 31-B

30-B 29-B

N CHAPEL

O P 40-HOLE LATRINE

Q BOMB TRENCH

R

S E W N

RUSSIAN COMPOUND IN THE INTERNATIONAL PART OF THE PRISON-CAMP

S

T

WARNING WIRE

DOUBLE-FENCE 8 FEET HIGH WITH GUARD PATH INSIDE

U

V GUARD TOWER →

NEW-KRIEGIE COMPOUND—
WITH BARRACKS 32-A AND OTHER ACTION SITES

TUNNEL FROM OUR BARRACKS
SOUTHWEST CORNER BAY

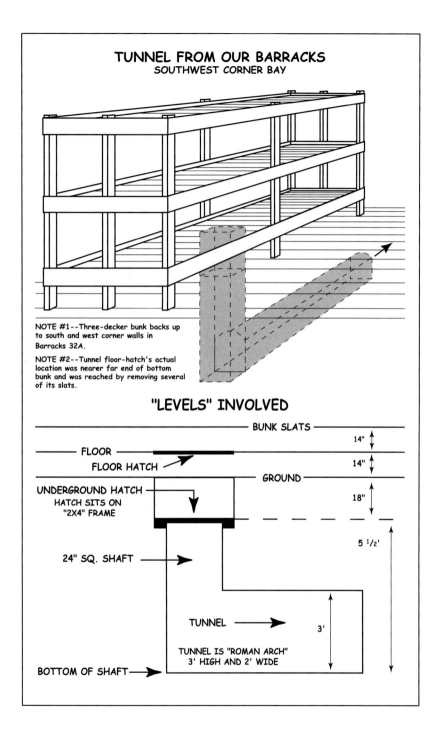

NOTE #1--Three-decker bunk backs up to south and west corner walls in Barracks 32A.

NOTE #2--Tunnel floor-hatch's actual location was nearer far end of bottom bunk and was reached by removing several of its slats.

"LEVELS" INVOLVED

BUNK SLATS

14"

FLOOR

FLOOR HATCH

14"

GROUND

UNDERGROUND HATCH

HATCH SITS ON "2X4" FRAME

18"

5 1/2'

24" SQ. SHAFT

TUNNEL

3'

TUNNEL IS "ROMAN ARCH" 3' HIGH AND 2' WIDE

BOTTOM OF SHAFT

sneezes, not even an occasional whisper. The discipline of the silence was absolute.

Off to our right shuffled a half-dozen kriegies carrying something we'd never seen with the thousands of Russian dead taken out to those woods: a coffin. They carried it on their shoulders across the field. *Who had made it?* I wondered. *When?* At that moment, far off behind us, came the sound of a bugle. The slow mournful notes of "Taps" moved through us like a whisper at first, a soft wind, and before long it caught us up, lifting, rising. The feelings evoked were complicated. It was not grief—we did not even know him or where he had come from. Had it been Meese or Wilkens, Sac, Pappy or Joseph, I would have felt quite differently. It was not even sorrow—we had all lost comrades, had seen our friends blown to pieces. I had felt the hammer blow of seeing men die and thinking in a primitive instant, *How was it not me?* Perhaps it was a sense of allegiance, empathy for a heart burst by too many days behind the wire? We all knew what it took to hold ourselves together; that kriegie's choice, desperate as it was, had surely occurred to many of us at one time or another. As the coffin bounced along the edge of the open field on weary shoulders, a sense of kinship grew among the imprisoned watchers. We had been calibrating our survival hour by hour, and yet the bewildered sergeant whose will had snapped had managed to leave us all and go out beyond the wire. I mourned him, and it was not my imagination that at that moment, as the bugler blew those slow, full twenty-four notes, the American prisoners of Stalag 17 closed in, a momentary family of mourners. Old and new kriegies, so distinct from one another for so long, were reminded that they were brothers-in-arms, that we were as dead as he; that he still moved somewhere among us. That burial brought with it a unity of purpose as powerful as that last morning watching the bombers fan out behind our plane in the moment before the Luftwaffe hit us. Only here, now, the enemy was irrelevant; the Luftwaffe, the Wehrmacht, all seemed of no consequence. Our allegiance to him mattered more to us than any rage we felt toward his murderers.

As the coffin was lowered into the ground, the last of the bugler's notes held. And then it was done. The detail walked away; the silent tribute was over. Talk began as men drifted back to their compounds. Walking later around the perimeter, I passed the compound where the Russian prisoners either sat or lay all about the ground. They demonstrated no curiosity in our dramatic ritual. Why would they? What had pulled us all together was an event that was happening to dozens of them every day.

That night I lay on my bunk thinking about those Russians, snuffed out and dumped without ritual. How little power we have over our own survival. Stubborn resolve can lead to its own decisions, but fate always has its own plans. While the others talked and told stories, I drifted back to the Topeka, Kansas, airfield where I had been stationed with the 333rd Heavy Bomb Group. The 333rd was a support group for B-24 flying crews in training. The airplane mechanics there worked to keep the bombers flying. The group was full of guys mostly older than me, in their thirties and forties (including quite a few regular Army). I was assigned to a squadron mostly made up of men from the Pacific Northwest. They had been loggers; they were broad-backed, patient, tough and reserved. Unlike other camps I had been in, these men did not smoke much or swear or fabricate adventures with women. They went about their work with a grinding stamina; they took me under their wing and made me a reliable B-24 mechanic.

Our two top men, Warrant Officer Waldron and his second-in-command, Master Sergeant Leckbee, were held in the highest regard. Waldron was a sort of John Wayne type who said little except when there was something that had to be said. Leckbee said even less. They apparently liked my work because quite soon they made me a private first class and then a corporal. In early June, reading our squadron bulletin board, I saw an order from Army Air Corps Headquarters. In plain English it advised us that all able-bodied B-24 mechanics were to report to squadron headquarters and sign up for aerial gunnery training. They

needed trained First Engineers to fly combat missions and were combing the bases that trained mechanics, like the one in Topeka.

I loved flying—the crews in training had let me ride with them on
the flights over Kansas—but it was not the love of flying that caught
my attention at that bulletin board. It wasn't even the fact that it was a
general's order. Since boyhood I had ignored seemingly senseless
orders, absurdly certain that my own common sense was a better guide
than those in authority. This order was different. Air Corps high command needed combat flight engineers. I had the training necessary to
be one. I thought I could make a difference in combat. It seemed a sensible order that needed to be obeyed, and to ignore it was not an option:
we were in a war, and so far, we were losing. So I went and signed up. I
didn't think about what would happen to the 333rd Bomb Group if
every one of the mechanics obeyed that order—nor did I think to ask
anyone else about it. The next morning, however, I was notified that
Waldron and Leckbee wanted to talk with me. I went to see them in a
dilapidated shed they used as an office. They offered me a chair, and
in his very low-key way, Leckbee expressed surprise that I had signed
up. Did I know that nobody else in our squadron had signed up? (I
didn't.) Did I understand that it would be damaging to the morale of
the others if I were to go ahead with this? (I hadn't considered that.)
Couldn't I see what a challenge it was to keep the squadron of mechanics together, and that if even a few mechanics took off for gunnery
school, it could lead to a damaging flight of talent? (I could.) Making
no headway, Leckbee looked over at Waldron, who stood there, his
great arms folded across his chest, listening. Waldron spoke up:

"Corporal Handy, is your mother living?"

"Yes, sir."

"Well, does she have any other sons?"

"Yes, sir. My brother."

"Well, what is *he* doing? Is he in the service?"

Only months before, my older brother had signed up to join the

Tenth Mountain Infantry, which served as the Army's ski troops. I told them this.

"Well," he said, "do you think your going to combat is fair to your mother? Should she have to face losing both her sons? And whether she likes it or not, do you think it's the right thing to do?" My mother would have mightily appreciated his logic. I suspect that better men than me could have made an argument out of it had one been required. I listened to them as I had my father about my enlistment, courteously but unmoved. I had a different plan and it was to obey the order. After some moments, knowing I'd already signed up and was not going to recant, they brought the session to an end. I was going to gunnery school and I was going to war.

Months later at a new base where we were picking up our B-24 to take into combat, I ran into one of those Pacific Northwest loggers. He told me that our former squadron, along with Leckbee and Waldron, had been converted to the "Twenty-first Airdrome Squadron" and sent to Africa to be an advance desert aircraft mechanic unit. They had been hit in a firefight; Rommel's troops overran them, and as the logger had heard it, all of them had lost their lives. I lay in my bunk and thought about those men. I'd been fortunate to get to know them and to work with them. In good conscience, they had logically decided to stay where they were and keep on with the indispensable war work they were doing to ready our bomber crews for combat. They understood there was no shortage of applicants for combat but that their work could not be easily surrendered to new, less-qualified men. They had made a careful decision and, as they saw it, a final one. They did not see that down the road someone with a fountain pen would send them into combat and death. I, on the other hand, had chosen to leave those men and take the road to combat. Those loggers were the better warriors, I just the luckier. What would I do with the life given me? The question had haunted me every day since being shot down.

When I finally fell asleep, I had a strange, discomfiting dream. I was woken once again by the gap-toothed airman who had rousted me out on the morning of our crew's last mission. "Briefing," he said, moving on to the next man before I could answer, "in half an hour." The morning procedures followed true to life in exquisitely slow detail, from dressing in my flying gear to eating my breakfast in the mess hall to walking through the drizzle to the briefing hut. The large room where we had our briefings was filled with its customary noisy anticipation and the smoke of a hundred cigarettes. The group was like any audience before a big show, small conversations colliding with one another, the crowd feigning the casual amid the unspoken tension of the task ahead. When the group CO came to the front and stood before the curtain that covered the great map of Europe, which was marked by the colored string of the morning's mission, I was startled to see that he was my father. When it was silent, he pulled the curtain back and everyone craned forward to get a good look. There was no map of Europe, just a blank space. And just as suddenly I was alone, staring past my father at a great empty wall. I woke up in a sweat. It was still dark outside.

WE DECIDED TO MEASURE THE TUNNEL'S length. We had still found no trace of the sewer line, and guys were getting grouchy about it. Heyburn's map had not been exact, so though we knew we had passed the anticipated location, we dug on. Wilkens had stepped off some thread that we could use to measure the distance, and I climbed down into the tunnel to see how far we had gone.

We had hoped to hit the sewer after twenty feet of digging. We had gone thirty.

I climbed up to face Meese and the guys. "No sign of the sewer at all, and we're ten feet beyond where we thought it was," I said.

"Was there ever a sewer line at all?" sniped Kozikowski.

"If Heyburn says there is, there is," I said sharply.

"Of course there is," said Meese. "We just can't find it. Could we just turn the tunnel right and go for the north fence?" he asked, looking out the window at some kriegies tossing a ball in the compound. "Maybe get us out into the open field?"

"It's over three hundred yards. It would take three more crews and months," I said.

"Four crews," said Tony Sac.

Guys were silent. Sanford argued persuasively that we should start digging deeper, as the tunnel might have passed over the storm sewer. Heyburn had been fairly certain about where we should expect to find the sewer, but he had said nothing about the sewer's depth.

"Hell, we can just dig a foot or two down and maybe we find we dug right over it," joined in Tony Sac cheerfully. Everyone agreed that heading off into a new direction was a mistake.

"Let's push deeper on what we got," said Meese. So we began to dig harder. We went down another foot and, for parts of the tunnel, widened it, even breaking into offshoots, blind fingers reaching through the dirt. We did not find the sewer pipe.

Two weeks later, a newsreader came in with an update. "At ease, at ease!" he shouted, and following the customary scramble to the windows and doors to be certain that the news could be read without risk, he climbed on the stool. He waited until signals confirmed the coast was clear and then announced in a grave voice that the Americans had crossed the Rhine at Remagen. It was a breathless moment for all of us. Normandy had stirred the hope with its immense promise, but troops crossing into Germany made that hope as tangible as an American jeep full of muddy GIs. We all knew for certain as we stood around the newsreader that we were going to win the war and that an American army would storm these prison gates. A round of soulful handshakes and clasped arms followed. Over the next few hours, however, there was a subtle shift in the barracks; an uneasy mood settled over us. When you live in the heat of resolve, when you burrow down into yourself to survive, you harden every part of yourself that is exposed to hope. You think of food and family and love as things to be measured and taken only with careful restraint. The news that Americans were on German soil stirred us all and, in the process, returned to us a risky kind of longing. With the Allies coming closer, our own circumstances became less predictable. We were in the hands of an enemy who was losing—what would they do with us? Some allowed themselves to draw and redraw timetables for freedom, postulate what the Nazis might do with us, wonder what the end of the war would feel like. Others were less optimistic. That night, talk in the bay was wary, anxious.

"They'll probably kill us or starve us at least," said someone.

Meese spoke firmly. "No way. The Krauts will begin to imagine life after this war comes to an end. If they kill us, all hell will break loose for them. No, it will be a dangerous time, we'll have to keep our eyes open, but if we stick together, we'll be fine."

"What's the White House saying?"

"What can they say other than to stay calm and be ready?"

Whether we would still be here or not when the Allies came was a gripping question to many, but not to me. All I could think about was our escape plan was now a bigger risk than it had been yesterday if freedom was coming closer. I got out of my bunk and stood alongside Meese's bunk.

"We'd better talk about the project," I said quietly.

"I thought about that."

"It's riskier by the day, I think," I offered. "The Americans are coming, the Russians, too. Who knows when or where, but it's going to be soon."

"We'd better talk with the team in the morning. It may be time to stop work for several weeks—enough time for the Rhine crossing to prove out, at least."

The next morning we met in the bay. Despite my own reluctance to relinquish our tunnel's purpose, I recommended the tunnel project's temporary shutdown. We should wait to see whether the crossing at Remagen could promise early victory. The tunnel was not worth the risk for the moment. GIs crossing the Rhine made escape a riskier proposition. How far away were the Americans? If we got out, where would we go? Why get ourselves killed if we were going to be set free in weeks? Everyone agreed. And after an awkward moment of silence, everyone broke up and left the bay. I was alone for a moment, save for Joseph, the ever-watchful owl in his blue heaven.

"Nothing will stop the American Army," said Joseph quietly. "Nothing."

"They have a long way to go," I offered.

Joseph turned his head and looked out into the compound. "When America wants something, it gets it." It was oddly phrased and made me wonder if he even considered himself an American.

"Well, the Nazis will have some say in how fast they get here, I think."

Joseph snorted. "America is like a great wind. It can clear away the storms that make good men shiver, but it blows away everything that chooses to stand against it. There is no such wind like it. There was a time when my people and the peoples of a hundred other tribes thought they could stand against such a wind. We know better. Every day the Nazis will learn this, too. Such a wind blows away good and bad alike without remorse."

I SOON REALIZED HOW DEPENDENT I had been on that tunnel. I wasn't sure what to do with myself. And just like that, summer fell away as completely as spring had left that morning when we first saw Stalag 17. It was as if the very day after our decision, I woke to the wind against the barracks walls, to the empty promise of nothing to do. The leaves in the grove of trees thinned with the approaching cold and the hillside burnt orange and red, camouflaging the tiled roofs. The changing of the seasons, another mark on the wall, unsettled me. Heyburn had thought we might be in Paris by Thanksgiving; some had convincingly speculated that war would be over by Christmas.

"The first one ended in November," said Sac on a crisp, tangy morning. "The Jerries always do things by the book. They'll hang it up in November, I'll betcha."

"Fat chance" said Sanford. "Hitler's crazy. He'll be swinging away as they dump him in his goddamned grave." The conversation was one we had had a thousand times—elaborate explanations of the complex reasons why all our troubles had to end within the month. We knew the Nazi infrastructure was breaking down. We figured the Jerries weren't much better off than our guards, who looked almost as bad as we did. Our bodies were hardening, and we were, in some ways, more resourceful than the hapless guards who worked so hard to act like veteran soldiers when they, too, were mostly simple men waiting for all of this to end.

Shattuck had begun painting small scenes on bunks around our bay. Tony Sac got the first one, a picture of his bomber. Everyone loved it, and Shattuck had to fend off requests from guys who wanted everything from favorite animals and camp scenes to places back home they remembered. Missing home was starting to be a theme that men no longer cared to hide.

I feared getting used to all this. The tunnel had afforded me structure, habit. Now I felt a bit lost, and it unnerved me. I missed the routine of having a task that broached no debate and precious little interference. When it was time to dig, I dug. I knew where I was and what I had to do, and no one could interrupt me. No doubt others felt the same way: it gave us a reason to make use of every single day. I renewed my vows to wash my clothes more regularly, walk the perimeter more often and improve my relations with others. I knew how to keep quiet, but my own instinct to judge was still strong, and I could occasionally be more caustic than I had intended. I didn't much like suggestions as to how certain things might be improved if they differed from what I thought was required. I was beginning to see how headstrong I could be and how I could rub others the wrong way. I did not know it then, but my stubborn resolve would cost me dearly in my final attempt to escape from Stalag 17.

PART III

FALL

> *She builds not on the ground, but in the mind*
> *Her open-hearted palaces.*
>
> —ROBERT LOWELL

I NEEDED TO go see Heyburn to tell him that his tunnel was on hold. We had not spoken for some time and I had given him few updates; talk of the tunnel was not worth the risk. Besides, until we hit the sewer, what was there to talk about? Now, though, he needed to know that we had not yet found the sewer. I had a gnawing sense that we had started the job and not finished. I was disappointed in myself and worried about what to tell Heyburn. I went to Meese, who listened to me and shrugged. He would have none of it.

"Everyone did their best. Some things just don't work out, that's all. Anyway, we could keep going, but the risks outweigh the rewards. This war is going to end soon and it's no time for impatience. Listen, the biggest troubles you get in life often come at the beginning of things and the end. The Russians and the Americans are on the move, and there's sure to be trouble."

"What kind? What do you mean?" I asked.

"All I mean is that whoever gets here first, the Germans aren't going to hand us over to them with dry sheets and fresh towels. We have plenty enough to worry about."

He may well have been right, but I still felt bad. Had another team leader set the parameters, I wondered, might the tunnel have worked? What if we had dug lower sooner? Had I misread his map? Meese put his hand on my shoulder.

"If you're bold, you'll make plenty of mistakes in this life. When you make 'em, you'll step up and shoulder the blame for your share. But this isn't one of those times. Learn the difference between a mistake and a hell of a good try. He'll understand. Don't worry so much. You may owe it to tell him we aren't digging, but don't give him an apology when none is needed."

I went looking for Heyburn. The old kriegies still seemed like citizens of an entirely different, almost hostile place. They always looked older and a good deal more stretched than we were. A guy with a pockmarked face shadowed by a cap stepped in front of me.

"Hey boys, we got ourselves a hairy ass here." His friends laughed. "What are you up to, hairy ass?" I stopped, surprised, and while I was thinking about what to say, he went on.

"You too good to talk to us, hairy ass?"

I stepped around him and heard him say to his mates: "These assholes have it so easy." Then he said something I didn't hear, which made his friends howl with laughter. I kept walking. How is it that men are so strange to one another? We were all Americans—in the same fix—yet it was still like being in a rival gang's neighborhood. I found Heyburn standing on the edge of a group. The talking stopped as they all turned to look at me. Heyburn grinned and said, in a voice loud enough for everyone to hear, "Hey there, Handy, how the hell are you?" and the talk started up again as if I were invisible. They were talking about escapes, and a burly fellow held forth like a ragged Santa Claus to a roomful of urchins:

"Some of you guys know this because you were there and know it's true, so shut up. There were these two British POWs—we were all mixed in together at Moosburg—and they managed to cop themselves some Russian clothing."

"Oh, not this one again," growled somebody. Santa ignored him. "Now beats me how they figured this one, but those Brits got balls, I'll say that for 'em. They got a hold of some whitewash and began to paint a line down the center of the camp's main road. I suppose the guards figured somebody had authorized it, so when those two passed through the front gate, no one batted a goddamned eye. Running a white line right out the front gate and down the road."

"Did they get away?" somebody asked eagerly.

"Naw. They were so surprised to be outside the camp that they started laughing and slapping each other on the back, and the Jerries know them poor Russian sons of bitches wouldn't know how to laugh if they was being tickled to death. They got 'em both before they could reach the woods. Thrown in the cooler for a goddamned age."

"I'll tell you one I saw in that camp with my own eyes, I swear to God," said another man. ("The time-honored words that precede a whopper," whispered Heyburn to me.) "Some American GIs—you remember this, Harris, don't you, one of them was from your home town, right?" The one called Harris nodded sagely.

"Goddamned right he was. We called him John Henry 'cause he was so good with his twin fifties."

"Well, anyway, they swapped some smokes with these poor-assed Russians for overcoats, got themselves a ladder, tools and pieces of barbed wire. They pretended to be a repair detail. I swear. Man, those guys worked all day, cutting and repairing wire up and down the fence. Every piece they cut, they repaired. By the evening when we were at roll call, I could see that they had worked themselves outside the fence, outside the damned camp! Guys were whispering up and down the line, 'They're outside . . . ' Well, the Krauts had been seeing these guys screwing around all day and paid them no mind at all. Figured them for a bunch of ratty bastards doing their typical half-assed job. At the far end of the roll call line a fight broke out, and it seemed a pretty mean one. I was surprised 'cause I had not seen two kriegies going at it like that since we got in here. They were going so hard the Jerries had to come in and break it up and threaten everybody. It was only when I realized the two guys who were fighting were crewmates and buddies that I got it. Sure enough, I looked back at the wire and that work crew was gone. The ladder and the tools were lying in the grass like clothes left at a skinny dip. They'd made it, all three. That night we were all so damned excited we couldn't sleep. I was even a little sad," said the guy reflectively.

"Yeah, but not as sad as when those poor bastards got dragged back to camp," said someone in the back.

"Ain't it the truth. They had been worked over pretty bad, that's certain. They dragged 'em by us to show 'em. Their boots left a trail in the mud all the way to the cooler. But you know one of those guys—your buddy, wasn't it, Harris?—had his eye swollen shut but gave me the biggest shit-eating grin I had ever seen."

A third man spoke up. He was tall and bald and looked older than everyone else. "Sometimes it's the damnedest luck. There was another GI we knew at Moosburg who got away after the first few days he'd been there. I'm not sure what he did, but he got out. He walked all night and was careful to stay off all the roads and steer clear of the villages. He was damned near Switzerland when he came to a river. It was deep and fast, and so he walked along it until he found an old wooden bridge. There was a little boy throwing rocks into the river and the GI, knowing that a kid's curiosity was trouble, just walked over that bridge and never gave the kid a glance. When he got to the other side, though, he looked back and saw that the kid was gone. It wasn't but ten minutes later that he was stopped by a policeman with a revolver as big as a cannon. That night he learned that the little boy had run home and told his folks that a man had crossed the bridge and his shoes had made no sound at all. Well, the boy's daddy knew that no Germans had rubber-soled shoes. His brother was the local cop, so that was that."

"Sometimes," countered Santa, "the luck is so bad it makes you want to cry. There were three guys who got out at Moosburg and made it to the Swiss border. They just snuck right past the German guards one night and boom, Switzerland here we come. One of them was kind of jumpy and figured that folks near the border might be Nazi sympathizers, so he convinced the other two to keep walking. They went all day and night, as far into Switzerland as they could get, and every mile made them happier and happier. The next morning they come to this beautiful little village, one of those Swiss numbers with colored shutters and flowers in the windows. They walked down the hill and into the town like cowboys on coffee break and strutted straight to the town hall where they announced they were American POWs needing sanctuary. There was an old man who listened carefully to them and then politely excused himself. When he came back he had a dozen German soldiers with him. Those boys hollered bloody murder about Swiss neutrality when one of the locals came forward and said, 'You are not in Switzerland, sirs, you are in Germany.' Those poor guys had walked right through the narrow corridor of Switzerland and right back into Germany."

Heyburn chuckled next to me. "Lord, I have heard these stories a thousand times." He turned and took my elbow. "Let's go for a walk." We walked outside and followed the line of the warning wire in his compound for several minutes of silence.

"It sounded like guys were escaping Moosburg left and right," I offered.

"The Jerries didn't know as much about Americans and their appetite for the open road. But they caught on fast enough," said Heyburn. "You look good," he said to me after a few moments. "That first day you boys looked like deer in the headlights, but I knew you guys would do fine."

I said nothing. We walked. Heyburn chatted amiably. He told me about some of the guys in his bay and the usual local adventures that kept every prisoner's mind off worries and schemes. Little things occupied us, brought us pleasure and made us forget our troubles. Heyburn tried out a few and I tried just as hard to enjoy them, but he knew I was struggling.

"Look here, Handy. You are awfully down at the heel. What's on your mind?"

I tried to think of the best way to say it and then just said it. "The tunnel's a dead end. We can't find the pipe, the guys are tired."

"What happened?" he asked. I told him the whole story from the beginning, the hatch, the digging, and the evacuation of the dirt. Everything. Heyburn was quiet, but he seemed very interested in all the details. Every now and again he would shake his head and say "Wow" or "Pretty slick." When I had finished, I added my own apology. I was sorry that he had given me a challenge that I had not met. Sorry, too, that I couldn't spring him from the stalag considering how long he had been here and how much he had suffered. He was quiet for a long time.

"You didn't do it for me, Handy. The sooner you figure that one out, the better."

"I didn't do it just for you, I know." Along with the rest of the guys, I had also done this as a duty—something American soldiers were told to do—and of course to escape myself.

Heyburn smiled. "You don't get it, yet."

"Get what?" I said, pressing him, a little puzzled.

"It's more than the duty, though that's important enough. It's what we have to do to stay alive. How we keep hope so real and hard that we can't forget how it feels. Like that omelet we once saw served for breakfast, remember? Don't mind me, Handy," he added with a shrug. "You guys did a good job and you made a damn good run at it. Thanks for trying." We spoke a bit longer and then I headed back to my barracks.

"Hey, Handy," Tony Sac called to me as I came in the door of 32A, "wanna hear the damnedest thing? You know McManus's crew? You know the little guy from Pennsylvania? Well, he just taught me to knit and chew tobacco at the same time. At the same damn time! This is one weird war where I learn stuff my grandmother and grandfather knew from a guy who is smaller than both of 'em."

· · ·

"CMON," THEY CATCALLED, "C'MON. TELL US one. It's time. It's been weeks." They hounded him, knowing he was going to tell them a story even though he pretended he wouldn't. The ritual was always the same: the lights went out, men grumbled and settled into the dark; they coughed, belched and traded sharp exchanges; and then, like clockwork, they waited for the soft, cool voice of Pages to fill the dark. He was a man who loved books, and somewhere along the way somebody had discovered that when he told the story of a book it was better than reading it. You would see him walking the perimeter of the camp with a few guys trailing him, and he would be telling them about Mr. Micawber or the Count of Monte Cristo, and they would be asking questions and pressing him for details. He always knew what his listeners wanted to hear, so most of his stories settled on the detail that brought us all the greatest pleasure: food.

"Now this is a love story, fellas," said Pages. "About the Hatfields and the McCoys and the love affair between their children, Romeo and Juliet." Immediate reactions, groans, annoyance from the listeners in the dark.

"We all know that story, there ain't nothing exciting about Romeo and Juliet."

"Romeo, oh Romeo," catcalled someone, and everyone hooted and laughed. Pages continued as if he had heard no complaint at all. And he told us a story:

"Boys, most all of you know about the Hatfields and the McCoys and how they hated each other. It was a bad hate, and neither family could ever remember how all the hating got started. That is the thing about hate—it feeds itself just fine. Folks knew there was no interfering in it. If a Hatfield was shopping in town and found himself in a side street with a pair of McCoys, he would have to fight for his life. If a McCoy fell asleep on a picnic, it was sure to be a Hatfield who would wake him up with a boot to the head. But all that hating was going to birth one of the strangest love stories you ever heard. So settle in and listen when I tell you about the night the Hatfields had themselves the biggest damn wingding of the year. Old man Hatfield had the idea that he would marry his youngest daughter, Juliet, to Poot Wilson, one of the most successful farmers in the whole county. Folks came from all over. One of them, in disguise, was Romeo McCoy. He loved the niece of old man Hatfield, a girl name Rose. He wanted to see her up close, maybe even sneak a dance with her. And so he did. And man, it was a party."

And Pages began to talk about the food, table by table, plate by plate. The dark was so quiet it was as if the whole barracks were listening. The Hatfields had laid it all out and so did Pages: smothered ham, sprinkled with sugar and browned all over with baked sweet potatoes topped with butter; roast leg of lamb, plump, moist and served piping hot. Trays of fricasseed chicken surrounded by dumplings awash in giblet gravy. There was pork and parsnip stew, stuffed onions, corn chowder, fritters and stuffed eggplant. Men called out: "Desserts, Pages, what have they got for dessert?"

"Lord," he laughed, "why the desserts were the main attraction. That's what folks really came for. They had chocolate soufflé and rhubarb Betty, pineapple custard with vanilla ice cream, lemon meringue pie, burnt sugar cake and oatmeal drop cookies."

"My ma made cookies like that," said a wistful voice in the dark. "She used to drop one teaspoon of dough after another onto a greased tray and my brother and me would watch them turn brown and swell up fat."

"Yes, sir," said Pages, "that's the kind they had. Just like that. And you could eat all you wanted and there was no end to the food. The more folks ate, the more the servants brought out. Plate after plate."

"Was there any plum pudding?" asked Beast.

"The plum pudding, I forgot to mention that. It was hot, sweet plum pudding. They made a hard sauce with butter, sugar and a rind of orange for flavoring. You could have vanilla ice cream with that, too."

"Not me," said Beast. "Just the hard sauce."

Some guys asked for their favorite dishes, and Pages would let some of them be served and others he suggested would come later, at the wedding itself. ("Hearing what they had at this party," said someone with admiration, "I can't wait until the goddamned wedding.") But after a while, the listeners had their fill and asked about Romeo and his girl.

"Well, Romeo wasn't hungry, at least not for food. He wanted to see Rose and he searched everywhere for her. There were lots of women, long-legged, high-hipped, big-breasted gals from all over." When Pages got to the moment when Romeo saw Juliet, he paused for effect. Some were already sleeping, but others were up on their elbows, their shadows rising and falling on the camp searchlights.

"Romeo looked across the dance floor and saw her standing shyly off to the side. She was pale but glowed like the moon. Her smile was a sudden thing and lit those around her. The awkward way she laughed made him weak with loving her. She was like no one he had ever seen before, and just like that, his whole life turned. Everything he had thought only seconds before seemed silly and useless. He wondered what he had been doing all his life not feeling the way he did at that very instant. 'Have you found Rose yet?' his friend whispered to him. 'No,' he said, as if far away. 'Hey, boy, have you seen a ghost?' and then his friend followed Romeo's eyes and saw the shy girl at the end of the table. 'Aw, now don't even think about it. That's Juliet Hatfield. Her father'd kill you if he thought you were even thinking about his daughter.' But Romeo was already gone, moving through the crowd toward her like a man walking the plank and glad of it."

"Tell us more about the food, Pages," said a voice, and a half dozen other voices hissed in the dark to shut him up. "Go on," they encouraged Pages, "tell us what happened with the girl."

"Well, he found her and introduced himself, and she looked kind of timid at first but her eyes stayed on him so long and hard without blinking that Romeo thought he was going to pass out. 'Do I know you?' she asked. 'Now you do,' he said. 'And forever.' And fellas, that was it—she saw him and he saw her. And you all know that being seen is the greatest moment in this life. Love, boys, is a fine thing and worth fighting for." Pages was quiet.

"Well?" cried out his listeners.

"Well, somebody saw them talking and came over and took a swing at Romeo and all hell broke loose. And before long there were knives instead of fists. Someone got a blade into Romeo's friend and he fell to the ground. Romeo took him in his arms and asked after him.

" 'You know,' said his pal with a chuckle, 'it's not as wide as a barn door and ain't as deep as a well, but it's killing me sure,' and then he fell dead. Well, that was it. Romeo took up the knife and howling like an animal, he went after the guy who had killed his friend. He ran that fellow clean through, stomach to back, killing him so fast the fellow didn't even have time to close his eyes."

"My waist gunner died like that," said someone softly.

Pages went quiet again. We all lay there remembering. And then Pages began again in an easy, conversational way, as if he were winding the story up. "Well, Romeo would've killed every male Hatfield he could get his hands on if he hadn't been grabbed and hustled off."

"And then?" said someone when Pages had gone quiet again.

"I'm beat, fellas."

"Can't you at least tell us about the wedding? It must have had twice the food!" shouted another voice.

"Naw, the wedding was small," said Pages. "No guests. Old Romeo and Juliet got together with a priest and made no fuss. Then they went off and had a picnic by the river with cold chicken, little toasted cheese sandwiches, asparagus salad, hot cranberry muffins and lots of other stuff. And they lived happily ever after, having a whole bunch of kids who later became kings and queens of England."

There was a volley of complaint as voices pleaded with Pages to press on with more picnic details.

"No. No more. Hit the sack and go to sleep," said Pages in a voice that brooked no further argument.

A deep quiet fell over the bay. Like any good storyteller, Pages had stopped when his listeners still wanted more. No doubt they would plague him to finish tomorrow. I wasn't certain why he had chosen to tell such a story. During flight training, all anyone ever spoke about was women. Most of us were still teenagers and knew nothing about women, but the air was filled with boasts and brags, speculation and laughing. The nearby towns were filled with potential sweethearts, waiting to claim you. Here, though, there was never any talk of women; there were no extended descriptions of their attributes or reminiscences of their allure. If romance was frowned on as a subject, sex was utterly forbidden. Occasionally, guys would report on the presence of Russian women in the neighboring compound or a wide-hipped peasant skirt tilling a nearby field, but the reporters were always restrained, their descriptions limited. Did Pages stop because he knew we could not bear too much of it? Hope had to be carefully measured and longing was restricted to those things that were not impossible. Men could get lucky with food or an unexpected parcel or a day of uneventful rest. But thoughts of women would only leave them frustrated and despairing. I wondered if Pages had stirred Romeo and Juliet into our dreams to remind us that the world was still out there, waiting. I thought about how much pleasure his stories always brought us and thought of Axel Jack's omelet. Were we becoming old kriegies now, dreaming of the things we couldn't have? Omelets and tunnels. Keeping hope real, Heyburn had said, even if we feed ourselves on dreams. I began to think I understood what he meant.

I fell asleep that night among my own ghosts of home.

THE WORD GOT AROUND TO OUR compound fast, whispered from bay to bay like all the best rumors: hot showers. I had not only forgotten what one felt like, I had forgotten to want one. In April, when I first arrived, we were shuffled through some hot water before we were deloused, but now, six months and dozens of cold-water washes later, we smelled like cattle. Some men couldn't stand cold water and never washed at all except a splash across the face. I was a New Englander, used to the cold and happy to scrub myself down with chilly cupfuls of water from the tap. My skin would tingle and fool me into feeling clean for a while, but hours later I could smell myself again, as if I had just climbed back into my old familiar stink. In the end, it didn't matter, since none of us could even remember how to smell. The promise of a hot shower changed all that. We all squirmed in anticipation, and the smells we had taken for granted now seemed unbearable. The Germans were going barracks to barracks, rousting us out systematically and herding us on to the shower facilities.

When the turn for 32A came (two days after the first rumor got started), we were taken up the hill to a fenced-off area next to the showers and we waited to go in. It was most everybody from 32A, probably all 143 men. If we were impatient to scrub off the layers of dirt that lined our skin like wrinkles, we were in no hurry. We had hiked up a small hill to the showers and we liked the outing. The fourteen of us from our bay made the most of our limited freedom as each group ahead of us passed into the showers where about twenty showerheads squirted hot water. Talk went on. Someone began bragging about his home state to kill time, and as always, it turned into an all-hands debate. Guys were full of facts and justly proud about the state they'd lived in all their lives. It was all of no account to me. Indiana's virtues seemed little different to me from California's. I had moved five times from state to state and had come to feel that home was not a matter of geography, but simply where my family was. We took our home with us, sometimes unexpectedly but always with a sense of adventure. My checkerboard life disqualified me from the debates.

"How 'bout you, Handy? What's the best thing about where you're from?" asked Koz. "I'm from nowhere," I replied, a little too enigmatically. Everyone looked at me blankly and the conversation rolled on without me. Max, who appeared to be the head guard for the shower waiting area, soon diverted my attention. He was particularly obnoxious today and came across like the worst of the Nazi military I'd encountered so far, inhuman and vicious. His interest in us grew as we waited and stood passively to go into the showers. The conversation drained away as one by one we all recognized that Max was getting louder and more vicious. Our wariness seemed to aggravate him.

He walked over to a kriegie who stood quietly in line. Max was considerably smaller and looked a bit foolish next to the kriegie, whose big thighs and broad shoulders suggested the build of a football player. Max, with the unerring instinct of the bully, chose his target well. The kriegie had a shrunken look about him, hooded eyes. A terrible weariness. He barely stirred when Max poked him hard in the ribs.

"Leave him alone," said somebody defiantly.

"Yeah, cut the shit, you pint-sized asshole," said another.

Max turned and faced us with an intensity that backed us all down and made him more than ominous. Then, as if on a dare, he turned and shoved the kriegie into the shed wall. The kriegie's head smacked the tin and he fell. Others helped him up. Everyone started muttering, and a few of us moved forward. I hated bullies and had always sought to defend the underdog. I swore at Max, louder than the others, and he turned toward me. Then he simply pointed at me and smiled. And that was that.

Within a few minutes we were rounded up for the shower trip and began ambling in twos and threes toward the shower building's large door. I stood in the hot water for a few delicious moments, the dirt washing away like forgiven sins. Then we were herded out and we collected our clothes. After dressing, I was the last out, trailing the others, when suddenly I was grabbed by my left arm and yanked about ten feet to a little shed. I was thrown through its rickety door before I could even react. My attacker was strong and he spun me around. It was Max. The shed was shadowy—it had only one small window at the back of its perhaps ten-foot-square floor—but I could see excitement in his face. He drew a large pistol from his holster, moved the barrel to his right hand and swung its heavy butt hard into my head. He hit me two or three more times before I blacked out.

I woke what seemed hours later to the hard, white burst of sky and felt myself being carried under the armpits. My feet wouldn't move; I tasted blood, and a loud ringing was all I could hear. I couldn't turn my head and wasn't sure what had happened. Someone was carrying me, and then I heard the voices of my own mates. A small group from 32A surrounded me and walked me the few hundred yards down the hill to our barracks. The water in the washroom hadn't yet been turned off for the day. They got the blood washed off my face and someone handed me a rag.

"It's bleeding bad," he said. "Staunch it with this. You got one hell of a pistol-whipping. We'd better get you to the infirmary."

"No," I countered. "Thanks, but I'll be OK. Let me be for a bit." My companions shrugged, assuming, I suppose, that I did not know how seriously I had been beaten. I went back to my bunk to lie down. There seemed quite a commotion with people asking me what happened and telling one another. I could remember little. I only saw the shadow of Max against the light of the doorway. The fever in his eyes was enough. Had trying to kill me really brought him such joy? My tongue felt swollen and my jaw hurt, but I just wanted to forget it, think about something else, and maybe get some sleep. For a while I lay wide awake—the sound of clogs up and down the aisle like cannon fire. In time I drifted off.

Waking hours later, I was told that Shattuck wanted to talk with me. When I got to his bay, he put his hand tentatively on the side of my head like a man touching fresh paint. He said, "That's grim. He beat the shit out of you. When you're up to it, Handy, I want you to go up to the White House about this. Report it. Report this goddamned guard." My ear rang and my head hurt.

I went up to the White House and was told to report to our deputy camp leader, Charlie Belmer. I had never met Belmer but knew that after Kurtenbach, he was one of the most highly regarded among us. With much courtesy and even a word of thanks for my visit, he made notes on my report about Max and said, with what appeared to be a flicker of sadness, "You want to press this?"

"Shattuck says I should."

"Do you want to?"

"Well, I don't care that much, but Shattuck really feels I should." I couldn't help but sense there was something Belmer wasn't telling me.

"I'll get back to you," he said and rose to his feet. "Thanks," he said.

A day or two later, I got word that Belmer wanted me to go back up to the White House. He was waiting for me along with Kurtenbach, our camp leader and Man of Confidence. Despite all that I had heard about Kurtenbach, I had never met or seen him before either. He was friendly and calm and shook my hand strongly, saying, "Tough deal, Handy. I understand he roughed you up something fierce." Without further discussion, we all walked across the compound to the office of the camp commander, Major Eigle, the German Luftwaffe officer who had stood before us that first roll call. Like the tall pilot, he too had a wooden leg; everyone in camp called him "Peg Leg." The name's mockery was good-natured and carried little venom. He had never done anything to directly insult or injure us, and we didn't blame him if some of his guards were morons or sadists. Kurtenbach maintained that he behaved well and that was good enough for all of us.

We entered his office. Peg Leg sat behind a desk while several officers and the square-headed Max stood at the side by the window. Max was sweating, his hands at his sides, fingers twitching. Peg Leg offered us chairs, but Belmer refused on our behalf and commenced speaking through an interpreter. Kurtenbach knew German and spoke it well, I had been told, but he simply stood and stared at the German officer. Belmer recounted my beating, stressed that it was an ambush without provocation. He claimed I had been badly injured and my hearing may have been permanently damaged (it was). He summed it up with righteous anger: the behavior contradicted the essence of the Geneva Convention and we wanted the strongest possible punishment brought to bear.

I looked at Max, who was in a real sweat. He watched his commander like a child whose parent is being told of outrageous behavior at school. Every time that Peg Leg shot him a glance, he shrugged and rolled his eyes as if to imply this was all a good deal of nonsense, a misunderstanding. I almost pitied him. At one point he spoke out directly and at the same instant patted me on the back, as if to say "No harm done. He's a good boy." I didn't like that and started to bristle when I felt Kurtenbach's hand on my arm. Peg Leg rose to his feet with the kind of certitude that announced he had heard enough and had made up his mind. He turned to Max and began to shout. They told me later it was something like "If I hear any more about stuff like this, you will be sorry." Then he spoke in a voice of disdain and disgust. Max came toward me, head bowed slightly, and offered me his hand. I looked at him. He seemed humiliated and I could see that his hand was trembling. His skin was clammy and moist to the touch, and only when he stepped back and I saw the relief in his face did it occur to me that that same hand I had just shaken had cost me the hearing in my left ear. And that was that. I was sent back to my barracks.

Tony Sac greeted me at the door and put his arm around my shoulders.

"You're in it now, Handy."

"What do you mean?" I asked, startled.

Tony Sac sat on his bunk and was quiet for a moment.

"No offense, Handy, but you're kind of a babe in the woods. Don't get me wrong—you're tough and all, and smart, but you don't know shit about how the world works. I mean, the guy nearly killed you. That's a tough break. And he'll get his, make no mistake. In Brooklyn, guys make a point of remembering. We'll all make a point of remembering Max when the time comes. But never," and he looked at me with a scolding eye, "never let someone else try and even the score for you."

"Why not?" I countered, not really understanding. "Maybe he'll hold back on the next guy because he's scared of what could happen to him."

"Oh, yeah, that's true. He may not do anything to the next guy. The point is, Handy, he sure as hell will be looking to do something to you. So keep your eyes open and watch your back. He's a sneaky bastard. Guys like him don't forgive or forget. When he's around, you stick with your buddies."

Later that night, lying in my bunk, I couldn't sleep. The slats beneath me were out of place; the palliasse needed redistribution of its wood chips and cardboard stuffing. I had been stupid to go to the White House. Tony Sac would've set me straight. Remembering again Belmer's fierce demands in Peg Leg's office, I began to realize that there was more to this meeting than I had realized. My beating was yet another piece in an ongoing chess game between prison leadership and the Luftwaffe officers. There was a kind of theater to it. It was not my rights anyone sought to protect or my well-being. My ear rang and my jaw ached. Max and I were of no account at all. Each of us was a pawn in a drama that had nothing to do with either of us. Whether we lived or died was a matter of luck or timing or fate, and we hadn't a clue which one. Tony Sac was right, though; if Max had a moment, he would want to play out his own part. He would exact his revenge as if that were all that mattered. I determined again to keep my distance. We kill you; you kill us, the Luftwaffe interrogator had said to Beast.

ONE SUNDAY AFTERNOON, ALL HELL BROKE LOOSE. The Jerries pulled us out for a roll call. "What's up, Schultzie?" somebody called out. The guards were tense. They said nothing to us. It was as if they were scared. They kept us out and recounted for hours. Something was up.

"Handy, go see Shattuck on the double. He wants to talk with you and right now." The kriegie with the message was agitated.

Trying to steel myself for some bad news, I almost ran up to the front end of the barracks. Shattuck wasted no time:

"Something big's happened. Kurtenbach wants to know whether the tunnel can hide five men. He needs to know now."

I was stunned. What was going on? I wanted to ask how our tunnel got center stage, but Shattuck's manner was one that demanded answers, not further questions.

"There's enough room down there, if that's what you mean. But how long would they have to hide?" I asked.

"All day. Days. I don't know. The Gestapo's looking for one of these guys and will likely tear the camp to pieces trying to find him. Even Peg Leg is scared to hell they're coming."

"Well, we were only able to dig for a few hours at a time. You have to come out for air. Meese and the others will tell you the same."

Shattuck was annoyed.

"Handy," he said with impatience. "We need to know right away if that tunnel can keep these men safe. The White House needs to know right away. Get back to me within twenty minutes. Yes or no. Hurry." Then he turned away—as always, his simple gesture of dismissal.

It was a rainy day. Our guys were lounging around the bay. The tunnel team hadn't met since our decision to discontinue work several weeks earlier, and getting together seemed to everyone's liking. When they heard what Shattuck had asked, no one spoke. Meese frowned, Wilkens braided string into yet another strand of rope. In the next bay there was laughter and someone sang off-key. And then everybody in our bay began to talk at once: about the risks, solutions, damnable timetables and general impossibility of using the tunnel as a long-term haven. Finally Wilkens's voice, with its loping drawl and easy rhythm, cut through the noise:

"They must have no other spot to hide 'em, so it's our tunnel sure. Let's all agree on that. Whoever these boys are, we're going to put them in our tunnel. Now the space is big enough to take them all, but there isn't enough air down there for them all to breathe with the hatch closed."

"So the problem is getting air in there," someone said.

"No shit, Sherlock," piped another voice.

"Well, that's one of the problems," I threw in. "The other is getting the air out. We're going to have to figure out a way to move the air efficiently down there. That'll take some doing."

"Shattuck needs an answer," said Meese, looking straight at Wilkens, who looked back at him long and hard before nodding. I had a sense that a question had been asked and answered between them with no words at all.

"Go tell Shattuck we'll do it. Tell him to let us know when, and we will be ready," said Meese.

"Yessir, go ahead and do that," said Wilkens absently. "We'll get it figured out one way or another." He continued to braid his string as if we were all sitting out on a summer porch. As I got up to go to Shattuck's bay I heard him tease the others softly: "Now, my merry magicians, we've walked this road together before. I need all the soup cans you can get your hands on in the next half hour . . ."

When I came back, Wilkens had the team busy. Meese, Dailey, Thompson, the Sac brothers, all were at work. They had already built about four feet of pipe, bending back the lips of the tin cans so that they would all slot together. Calling for a break, Wilkens gathered us around him and described his plan.

"We'll pull down the inside sheathing boards behind the bunk—that corner bunk covering our floor hatch—and then work this half-inch-diameter rod down into the ground hidden between the inside and outside sheathing boards. There's six inches of width in there, so we'll have plenty of space. But we'll have to start our rod right in the center of that space." Wilkens was the teacher now and we were his rapt, dutiful students. "This pipe we're putting together out of soup cans will fit snugly through a three-and-a-half-inch hole. But to make sure that pipe hole stays within our six-inch-wide hidden space, where the Jerries won't see it, we have to center it in there. The idea's to get this half-inch-diameter rod down through a reamed hole the diameter of the soup cans. We'll go down four feet or so of ground through to the tunnel ceiling. Meanwhile, one of you diggers will man the tunnel and let us know when our rod breaks through."

"Yeah, what about a cave-in?" asked Thompson and Tony Sac together.

"No worries," Wilkens answered. "We'll work it down gently to avoid a cave-in. Once the rod's through and has given us the alignment, you diggers will work from inside the tunnel, using a pipe and some other equipment I've got here. You'll ream out that hole working from the bottom. That's how we're going to stay clear of cave-ins. Coming down from the top could be bad news."

Wilkens stopped and took a breath. There was an unusual silence. Then Kozikowski, from his upper-bunk perch, said, "Wow!" There was a general sigh of relief.

"So you get the idea, fellas. I knew you would. The stalag's greatest tunnel team is back in business!" Wilkens went on, beaming broadly. "The pipe will stick up a couple of inches above the ground, but out of sight after we nail the wall boards back in place. Down in the tunnel it'll be level with the ceiling. Then we'll make another cut-through for another pipe a foot or more away."

"A kind of exhaust pipe?" asked Kozikowski, excited now.

"Yeah, Koz, exactly. Exactly. Good air in, bad air out. But there's one more problem, and it's the big one. Anybody know what it is?"

"Sure," said Tony Sac, always able to enter a discussion at its key moment. "We need a pump, something to move the air in and out."

"On the money. We need a pump—and a quiet one. I've got an idea. While you guys are putting together the air pipes and getting them in place, I'll see what I can do."

"Handy, what did Shattuck say?" It was Meese. I hadn't yet said anything about Shattuck's reaction to our telling him that we could pull it off. Wilkens looked at me expectantly.

"Shattuck's happy. He wishes us luck and Godspeed—but not to forget we've got to have these guys in that tunnel early tomorrow morning."

"Plenty of time," said Wilkens, though he was no longer smiling. "Let's get a move on." It was the first time I had ever seen Wilkens tense.

Wilkens's briefing had taken twenty minutes or so. We still had more than six hours to work before curfew would shut us down. Everyone got back to work in high gear. After taking meticulous directions from Wilkens, Dailey and Sac started on the air pump. Meese and Thompson cleared out the workspace over the tunnel hatch and began prying loose the wall sheathing that would give them access to the ground space where the air-pipe shafts would go. We opened the floor hatch, and then the tunnel, to get ready to work down there. Meanwhile, the word of what was afoot moved quietly through the barracks and a "Jerries watch" was fast in place. Luck was with us; it was a lazy afternoon and no guards came by, no special roll calls. Wilkens's plan worked. By early evening all was done and ready except for the delicate "butterfly" air pump. Wilkens was having trouble with the finishing touches. It had to have a crank the hidden men could turn without a sound, and to get it in place turned out to be a challenge. Wilkens spoke to no one. He worked as if he were utterly alone. We gave him a wide berth.

That night around eight o'clock, approaching curfew, I was called up to Shattuck's bay to meet the men who were to be hidden. There were four of them together, looking a little shell-shocked, but it was a tall, intense one standing a bit apart from the others who particularly caught my attention. As it happened, Shattuck singled him out.

"Handy, this is Grey. He's the guy the Gestapo is so keen on."

Grey shook my hand. His grip was powerful and very confident. He was a big man with high, wide cheeks and wary eyes. He seemed rugged and looked me in the eye as if searching for some clue about me. Shattuck introduced three others, all Russians. They looked scared and barely acknowledged me. The last of the five, a tall, stringy fellow much older than us, Shattuck ignored altogether. The man said nothing and seemed utterly disinterested in the proceedings.

"These men will stay with us in 32A tonight and they'll go in the tunnel at five-thirty tomorrow morning," Shattuck said, adding, "we've got to be ready for an early roll call." Then his face hardened as he queried, "You guys will be set?" Shattuck spoke to me at times—and to others as well—with a touch of hostility, but I was learning not to take it personally. He always seemed to have a lot on his mind, but today, I knew, was special.

"We're already set, except for the butterfly air pump Wilkens is making. He'll be finished in time."

"Great. Take these men with you, bunk them down and get them in the tunnel before dawn." I turned to walk out and Shattuck called my name. I went back. Shattuck came very close to me and his voice dropped into a whisper.

"All hell is going to break loose tomorrow, Handy. If the White House is right and it's the Gestapo, these barracks are going to crawl with ferrets, guards and dogs. They'll tear the place to pieces. I don't know what it is about our friend Grey here, but he's hot and they want him. So warn everyone it could be rough. If these guys are found, they're dead, and the ones who hid them could end up the same way. So good luck."

The five refugees had been standing just outside Shattuck's bay waiting. I brought them down to our bay, introduced them, and asked Dailey, who was not involved in the air-pipe work at the moment, to find places for them to bunk that night—and to let me know where they'd been put. We agreed that Alex, the youngest of the three Russians, would bunk with me, since I had the space.

Meese and some of the other guys had already begun on the details of getting the sheathing boards back in place undamaged. Meanwhile, Wilkens had been working on the crank for his air pump in his lower-bunk workshop. He got some help from Meese and Thompson once they returned from closing up the wall. I looked over their shoulders and caught Wilkens's eye.

"Give me a few minutes more," he said. "It'll be ready to take down in a few minutes." The plan was to have Tony Sac and me go back down into the tunnel and install the pump inside the pipe that would serve for air intake. We'd left the tunnel open after finishing our work underground to get the two pipes in place, and we were now ready to go. Soon enough, Wilkens called us over to his bunk; his face lit with satisfaction, he demonstrated the workings of his pump. He explained how to lodge it securely in the pipe in a way that the stowaways could best turn the crank.

Well before the Germans cut the lights, we were done. The five men were bunked where we could find them quickly before daybreak. I lay on my top bunk too full of thoughts to sleep. I gave Alex, my Russian bunkmate, the lion's share of my blanket and overcoat because he was shivering worse than I was.

In the middle of the night, I sat bolt upright. We had made a great mistake. I felt like a fool. Why hadn't I thought of it before? The dogs. We hadn't considered the Gestapo's dogs. Once under our barracks, they would surely smell the hands that packed the dirt over the hatch and crawl right up to the far ground concealing the cover of our tunnel shaft. I blamed myself for not having considered the obvious; we were ten independent guys working together as a team with no one bossing anyone else, but in fact I was the team leader. Our bomber crew had worked together in the same way, but Tedrowe had always been in charge, had always been the one who took responsibility if things we did went wrong. This was my mess, not theirs: was there time to fix it?

Somebody was talking in his sleep. Giving Alex the hush sign, I swung down to the floor and moved over to Wilkens's midlevel bunk. Like me, like perhaps most of us, he was still wide awake. I spoke to him, told him the problem. He was quiet for a long moment. Then he started to laugh.

"What's so funny?" I asked.

"You look like you need to take a shit." He kept looking at me, laughing.

"No, I'm fine," I whispered, somewhat puzzled.

"Really? I don't think so. I think you need to go to the crapper. Right now."

"Wilkens, *what* are you talking about?" I said, getting a little tense.

Wilkens seemed to catch himself. His humor went as quickly as it had come.

"Lime," he said.

The moment he said it, I understood. The Jerries dumped lime in the outhouse to kill the smell. It was a great idea. I had not caught his humor, and he poked me in the shoulder with a forgiving smile.

"The lime can in our one-holer's almost empty," he said. "I was down there awhile back. So you'll have to go out to the big latrine. You can use my undershirt." He swung down to the floor. He took off his heavy shirt, then his undershirt—the standard GI clothing the Red Cross got from our military and funneled through to us, except that his undershirt was a cold-weather type with sleeves. Reaching into the darkness of the workshop below his bunk, he located a foot's worth of string and then deftly tied the undershirt's bottom tightly together.

"Look, Handy," he explained, "the bottom's as good as sewed up. Just put handfuls of lime—as many as you can—through the neck opening. Hold the shirt up by its arms—I'll tie them up, too—and when you've got a shirtful, put it inside your coat and tie the shirt arms tight around your waist. Your coat's bulky enough to cover the bulge." He caught my elbow as I headed back to my bunk. "Good thinking, Handy. It never occurred to any of us and wouldn't have until those dogs started howling."

I thanked him and wished him a good night's sleep; he'd earned it. I pulled my heavy GI overcoat off Alex and signaled him to stay still. I set off. It was a beautiful, crisp September night, but I saw no stars. Neither the tower guard nor his counterpart who walked the fence showed any special interest in me; I wondered for a second how it was that they weren't all over the place lying in wait for any unusual activity. Was all this as important to them as to us? Once in the latrine, I breathed a sort of sigh of relief at finding the lime barrel well stocked. I brought up one fistful after another until the shirt was filled. In a little over five long minutes I was back in my bunk—the overcoat on top of Alex once again, the lime supply tightly tied and stuffed under Wilkens's workshop bunk. There wasn't much sleep in our barracks that night. The watch my mother had given me had a radium dial and I watched the hours creep by. At 5 A.M. the bay was already stirring, and at first light we got to work. Dailey and Meese shared the rounding up of the other four refugees—Alex was already on deck—and I went up to Wolf's bay for the start-up there. Likely they hadn't slept much either: the far lower-bunk slats were already removed and the floor hatch open. I'd brought along the makeshift sack of lime. We waited for the arrival of the five hunted men.

In a couple of minutes Meese brought the five to Wolf's bay entrance. No introductions. He told me his thoughts on who should go where in the tunnel and we went with that. Below the open floor hatch the morning's dim light was enough to reveal the open shaft—we'd decided not to cover it after getting the air pump in place. Meese put the three Russians in first, and then Grey—the mystery man having opted out altogether for reasons that were not explained to me. Grey would be the one to operate the air pump. There were many whispered wishes of good luck as they went down. Both Meese and I gave a thumbs-up sign to Grey as he took a final look at us from the bottom of the shaft and then we sealed them over. I slid down for our last job: filling our piled-up earth into the two-foot-square hole above it. From under the bunk, Meese emptied Wilkens's lime bag little by little through the open floor hatch and down into the earth as I pushed it in over the shaft cover.

Stirring the lime into the earth with my hands as we went along, I offered up a crude prayer that the mixture would be strong enough to keep the dogs from smelling human flesh but not so strong as to discolor the earth so that the Gestapo would detect the difference in the beam of its heavy-duty flashlights. At least there was some encouragement in the thought that the ever-narrowing space from barracks floor

to ground level—thanks to the hillside our barracks was built on—
would stop them a long way from our shaft cover's limed earth. All this
took us about ten minutes. The rest would be up to the dogs. Were they
trained to look for discolorations in the earth? With the limed earth
finally in place, I packed it down at the top to make it look like the
undisturbed earth around it, and came back up. We closed the floor
hatch, swept mud under the bunk, put the slats back in place and that
was it. They were underground.

Moments later a large number of guards came bursting into the
barracks, rapping bunks and rousting everyone out with shouts and
cries of *"Schnell! Schnell! Raus!"* They insisted we take everything with
us that we wanted to save, everything we wanted to keep, and go out
into the compound. Whatever was left behind would be taken. None of
us knew what that really meant.

I was standing by my bunk, watching Dailey and Thompson argue
about what they would carry out, when one of the regular guards hov-
ered around the bay. I recognized him: he was low-key, shy and often
looked like he was going to say something and had thought better of it.

"This is a bad day for all of you," he whispered in a timid, hesitant
English. "Us too. We come to take everything. All you have, your
things, whatever you leave here, you don't see again. I am sorry. It is not
up to me." His voice caught me. It was quiet, melancholy. I had never
heard any of the guards speak in such a personal way, either with any of
us or even with one another. He stood by awkwardly as we gathered our
things. His eyes were blue and sad, as if he were waiting for us to tell
him it was OK. We all ignored him and, soon, he left. I put my few
utensils, canned food, D-bars and clogs in a Red Cross box, tucked my
journal under my shirt, the pencil in my pocket, put on my overcoat
and was ready to go.

We were herded out into the compound, and not since the murdered sergeant's burial had I seen so many men. It seemed as if all the
barracks in our compound were emptying out at the same moment,
men coming out into the morning air cursing, laughing and stumbling.

The guards then lowered their guns to waist level and threatened all of us to get back.

"Man," said Tony Sac, "it's starting." The search was on.

It began in the eastern end of the camp and worked west toward us. Kriegies in each compound were roped off into the back third. They were keeping us as far away from the barracks as possible. No one in our barracks spoke; we all understood that we had to know nothing. Prisoners in other barracks were pissed and wanted to know what the hell was happening, and we had to mimic them. We had to be annoyed, but also unfailingly casual. To act differently would alert the guards, who were already very savvy about detecting behavior that was out of the ordinary. So we mirrored the other kriegies, cursing and mocking one another as part of the old routine.

We could see the Gestapo officers dressed in black, standing outside the barracks in the compounds east of us, directing the guards. Their body language set them apart, even from a great distance. They demonstrated a chilling economy of movement while Luftwaffe and Wehrmacht uniforms scurried all around them like servants. Before long we heard an odd sound, a tapping noise.

"They're using rods," said Pappy, pretending to tie his boot. "Tapping the floorboards. They're looking for a tunnel, or at least a hatch." The tapping, distant at first, grew louder as they came toward our barracks. Guards would come out of a barracks and we saw them carrying long iron rods.

"What did these guys do?" I wondered. "Why're they so damned important?"

"Beats me."

Tony Sac ambled up. He had a ball that he tossed lightly from one hand to the other. Everyone was trying so hard to look normal. "I was working with Stein all day on sorting the Red Cross parcels; ya know, he's the guy who manages our parcels. Well, we were working together. He and I have gotten friendly—I like him, he's good people. So he says to me I need help. I says what gives, and he says I need pants and coats, and I says what's the problem, and he says they got some guy in camp that the Gestapo wants bad. He's escaped from a lot of camps and sabotaged a lot of Nazi facilities. And then Stein leans close and whispers, they want him dead. What the hell is he doing here? I asked, and Stein says beats me, but we got to hide him and I hear they want to use your barracks. Stein knows about the tunnel but he's as quiet as the grave about it. And I says, no way, that ain't gonna happen. We ain't finished yet. We're still working on it. Then some guys come in and Stein clams up and so do I. So I made my way back to 32A and by then you guys were already meeting."

"If they find them . . . ," I started to say.

"They'll kill them. No doubt," said Pappy, finishing my thought out loud. "The Gestapo doesn't care about kriegies. There's plenty of us to go around. No, they really want this guy, and if the Gestapo wants you, it's to skin you alive."

Some kriegies nearby broke out in song. They were not from our barracks, and their giddy voices brought me some relief. They didn't have a clue.

"You know something?" Pappy continued. "The fact that those guys are alive and hiding means they're playing with house money. By all accounts they should be dead by now. So they're lucky to be in the game. It's the boys in the bay with the hatch I worry about. They didn't ask for any of this. The Gestapo will want to make a point of them, too." I winced at the thought. I felt as if I had gotten them all into this.

"Peg Leg's not a bad guy. He wouldn't kill them . . . ," I suggested hopefully.

"Peg Leg hasn't got anything to do with it," answered Pappy. "He won't have any say in the matter."

Sac passed us, walking slowly along the fence, distracted. He was looking for his younger brother.

"Pee Wee?" he called out, using the forbidden nickname. I had seen so little of him compared to Tony Sac, who was in the middle of all our tunnel activities. Tony Sac was always moving through the camp, always overhearing various schemes and offering practical, savvy assistance. He had become invaluable in managing the dwindling Red Cross stores. But his older brother had grown steadily quieter, more solitary, and he kept to himself. Tony Sac cuffed him lightly and, draping his arms over his brother's shoulders like a protector, whispered in his ear.

Pappy stood up and stretched in a bid to appear casual.

"See you in a bit," he said and strolled off. I watched him and admired his quiet confidence. Later he became our barracks chief after Shattuck took over the whole compound but agreed to do it on the condition that he wouldn't have to leave his bay mates and move to the barracks chief's solitary corner. He had about him an aspect of leadership similar to Meese. A steadiness flavored by a genial enjoyment of other men's company. I remembered his crew mate Bob Watson recounting the moment they had been shot down. Watson had been badly hit by flak and temporarily knocked out. When he came to, Pappy was holding him by the collar and shouting at him over the noise of a burning plane:

"Your chute is on, can you hear me? It's on. Put your hand on this ring here. We're going to bail out. Don't pull that ring until everything is quiet, OK? As long as you can hear the engine in your ears, Watson, don't pull that ring. OK? You do as I say and we'll tend to your wounds when we get to ground. OK?" Watson bailed, waited, heard nothing and pulled the ring. Then he passed out. Pappy, he said solemnly, had saved his life. When his crewmate's testimonial got back to Pappy, he shrugged and, with the hint of a smile, commented: "Can't a guy make an honest mistake every once in a while?"

I stood awkwardly, trying to ignore that the guards were now only two barracks away. Across the compound, men were sitting on the dirt, standing about in small groups; others roughhoused good-naturedly. Among the hundreds of men packed between the rope and the fence, only the men of Barracks 32A knew the Gestapo's purpose. Anyone from our barracks could, with a slipped word or one too many nervous glances, spill the secret. I could see men from my bay trying to drift casually amid the crowd, but I knew their stomachs had to be tightening up, like mine. Had I been a guard, could I have seen our forced laughter or faked smiles? Would I notice all those eyes stealing glances at the Gestapo agents? I made myself look away. I looked toward the hills that had so often brought me solace. The little tile-roofed houses above the terraced farms seemed so peaceful that for a moment I forgot everything else. Who lives on those farms, I wondered. Were they Nazis, or, more likely, did they fear the Gestapo, too? Would they search for us if ordered? Did they ever think of the prisoners starving slowly below them when they drank a cold glass of milk or ate a piece of well-cooked meat? Would they have helped us if they could, or would they, like their small band of countrymen in that field, have preferred to beat us to death? Probably not, it struck me standing in the compound with the Gestapo combing the barracks. I was coming to believe that it was likely the people up there were no better or worse than we were.

I turned back and saw Sanford talking to Meese, who listened to him with a distracted smile. Then, as I watched, Meese's smile faded; he looked pained. With a well-rehearsed casualness, he worked his way toward the restraining rope. The Gestapo had now come to *our* barracks. They went inside and began tapping the floorboards with their steel rods. Of a sudden I wondered—all the men were wondering—how the Meese/Wilkens trapdoor—a masterpiece of invisibility—could, after all, now escape detection. By the guards, yes—but by the Gestapo? We could hear the tapping, but we couldn't look. I found myself listening to the tenor of the knocks exactly as the Gestapo must be doing—testing the floor with my every breath. Does that one sound different? That one? Would they move the bunks? What did the men hear in the tunnel? The knocking seemed endless until it suddenly stopped. The silence shot across the compound like a gun. Meese was squatting down, his back now to the barracks, his face looking up. And then the Gestapo suddenly appeared in the barracks doorway, iron rods in their hands. They hadn't found our trapdoor! Overwhelming inner joy gripped us, but it was short-lived. The black-suited agents, now joined by two ferocious-looking dogs, disappeared *under* the barracks, through a door at the downhill end where the crawl-space clearance was four feet. Some of us absorbed this impending disaster while twisting around in feigned horseplay, others while casually turning their heads. There were over a thousand other men in the compound who, of course, had no idea what was going on. They were genuinely laughing and talking. But for our 143 teammates the tension was like a volcano ready to explode—and we *had* to keep the lid on. Seconds were minutes; minutes were hours. We prayed.

"Jesus Christ awmighty," said Beast, who had come up alongside me. "Jesus Christ awmighty," he kept whining, each time growing more distressed. I shushed him like a child, trying to appear as though I were joshing him. I was wishing I'd had another pound of lime to put into that dirt.

"Aw, fuck, I can't stand it." Beast was getting more and more agitated. "I gotta help those bastards. Those fucking bastards." His eyes were watering. He began to shoulder his way forward.

"Beast," I said, getting worried. "Beast! Listen to me. We can't do anything. We gotta wait. Beast."

But he could not hear me. He started moving to the rope, cursing, breathing hard. It was then that I realized how big and strong he was. His arms were massive and my hand barely caught his biceps.

"Don't fuckin' touch me," he growled, moving forward through the crowd. "Those fucking Nazi bastards."

"Meese!" I shouted.

Meese turned and saw my look of alarm. Then he saw Beast. He sprang up from a crouch and stood in front of Beast, who momentarily stopped, as if woken.

"Beast. Listen. I need your help. See, those guys are fine as long as the dogs don't bark. Get me? No barks and that means they haven't found anyone. Got it?"

"No barks," Beast repeated.

"Right. No barks and those goddamned Jerries have nothing. Now if we hear the barking, I'll need you to help me figure out the next move."

"Right," said Beast. "We wait for the barks."

"Right," said Meese, patting the huge man on the shoulder. "Right. We wait for the barks."

We were still suspended in a trance when someone behind me said, "Look—look!" I couldn't for a moment, and then I did and saw a black-suited Gestapo agent hunching his way out from under the barracks. The dogs and their handlers followed. It was as if all of us gasped at once, though there was no sound at all. The dogs, empty-mouthed and agitated, came out straining their handlers' leads. It was as if, in that single moment, we had won. The Gestapo agents moved with the efficient frustration of authorities thwarted. Moved to tears, we had to show boredom. One tear now—one hint of interest—and all would be lost.

"No barks," said Beast with a sloppy grin.

"No barks," answered Meese. I continued to feel a kind of joy I had never before known: these men whose fates we had taken into our hands were going to live. We began to talk in a cautious excitement, looking out at the hills, not at each other.

"How did they not find it?" said Tony Sac wonderingly.

"It was the beautiful bevel Meese put on that hatch," I muttered.

"It was good goddamned luck, that's all," said Meese in a soft voice, talking to no one in particular.

The sun had set before we were allowed back into our barracks. The place was a shambles, palliasses thrown all over the place, the stove knocked over, bed slats lying about. We began to pick up and put the simple place together again.

Meese pulled me aside. "I hope to hell that air pump worked. They've been down there a long time." I knew what he meant and wished that right then we could have pulled up the hatch and gotten the answer, but we knew we would have to wait. The ferrets would be all around. I wondered if the tunnel ceiling had held? Did they panic down there? Soon enough, though neither Meese nor I had said a word about it, men began to realize that the ordeal was not over, and soon it was quiet in the bay. It was as if we all wanted to hear them breathing.

A little before curfew, we got them out. We opened the tunnel shaft, and after a moment that passed so slowly someone whispered "Come on, come on!" the four of them climbed out of the tunnel shaft like ghosts, one by one, exhausted, cramped, grouchy, but *alive*. It was a joyous moment. Later, after the lights went out and the talking died down, a low whisper was passed bunk to bunk, bay to bay:

"Another search tomorrow. Same drill."

So it was. The Gestapo came back and commenced the second of what turned out to be three searches. The American barracks were emptied and the kriegies were again penned in at the back of the compounds. Once again the black-clothed Gestapo agents came with their dogs and their rods, and the knocking was as loud as the barking was silent. The second day's search did not seem as rigorous or intense, and the third day even less so. On the afternoon of that day, two guards followed by a black-suited Gestapo agent came to the back end of our compound, where we were milling around in our roped-in confines, playing games and throwing stuff back and forth to each other. Nearby were the kebos, the big wooden buckets they used to feed us, one of them still topped by its heavy wooden cover. The two guards, one of them Schultz, yelled at us to get away from the covered bucket. Approaching it carefully, they took the cover off and looked inside, clearly wanting to see whether anyone was hiding inside. We couldn't let on that we had any idea what they were doing, but someone shouted, "Hey, Schultzie, if you're hungry, come back at suppertime and we'll set you a place at the table." Everyone laughed, but not just at the joke. Finding the Nazis hunting for a stowaway in a food bucket was funny; but it continued to make us feel the winners in a deadly game of cat and mouse.

After that third search, the Gestapo gave up, but not without exacting some revenge. The guards came out with bundles of clothes, personal items, everything anyone had left behind or near their bunks. The sad-eyed guard who had warned us was true to his word. When we got back, most everything was gone. Wilkens had thrown his tools into the tunnel, but the rest of us lost whatever we had saved or stowed away. I had kept my journal with me, had worn all my clothes and brought along D-bars and canned stuff, so I was none the worse for the pillaging. Complaints were rampant and promises came down that the White House would do what it could to get things returned.

That night Tony Sac joined Alex and me on my bunk. He was excited and spoke in such a fast whisper that his words came out in a great gush of enthusiasm.

"I feel like a goddamned genius, don't you, Handy? I mean, the Gestapo went after them guys with rods and dogs and turned the place upside down and those fellas are snoring the night away right now. It makes me feel big as a goddamned mountain. Top of the damned world."

"I sweated those dogs, I'll tell you that," I said.

"Yeah," he answered excitedly, as if I had reminded him of something else he wanted to tell me. "Some kriegie kept saying to me, 'The dogs! The dogs!' He kept poking me in the side and saying 'They're going to find it. They're going to *find* it!' I said, 'They're *not* going to find it'—but I was bullshitting him. I was bullshitting myself. The only thing I really thought was they'd find those four guys dead—or the Gestapo would find them alive and kill them right there. But he kept saying, 'They're going to find it'—so now I said, 'Shut up! They couldn't find an elephant in a closet! The dogs ain't much smarter than the Gestapo, and they won't find shit.' But I was saying to myself, not to him, 'Christ Amighty, those guys are dead; they're dead!' Then when the Gestapo came out with nothing, well, what a sight! And the guy said, 'You were right!' I said to him, 'I told you; of course I was right; you shoulda believed me!' But I said to myself, 'Gee! Oh boy! Oh boy!' "

I stretched out on my bunk and listened to Alex breathe. He was fast asleep and his body twitched. The tunnel had frightened him and he went right to the bunk to sleep. I felt such joy but, even more, such debt to the heavens: our big win had been against such heavy odds. At that moment I could think of nothing more than that the tunnel we had dug had saved those men's lives. Yet I did not even know these men. Had never seen them until the day before. What would have happened if the Gestapo had found them? Who else would have been punished? I remembered standing in the bay with Sergeant Wolf and how I had lectured him about his duty. My words seemed so hollow to me now, as if I had prattled on into a great wind. Wolf had rightly seen the future, had correctly realized it was not my neck I was risking, but his and those of the men in his bay. It occurred to me that we sometimes speak words with a sense of righteous indignation and that those words set in motion events that spin far past our ability to influence them. Once spoken, those words cannot be recovered, and others must live with the consequences of them. I had put Sergeant Wolf at risk with my own words, with my blind assertion that the risk was a matter of duty, even though the risk was not mine and the duty had to be his. Wolf had chosen to live by that sense of duty and had helped save the lives of four men at great risk. I thought too of Sac drifting over to his brother and how worried we all were about him. He was sensitive, and camp life was increasingly a trial. I remembered a moment some weeks into our crew's combat flight training when he pulled me aside after we had completed a long practice mission. He spoke like a man who had made up his mind after great deliberation.

"Handy, you know more about this plane than I do. I want you to take my place as first engineer." He was our First Engineer/Top Turret Gunner, but had rightly read the difference in our know-how about the four-engine B-24. Trained at Ford's Willow Run "24" factory and then assigned to eight months' work on the plane as a mechanic in Topeka, I had some solid experience with the B-24. Sac had none. All the same, surprised that he would take such a step, I encouraged him to reconsider. It meant lower pay for him as well as becoming my subordinate, but he stood firm. So I agreed, and with Tedrowe's approval confirmed, we made the switch. The crew immediately supported Sac for the quiet way he had determined what was best for the crew's effectiveness and treated him with an elegant respect that spoke well of them all. What makes all these men do what they do? How do they know the shape of such bravery when they are still so young, still ignorant of so much? I listened to Alex breathe well into the night. I couldn't sleep at all.

OVER THE NEXT FEW WEEKS, THOSE of us who had built and maintained the tunnel began to get to know Frank Grey. Shattuck had put him in a bay where there was space—he bunked with Paul Knight, a good man, a Californian—but as soon as the searches were clearly over, he came to our bay and made a point of thanking each of us for the tunnel that had saved his life. He admired Wilkens's air pump and made us laugh with stories of being underground with the three Russians, who always wanted to smoke their rope-filled cigarettes. Although cautious and tense—always on the watch for another search—he began little by little to get around the barracks and thank everyone. He was now known as "Wolf." He had been the first to point out that calling him Grey could tip the Jerries, there being no one else by that name in our barracks. I was pleased that we changed his name to Wolf, a kind of subtle homage to the tough sergeant whose turnaround had started the tunnel that saved Grey's life.

Bit by bit, Grey's story took shape. Thinking I was the tunnel crew chief—Shattuck had said that when we met—he decided to tell it to me first. Or perhaps he had some other reason. I don't know. He was an impressive man, often affable, but he held his cards close. It was now some time since the last Gestapo search and Grey, sensing they'd given up, had begun to go outdoors. We took long walks around the compound and gradually I came to know some of the key parts of his story. An army regular (he was now twenty-six), he had signed with the Air Force at age sixteen, five years below the required age. I asked him how he had gotten around it and he demurred, like a magician unwilling to explain his tricks. He bailed safely from a crippled Flying Fortress on a mission to Schweinfurt's ball-bearing plants, was quickly captured and, almost as quickly, found a way to escape.

"Always make your move early. Every hour that passes, it gets harder to escape. You want out, you have to move fast and in those first hours!"

That raid had been flown on August 12, 1943. Now, thirteen months later, he was able to recount a series of seven inspiring escapes. He told his stories without hyperbole or any apparent exaggeration, almost like a man explaining how he got to work each morning. He lingered over details that he found interesting but passed over moments where additional information might have made him seem almost heroic. He was a good storyteller, and kriegies liked to get him to talk. After several of his escapes, he had told me, he had committed acts of sabotage—the best being the nighttime release of heavy guns from German freight cars headed for the Russian front.

"That's the one that pissed them off the most. Gestapo wanted any ass after that one."

"How did you get caught?" I asked.

"I wanted to get to Yugoslavia and fight with the partisans there. I got caught about two weeks before they dumped me here. They figured out that I had a dossier with the Gestapo and those assholes were thrilled to turn me over. A Gestapo agent laughed at me. 'No more trouble from you. You go to Buchenwald,' said the bastard. I threatened to break his nose and they threw me into a cell and gave me nothing to eat for a week." I had not heard of the Nazi death camp. I asked Grey what he knew about it and why they would send him there.

"Don't know. But judging from that agent, I knew I didn't want to go there. Some time later, they put me in chains and threw me into the back of a truck. A guard pointed a gun at me the whole way. He didn't blink once, so I couldn't escape." Grey poked me as if to remind me he was teasing, but I was riveted by his story.

"They unloaded me here at Stalag 17 until they could route me to Buchenwald by train. The guards stood around the commandant's office looking confused. It was Sunday; no one was around the office. So they put sealed orders on his desk and turned me out into the camp. I couldn't believe it. The orders basically said let this guy out of your sight and we'll skin you alive. But being Germans, no one would open the orders without authority. They waited for the boss, the idiots. Now here I was, walking in your camp. I didn't have much time. I got to the White House and filled Kurtenbach in. He's smart enough. Unusual for a guy in charge, I'll give you that. He started making plans. We both knew that the Gestapo was gonna turn the camp on its ass. I had two crewmates in camp with the old kriegies and he sent me to 'em. About half an hour later the alarms went out, whistles and dogs and all that German bullshit. They were having a surprise roll call. Guys were wondering what the hell was going on, but I knew. Someone had opened those orders and figured they'd made a hell of a mistake. I skipped out fast. Straight to the barracks one-holer. Got right down into it and waited it out. The poor sons of bitches who had to pull me out and get me clean, bless 'em. After that Kurtenbach introduced me to Rich Hoffman, who took me to that makeshift theater you got made of cardboard, and I hid under a false floor that night. Then they brought me to your barracks along with those Russians."

I listened, didn't talk, asked few questions. He asked me about the tunnel and I told him how it came to be there. He asked about the Russians; I told him we'd learned that after killing a German guard they'd been hidden by our men. That had been at Stalag 7A over near Munich, where our old kriegies had been until they came here a year ago. Getting the Russians through undiscovered had been a challenge and required some ingenuity and a generous dose of luck.

"Nothing is luck," said Grey sharply. "Nothing."

Grey lived in our barracks, along with the Russians, for many weeks, needing always to be near the tunnel. Eventually the Russians left us, returning to their camp, but Grey stayed on. He was well liked, but he was distant and often aloof. Few enjoyed his confidence. His bunkmate, Paul Knight, and several men from our bay, in particular

Gene Meese, kidded him and often swapped stories. His relationship with me as time went on was good, but it was strictly business. He was a loner and had found in me, I suppose, something of a kindred spirit. I did not have his intelligence, his street skills or his unique ability to be in the right place at the right time, but I could keep my own counsel and was well able to watch and listen. As the fall began to fade, tension about the Gestapo began to ease, and Grey's crewmates were after him to join them in Barracks 37. He declined. He figured the Germans knew that his crewmates were over there and were watching Barracks 37. Perhaps, I speculated, the Gestapo had given up on the American escape artist and had closed their books on him. Grey would not take that chance. He continued to stay close to us and to the tunnel.

There were big plans cooking at the White House. Kurtenbach and the others knew that Grey was the kind of guy who would take matters into his own hands if he thought enough wasn't being done to get him out. Someone told me our tunnel had stimulated some lively discussion about a new one. The barracks chiefs agreed that a new tunnel would be dug out of Barracks 29 in our compound, the one right up against the double fence that separated us from the Russians. The idea was to dig west below the fence and over to a building we called "the Russian Chapel." I don't know how it all got worked out, but clearly Kurtenbach named 29A's barracks chief the leader and asked Shattuck for strong support. I knew that because one morning after roll call he called me to his bay.

"We're going to get Grey out," he started. "It'll be a tunnel from 29A. Once on the Russian side, he'll be on his way. I want you to lead a digging crew. How about it?" Shattuck was trying to repair a tear in his coat. He seemed more focused on the coat than on our conversation.

"Sure," I answered.

"We're going to go around the clock. Three crews, six men to a crew. It will be dangerous, but we have to work fast and hard. You can pick your crew. The other two crews will come from the other barracks. It's an all-day operation until we get out to the Chapel."

I didn't know anyone in Barracks 29A, and when we went over, we got started without any talk. I thought of myself now as an experienced digger and relished the chance to prove it, so I dug for hours on end. Guys would call to me to come up and take a break, but I didn't. The other digging crews were the same; you dug until you couldn't anymore. They did not have the kind of shaft we had built, nor much width or height in that tunnel. We were trying to make ground as quickly as we could, so there wasn't much attention to security. At one point, they sent a guy into the tunnel with a piece of steel wire. The idea was to see how far we'd dug. He would push the wire up through the tunnel ceiling till we could see it breaking ground. I stood at the window with Shattuck and a few others looking out over the stretch of dirt running to the double fence, and sure enough, like a living creature, the wire poked cautiously out of the ground, wiggled for a brief moment and disappeared. "We're still short of the Russian Chapel by twenty feet," Shattuck said.

I don't remember much more about the digging except the thick oily smell of the tunnel project's butter burners and the sense that something elemental was draining out of me. Gene Meese and I hated the idea of using the unhealthy burners for light, but the 29A chief had insisted we use them so as to dig faster. I woke in the mornings with a heavy head and my shoulders ached and I could not seem to clear my head. I tried to eat more slowly, chewing my bread to mush. I did not eat any of the sugared sweets that came out of the Red Cross parcels, but for one typically blessed with a rugged constitution, I did not feel well at all.

Grey knew we were working hard for him. I didn't see him as much as I had before, but he always greeted me warmly when he was out stretching in the compound. Once we stood outside together and listened to Morrissey (they called him "Stoop") sing "Danny Boy," and guys got pretty melancholy at the sound of Stoop's sad refrain.

"I don't go for that," said Grey. "Sad songs slow you down. The sadder, the slower. And the saddest ones get you killed."

Sometimes he would catch me walking back after digging in 29 and he'd say in a low voice, "I appreciate what you fellas are doing for me. It's a matter of time before I get caught here, and I had better get a move on. I know what to do once I am over there and I'll be sure to send you a postcard."

It was Friday, October 13. I was not superstitious, but that day made me think twice about it. After being in the tunnel most of the morning following roll call, I had finally come out to rest, my eyes swollen from the burner. Sac had gone in with a crew after me, and he poked me as I passed him. "You don't look good, Handy," he said. Later, back in my bunk, I was drifting off to sleep when I heard the sound of the whistles. I sat up and almost immediately guys were running down the aisle.

"The Jerries found a tunnel in 29. They were digging a tunnel in 29. They got the guys inside and are going to shoot 'em all."

Sac was in that tunnel. So was Gene Meese. I ran outside. Men were pouring out of their barracks. There were guards all over 29. I saw Grey on the edge of the crowd.

"They knew right where to look," he said furiously, his eyes flashing. "There was no search at all. Just went under the bunk and pulled the hatch. Goddamn it. Goddamn the Jerries and whoever squealed. It was one of the Russians, I'll tell you that. Sergei, that sonofabitch. He's the one. Or some loose-lipped jackass. I told you the only way is to work alone." He was beside himself with anger, and I realized how much hope he had had for this tunnel. The utter despair on his face made me realize something else: my own. The tunnel was found and there would be no escape. Pappy came up.

"Meese is in there. And Sac," he said, rubbing his jaw, worried. The guards were shoving men around, but I couldn't see anything.

"They're lining those guys up to shoot 'em," said someone.

"No, you asshole. Not to shoot them. They're making them collapse that tunnel." He was right. The men were working at it as guards shouted at them. Then I saw Tony Sac leading his brother by the hand. Meese followed, his face dirty.

"What happened?" I asked Meese as he passed.

"Tony Sac staged some kind of fistfight with another kriegie and bought us time to get out. Just in time." Meese looked exhausted. I turned toward the barracks with a terrific fatigue. My body was in big trouble and I didn't know it. Within a few hours I found myself in Stalag 17's crude infirmary. I was there for more than a week.

PART IV

WINTER

> *I have it in me so much nearer home*
> *To scare myself with my own desert places.*
>
> —ROBERT FROST

THE FIRST SNOW came early, a white salve to the stalag's scarred ground. I stood in the doorway of the barracks and watched the men wander out into the compound, staring up at the fat flakes drifting down. It wasn't long before the first prisoner gathered up a fistful to test the consistency and the snowball flew. The guards ignored the assault against them, as did the Russian prisoners, and snowballs arched over Stalag 17 like ordnance. Everyone got whacked; even Schultz was hit across his broad back as he passed through the gate, shaking his head like a mildly annoyed father.

We suffered much in those first nights of winter, and no amount of midnight exercises, even when done every few hours, could stop the pain of muscles and bones emptied of warmth. The cold settled in as Austria faced its worst winter in decades. The old kriegies had said the year before was bad, but even they agreed that this was a winter to beat them all. Our last night in the boxcar had been the last cold snap for many months. Now the cold at night was almost unbearable. There was no advice, either from the White House team or from our own barracks leadership as to how to manage the nighttime freeze. No doubt the White House had bigger problems to deal with, as it had been many weeks since we had been given any Red Cross parcels, our primary source of food and nutrition. So Kurtenbach and his team were likely focused on all they could do to keep us from starving.

When it came to managing the cold, each of us was on his own. Men slept as close to their bunkmates as they could and often doubled up the blankets. They tossed and turned, and in the middle of the night, you could hear muffled arguments over ownership of a blanket's corner. I slept alone, in a ball, like a cat.

We were airmen, so we had considerable experience with extreme cold. At the high altitudes we reached during combat missions, most of us had run into the challenge of keeping warm. My worst trial by ice had come two winters before, at the Topeka Army Air Base in Kansas, where we worked long shifts—eleven-hour days, thirteen hours on the night shift—to keep our B-24 Liberators flying. The temperature out on the tarmac may have been 10 degrees, but the legendary Kansas winds made it 20 or 30 degrees below. I learned that silk gloves would help our fingers stay warm and still give us the maneuverability we needed. On the night shift, working inside the hangars, the temperatures were slightly more forgiving: barely above freezing. Relief came only with activity, and the night work gave us plenty of that. But if we finished before the closeout of the shift, we had to figure out how to keep warm and perhaps, too, get a few unscheduled hours of sleep. I'd convert one of the huge B-24 tires in the hangar's supply section into a hard rubber hammock. I'd wake up stiff, my body so bent out of shape that only a half hour's worth of steaming hot water back at the barracks could loosen my joints. No one had ever told me about either hypothermia or the needs of my own metabolism, and nothing had prepared me for the relentless cold of Stalag 17.

We dreaded those long nights. Sleep offered no sanctuary from the freezing, and many of us lay awake for hours, shaking, turning and cursing. The thin palliasses with their scanty cardboard and wood-shaving fragments provided no insulation at all. We kept the clothes on that we'd worn all day long, but on the worst nights even the heavy U.S. Army overcoats given to us by the Red Cross in Switzerland offered little help.

One particularly cold night I turned to find Wilkens standing alongside my bunk. He looked annoyed.

"Where's your cap?" he asked. Each overcoat had come with a woolen cap, and most of the guys wore them. I did not. I had always thought wearing hats was frivolous, almost dandyish. Before my father's financial collapse, he had bought me a boy's version of the hats he wore, one made of straw, the other of brushed felt. I hated them immediately and always found excuses to leave them at home. Even in winter while sledding, skating, skiing, I went bareheaded. If I had an irrational dislike of head cover, I had a justifiable dislike of sweaty hair. "I don't know," I answered Wilkens sheepishly, "I've got it somewhere around here."

"Well, find it," said Wilkens in an uncharacteristically brusque manner. "Find it now. Don't you know that if your feet are cold, you need to put on your hat?"

"No, I didn't."

"Well, havin' no hat on your head is no less stupid than havin' no roof on your house. Put your cap on and keep it on." I did and was amazed at the difference. The little wool cap became a most unexpected ally.

Winter was a time of struggle for all of us in Stalag 17. The spring and summer light was gone, as were the chances to lie out under the healing sun. In 32A it seemed worse: no tunnel, no teamwork, no adrenaline. We all settled into ourselves, our imaginations a refuge, expectations of liberation giving way to a fatiguing cold. Conversation was the only relief, and it came around at the small stove that barely heated our hands.

There was one small coal stove for each half of the barracks—for 150 men. Fuel was the constant problem. The ration of coal was very small and frequently nonexistent. Sometimes we burned scrounged wood in the coal stoves or anything that might cause a flame or a flicker of heat. Men took turns around the stove, hopping from foot to foot, rubbing their hands together like two sticks in search of a spark.

It was not long before guys in the barracks noticed that Young—the loner in the bay across from us—never missed a moment to take up a position around the stove. Though he was never taking another's place, it vexed men that he was so persistent in poking the fire's coals. Young was a man who knew a great deal about many things but broached no small talk. He did not suffer the kind of casual conversation designed to keep people's minds off hunger and anxiety. His unrelenting self-reliance annoyed many kriegies, so they teased him with an edge, always trying to draw blood. Though not aware of it, he played the part of the outsider to perfection and came to serve as a kind of strange, silent scapegoat. He spoke to no one and no one spoke to him, though often men would talk about him as if he weren't there.

"Some jackasses won't let the heat get out into the barracks 'cause they're so goddamned busy soaking it up before the rest of us can get it," somebody would say in a loud voice as he puttered around the stove. Young seemed not to hear anything anyone said to or about him. He wore his loneliness like a brand.

He had some odd tools that he messed with, and he stood over the small red coals like a wizard. When men tried to query him, he would grunt and turn his back on them. From my perch, I could tell that he was making things, and he followed a rhythm and a routine of a man completing specific tasks in a set sequence. I knew that Wilkens had made him some odd tools, including some elongated tongs. ("Old Young's as odd as a three-legged hen, but I like him," Wilkens said to me once.) I climbed down off my bunk and took up my place at his elbow. "What are you doing?" I asked.

"Casting." I could barely hear him. He was standing over the stove with an array of small hollowed strips of metal. He was carefully pouring the silvered metal into those molds and working with a methodical care I had also seen in the work of Wilkens and Meese.

"Looks complicated," I said.

"Not if you know what you're doing," he said in a way that was neither friendly nor aggressive, just words from a man in the middle of his work. "Move." I stood back and watched him. Before long, as if recognizing my interest was genuine and growing, he began to talk. He spoke to me like a wary teacher interested in what he had to teach but afraid of being liked by his student.

"Casting is procedure. And preparation," he said, carrying small trays of earth back and forth across the stove's top. "That means having the right materials. You have to be patient. To cast you got to have exactly what you need. I've been collecting stuff since the summer. The first thing is to make the form, and for that what you need is the right earth. Foundries use special sand. I got my soil by sifting through the stuff you dug down in your tunnel."

Likely he was part of our tunnel's earth-disposal crew; I hadn't known that. I thought back to the earth I had dug. I had had no idea that it would be of any use at all.

"The soil has to have a consistent quality," he continued, "not too dry, like sand, and not too oily, like clay. The sand won't hold the heat and the clay will bubble up when you heat it. You know if you put your hand into dry sand and pull it out, you don't see much left behind, but when you scoop up sand close to the ocean, you can see the joints on your fingers or the lines from your palm. Well, I'm looking for dirt that holds the impression of whatever is pressed into it. Yours was good for my molds," he said in a light voice as he finished his task. Then he stood straight and looked directly at me for the first time.

"I make these trays where I can pack the soil and then I press into it the form of the thing I am making. Got to be careful. Press too hard in one direction and you'll wreck the balance of the mold. Press too softly and the form won't take. You got to be careful and tamp it down just so." He went back to work as I watched. "Then you heat the metal inside the stove. Wilkens gave me an iron container he made out of an old ladle. I heat up the metal until it will pour into the form."

"Where does the metal come from?" I asked him.

"Toothpaste tubes. I pull out the liners, because you don't need high heat to melt them." His voice lost its easiness. He said coldly: "Some guys thought I was crazy for trading D-bars for empty tubes." It struck me, at that moment, what a lonely man he was. The camp seemed to consist of men who sought one another's company and those who did not. I seemed to move between the two groups, belonging to neither.

"Hey, Young," called a voice from a nearby bay. "Get the hell out of the way and let others use the stove."

"Help yourselves," he said as he finished pouring the metal into his mold. I looked down but could not see what it was.

"What did you make?" I asked. He was gathering his stuff, and I thought he would not answer me. As he moved back toward his bay carrying the molds, the silver metal jiggled like Jell-O.

"A crucifix," he said. "Some guy asked me to make him one." As he passed me, I could smell the molten metal in the molds made from my earth.

PAPPY STOOD IN BACK OF BARRACKS 29 along the fence, watching the Russians fall out for a food count. Some looked coldly across at us but most just stared ahead, their faces black-eyed masks. There was no talk between them, no jocularity, just an awkward, mournful assembling. "See that first line," said Pappy, "the one that starts with the guy on a crutch?"

I could see the man missing a leg. He leaned on a long stick and his stump wiggled blindly in the air.

"Now count over five guys." Another prisoner who had been behind me and heard Pappy's comment wedged forward into the conversation. "Yeah, I see him," he said. "A tall one. Standing straight.

Must be a fuckin' officer." The Russian seemed oddly formal, his hips thrust out as if poked from behind.

"He's no officer," said Pappy softly. "But he's dead." As soon as Pappy said it, I immediately recognized the shape as one no living man could hold, a clay figure bent by a casual hand. I could not see the details of his face, but men gripped his body on either side.

"Look in all the other lines," whispered Pappy, his voice sad. "There are dead men in every one. I've counted nine already."

"How can you tell?" I asked, looking hard at them. There were so many who looked dead who then startled me with a sudden gesture.

"See the plumes of breath? Just look for the ones who have none." And there, all along the line, the unmistakable sight of propped marble men.

"Can't the goons tell? I mean, how stupid can you get?" said the guy behind me.

"They count the feet. The goddamned guards don't want to have to look into anyone's face. It's easier on their consciences, I suppose."

"Why do Russians do this?" I asked. "Why don't they bury their own dead?"

"They need the bodies. For the food count."

"They'll eat anything over there," said the guy between us. "One of the old kriegies told me that there was a German commandant who toured the Russian camp one time. He had a small dog on a leash with a fancy collar. He was talking to somebody and the dog started sniffing near the entrance to a barracks. An arm reached out, grabbed the dog and the collar came flying out of the window. The Kraut was crazy mad and turned the barracks upside down, but that dog was gone. They probably ate it raw."

"But how do they keep them?" I said, still shaken at the sight of the dead, shoulder to shoulder with their barely surviving comrades.

"Winter keeps them," answered Pappy. "They'll come out with the first thaw. Hundreds of them brought out one warm spring morning. So many, they'll run out of paper bags."

"Damn," said the guy behind me, walking away. "They're animals."

"Who?" I asked him, not certain whether he meant the Russians trying to stay alive or the Nazis trying to starve them to death.

"The whole fucking lot of them," offered the guy over his shoulder.

Pappy and I stood there pawing the ground and rubbing our hands. The guards shouted and the Russians dissolved into a gray mass, carting away their dead until the next feed.

"Kurt told me the first camp he was in, the Russians suffered worse than here. It was a stalag near Lamsdorf, Silesia," said Pappy.

"Where's that?" I asked.

"Near the border of Poland and Czechoslovakia, I think. Kurt said there were Brits from Dunkirk, Canadians from the raid at Dieppe, men who fought in Greece and Crete. Apparently the Gestapo also dumped a lot of escape artists in there and tough cookies that they wanted to put away for good. A small distance from their camp was a Russian compound with maybe three or four thousand Russian prisoners, and Kurt said it was so bad you could hear them moaning and calling all night long." Pappy looked at the Russians as if at a wasted landscape.

"There were no food lines at all. They were being totally starved. It got so bad that the prisoners decided they would rush the wire. All of them at once. They knew most were going to die, but they figured it was better than all of them dying from starvation. The Russian lines were still within a hundred miles, so they thought that some of them might be able to get back. Hours before they did it, somebody snitched. Told the Nazis what was going to happen. The Krauts set up machine guns and opened up on them as they rushed the wire. Machine guns on either side. It was terrible. Those Russians died in rows, but they kept coming, and the bodies kept piling higher along the wire. Each wave made another human step closer to the top of the fence, and guys just climbed over the dead to crest the wire. The first to spill over were killed before they hit the ground, but they kept coming and the Jerries couldn't kill them all. A few got off into the woods. The British prisoners told Kurt that for the next few weeks the guards would only go into the village in groups. They were spooked that the Russians who had escaped were still in those woods waiting to ambush them."

I watched two Russians standing at the wire looking back at us. Did we look like scarecrows to them? I raised my hand to acknowledge them, and one mirrored my gesture, raising his hand in return. We stared at each other, our hands in the air for a long time.

"It's a world gone crazy, and we're all part of it," said Pappy to no one in particular. Then he walked away, too. I stood there for some time watching the Russians, trying to locate in their movements and behavior some parallel to our own. I winced at my summer notion of the dead kriegie as free beyond that wire. There was no freedom out there. That tiny grove of trees was just another hellhole. Beneath the tranquility of those trees was a savage waste of bones and rotted flesh. Men of so many nationalities stirred into that ground like a grisly mulch. What difference did it all make? The flags and coffins, the sound of Taps, the paper sacks and bony blue feet? What were we becoming behind this wire? How would we ever forget, or worse, remember? I returned to my barracks, winter heavy on my back, consoled only by the idea that every one of those dead and dying men had been part of an honorable crusade against the Nazis.

"DO YOU GUYS KNOW ABOUT THE Flame Keeper?" asked Wilkens to nobody in particular. "Well, you know how guys always bum lights off other guys, cigarettes lighting one to the other, like a torch getting passed. Well, do you ever wonder who lit the first one? I mean, why is it that though matches are scarce and you can almost never find a guy who has one, there's always a lit cigarette you can use? Always. Well, that's because the Keeper's the kriegie that every morning, before dawn, lights the first cigarette in camp and every night, after everyone else is asleep, smokes the last one. The Alpha and Omega. They say he's been in the camp from the beginning. Skinny told me that one of the guards swore the Keeper is a French pilot who was shot down over Paris. He was carrying his mistress with him to show her the city at night while he killed a few Germans, only they got shot down and she died in the flames. He never recovered. The Germans found him sitting by the smoke and wreckage holding her in his arms, and it took three Krauts to pry her loose. And he has never spoken to anyone since. Not a word."

"So how come he's the Flame Keeper?" Sac asked.

"He just is."

"You met this frog flier?" asked Beast.

"No. Nobody has. But he's here in this camp. He's the one who makes certain that there's always a lit cigarette in Stalag 17. Always. They say that on the day the Keeper wakes and chooses not to light a cigarette, well, that's the day we're starting for home."

Everyone was quiet and then Meese spoke up, his voice low and steady.

"The flame keeper in my family was our mother. I grew up in Plainfield, Ohio, a small mill town on the banks of the Little Miami River, a tributary of the Ohio. The mill made grain that got shipped via the Miami and Ohio rivers. The waterwheels were still in place when I was growing up, but the mill had been shut down long ago. My mother and father built a new house next door to my grandmother and my mother's sister. Another aunt, one of my father's sisters, had a farm farther up the hill, so we were all together. My own sister and I knew family was all around us, but we didn't see them so much. We had everything we needed in that house and we loved it. My mother had overseen its construction just three years earlier and was proud that it was the first house on our road with two stories and the only one with an indoor toilet. The year I turned fourteen, Plainfield was overrun by the biggest flood in its history. The rain fell in sheets, day after day. We'd never seen anything like it. My mother would stand at the window and say in a sad voice: 'The river is coming.' She was not well, and during those rains, she got steadily worse. I don't know what worried my father more, the rain, the river or my mother's health. She was a strong woman who was not used to illness, and none of us knew how to comfort her as the rain poured and poured, pooling in the yard, washing away her garden. Before long, she had to sit by the window. And then we moved her bed so she could watch lying down.

"When the water crested the banks, they carried my mother up to my aunt's farmhouse. My father had to go down to town, and my mother gave me instructions to stay and move as much as I could until my father came back. I helped my grandmother and aunt move furniture to higher ground. We carried chairs and boxes and lamps up the muddy hill to my aunt's house, and the rain soaked us through.

"By the time my father arrived, the water had already filled the basement and nothing more could be pulled out or saved. We went to work getting our first-floor furniture up to the second floor. It was a heavy-duty job and we got most things up just ahead of the rising water, which filled the first floor with more than three feet of water. We tried to move my grandmother's beautiful nineteenth-century piano with spiral carved legs and shiny black wood, but it was too heavy for us to carry up. The water had crept up the front steps and licked along the door and then, as if finally deciding to come in, had spilled into the house with a rush. The water slowly rose along the piano legs, and my grandmother, who knew it would be ruined, comforted us all. 'Things have a life, too,' she said to me. And then she sat down for a moment and played a lovely, sad song, the water nearly to the keys."

Meese paused. I thought I would have liked his grandmother.

"I remember my father standing at just about high water saying, 'I'm glad your mother can't see this.' It would be nearly three weeks before that water returned to the river, and during that time, my father, mother, sister and I lived with my aunt on her farm. Each day, as my mother grew worse, she would ask after the house and her things, and my father could not bear to tell her about the damage. She once asked me about my grandmother's piano and I could not speak, didn't know what to say. She smiled and changed the subject. She must have known my father and I worked together to clean out all the mud and silt. We worked with a pail and sponge, scrubbing walls and floors a little bit at a time. It seemed to us, though we never spoke of it, that if we could get Mother back into the house she loved, she might start to get better. I figured that if the rising waters had started to kill her, maybe a dry house could make her well again. Each day we would come back and tell her about how things were going and how one wall or another was dry and ready for a coat of paint. She would listen and smile, but she no longer cared so much. She was fading. The strangest thing," said Meese wistfully, "was that as my mother was dying, my sister and I were learning that we were part of a large and growing family. We lived in the houses of our relatives. We drifted from one house to another whenever it suited us, and whatever house we went to, if it were mealtime—breakfast, lunch or dinner—folks would smile and call us to the table like they had been waiting on us. We learned that we were part of something that was still there and always watching out for us. It didn't ease the pain of watching Mother die, but it made us feel stronger. We learned that our family could survive and keep on."

"Did your momma get back into the house?" someone asked.

"Yes, she did. We got her back there but she died soon after."

The silence that followed was long, respectful. Meese had said his mother was the flame keeper for his family. She had kept going, had persevered despite rising water and illness and had kept the faith in family alive. We needed the same kind of resolve in this hellhole of a camp. It was as if we too were flame keepers, keeping alive for ourselves all that was right and good about America. None of us would have said it aloud, but we all knew that persevering was about more than survival, it was an act of defiant faith.

It was still early, and before long others began to talk. "I had asthma as a kid," said Wilkens softly. "One night I had some kind of attack. I could not breathe. I was scared. My chest was in a vise. The doctor came and gave me pills, my daddy told me not to be so panicky. Hell, even my brothers told me to stop making such a fuss. Well, the more folks talked at me, the worse it got, and I started thinking I was going to die. My mother came to me and took me in her arms. She said,

'Now, hold on a moment,' and rubbed my head. 'You hear all them wheezes? Don't it sound like a big band with every kind of instrument?' And though I could barely breathe, it sure did sound like all kinds of high and low notes in my chest. 'Let's pretend,' she said, 'that all them players in the band is on the stage and one by one they're going to walk off that stage while the others keep playing.' And then she began to describe each player, the banjo man, the fiddler, the piano man, the washboard bass player and the one with a tambourine, telling me what each looked like and how they carried themselves. Each one left the stage one at a time, and before long, there was just one thin sound of one little wheeze left. My mother said, 'Hear that? He's the last. He plays no instrument. He's the singer and look, you see? His song is done. Watch him. He is going to blow out the candle,' and she blew softly over my face, and with that I was breathing as easily as a baby."

There were now more sleepers than listeners as Wilkens finished his story. I thought about my own mother. Winters when we were kids, she and my father would sometimes take us to an unheated farmhouse out in the hinterlands of New York State. We had one big fireplace for warmth, and my mother would cook us great stews with every kind of vegetable and tasty meats simmered in. And after dinner we would climb into the icy sheets on our beds only to be surprised by the small, welcome furnace of a hot brick warmed by the fire. She was a woman of depth and art—painting the door to my room blue, "like the door to blue skies," she said. Later she added wildflowers at the door's center, so I would always remember to keep my eyes on "the nature at your feet." On picnics she would magically produce little sandwiches, ripe fruit, cookies and wool sweaters. After getting back from rugged outings, we always got great mugs filled with hot chocolate. It was her singing, however, that was the best of all. We couldn't have imagined anyone singing with a voice of such unworldly beauty, with so much love and soul. She would sing to us on long trips by car, on family picnics in summer, at the piano from time to time, but the most important time was when she came to our rooms at night and sang to each of us, one by one. We each had to wait our turn, and our places, whether first, last or somewhere in the middle, changed from night to night. The waiting was often agony, but none of us ever begrudged the other's earlier place on my mother's evening journey. When your time came, you were always given your own song—a show tune, a folk melody, even an opera aria. She was altogether different from the woman we knew by day. No longer beset by the tasks and worries of managing the house or swimming upstream in my father's demanding social life, her whole attention seemed on us. She sang the songs we asked for, and a few song-filled minutes seemed like hours.

Lying there in the dark, her life came to me more clearly than it ever had before. She had begun with what she always said was an extended honeymoon. My father had taken a job in Akron, Ohio, near her family, and had bought her a small, cozy house. She loved the Thoreau-like simplicity of those first three years and spoke of them with a wistful sweetness. My father's work then took him to New York, and she found herself living in Westchester County, a place of horses, cocktails and smart talk. My mother, a reserved, quiet artist and singer, began to suffer.

The more the new life pressed her, the more she turned to her singing as her refuge. Her own mother had been a very good singer who had lived on the fringes of the operatic world most of her life and known many of the opera greats of the time. Through her mother's connections and influence, an overqualified voice teacher—a man with many leading opera singers as students—was convinced to take my mother on as a favored student. One day a week she took the train to New York City for her singing lesson, and it was that one day a week that kept her alive in the new world she could not bear. I remembered she once sang a beautiful aria to me. I asked her to tell me what the words meant and she said that they came from an Italian opera and the singer was lamenting, "I lived for art, I lived for love; why, why, oh Lord, have you brought me to this." Lying there in Stalag 17, I realized for the first time that she was singing about her own life. The thought dug into me hard. My being shot down must have broken her heart. Did she think I was dead? For a moment it tore me apart to think that her life, already tragic, was now worsened by my own fate.

"Hey Beast, what about your mother?" someone asked.

"She's a whore," he said to a hushed dark. A shutter flapped outside as the wind picked up. I listened for a while to the spooky, disconnected sounds of the stalag night and finally joined the other kriegies in sleeping the rest of the winter night away.

THE NIGHT BEFORE, WE'D ALL GONE to the windows and watched the bombers hit Krems. It was like lightning at first, brief, vivid flashes of yellow and white followed by a hollow thumping. Before long the horizon began to glow a sullen red and the guards shouted at us to get away from the windows and return to our bunks. On this morning, walking the perimeter, I saw Grey. He fell in beside me. We talked about the bombing. The Allies were moving across Germany. Grey looked troubled.

"What's wrong?" I asked.

"If I don't get out of here, this war's going to end badly for me. I've got a plan," he said, turning toward me, "and I want you to be part of it." I felt a rising excitement.

"First," he said softly, "we have to get into the Russian camp. Then, we'll get ourselves on a work detail. You can volunteer for work details over there. You like to cut wood?"

"Yeah, I've done a lot of it."

"Great. The guards don't give a damn about guarding Russians on a work detail because they know they'll always come back here for the food and the bunk. Always. There's nowhere else for them to go. The Jerries will kill 'em on the road or the Russians will kill 'em at home, so they're safer here than anywhere in the world."

"Why would they get killed at home?" I asked, startled by the comment.

"Those poor bastards. The Russians make it simple. Kill Nazis or be killed. Get caught or surrender, consider yourself a Nazi collaborator. And that means you may as well be dead. And your family ruined. What a solution, eh? Fight to the death, since if you don't, you'll die anyway. So the Krauts don't pay them the slightest mind. They need workers to cut wood, so we'll get ourselves a detail cutting wood. They take them down along the Yugoslav border where the big forests are. Then we slip off and make a run for it. I've got friends down there."

"We'll need to get the guys to cause a little confusion at roll call to buy us time."

"No," said Grey sharply. "Listen, Handy, never tie your plans to somebody else, ever. Don't ever stake your life on others doing their part. They change their mind or make a bonehead mistake, you're the one that pays the price. We're going to get some prisoners to switch with us. Some Brits or Aussies, guys that can speak English. They'll love it over here because most of them are privates and have to go out on work details. Their life over there stinks. Coming over here is coming to the other side of the Lord. It's better than Christmas. They'll take your name, your bunk, your clothes, even your Red Cross parcels, and none of the guards will notice a thing. But once we go, Handy, there's no going back. This kind of escape is a one-way street."

It all sounded pretty exciting to me, though I'm sure I didn't listen to him with much imagination. I didn't, for example, consider my comrades or barracks mates, or even the possibility of danger or even being caught. I was focused on only the most immediate, most practical details. "How will we get into the Russian camp?"

"Through the main gate."

"What?" I thought at first he was joking until I saw his face.

Grey immediately looked down and poked the ground with his boot in a way that signaled me to stop talking.

"Hey Handy, you seen Wilkens?" It was Beast. He looked at Grey and me for a long moment and then lowered his voice, "You guys up to something?" I looked at Grey, who squatted and rubbed some dirt into his meaty hands.

"No. How about you? Are you up to something?" he asked Beast with suppressed impatience.

"Fuck off," said Beast. He walked away, shooting us a glare over his shoulder.

"You don't talk to anyone about this, do you understand?" said Grey, glaring at Beast but, I sensed, feeling a bit sorry for him.

I shrugged off Grey's commanding tone. His intensity and will worked to dominate others, but I felt he meant no disrespect, and anyway, I knew he and I had developed an understanding. Even if I was something of a junior partner, I was determined to be as resourceful as he was, only in my own particular way.

"How do we get through the main gate?"

"Walk through it. It's that simple. You guys in this camp, you make things too hard for yourselves sometimes. Building a tunnel, involving dozens of guys, it's a recipe for disaster. Somebody's bound to talk or do something stupid."

"That tunnel saved your life," I said, unduly defensive. He noticed it right away.

"Don't get me wrong, Handy. Sure the tunnel saved my life, but nobody gets out of prison camps with a goddamned tunnel. You had one tunnel that saved me and another one that just lost me a lot of time. I'm not knocking the effort you all made for me. In my book you and your guys were heroes. You rigged up that tunnel in nothing flat to keep me—and the Russians too—alive and saved my ass from the Gestapo. But the tunnel hasn't gotten you out of here. You get out of prison by doing the simplest things and doing them at exactly the right time."

His criticism seemed wrong, but I appreciated the wisdom of what he was saying. He could teach me a lot. "So," I asked, nixing a debate about tunnels, "when is the right time?"

"During a winter storm. Heavy snow. The only time you bribe a guard is when he's damned sure no one else will know. In a snowstorm, the tower guards can't see the main gate and the guard at the gate will know that, too. We buy him off—D-bars or cigarettes will do the trick, and we've got to show him we've got replacements so he can't be blamed for missing prisoners."

"Why not just one replacement? One guy. You're on the run over here and the Germans don't even know it. We get a guy to replace me and no one would ever know you were here."

"Think it through, Handy," said Grey, with a touch of impatience. "To get assigned to a work detail—one that gets us to the Yugoslav border—we each have to take the place of an English-speaking prisoner over there. That's not hard. Brits, Canadians, Aussies, New Zealanders, they'll all do anything to get over here. They're treated better here. What's more, the guard has to think that we're just going over to trade and will soon come back. He has to see two men coming back. So they're Brits; he won't know the difference or even care."

We walked along, my mind swirling. It sounded astoundingly simple and was something I'd never even considered. We'd spent months tunneling and he had a better way; he was just going to walk us through the main gate during a heavy snowstorm. Simple. It was also the first time I'd considered the concept of bribing a guard. Trading with them for tools or items that a kriegie might use to make life a little easier in camp seemed almost like basic commerce. But the notion that you could ask a military man to let prisoners move through the camp illegally for cigarettes or chocolate—that stunned me.

"Why would a guard take his life in his hands for a bit of chocolate?" I asked.

"Handy, you have no idea what life is like for that guard. He would no more eat that chocolate than you would, because he knows it has a trade value that could give him something he or his family needs. It's not a sweet tooth, for Chrissakes. It's desperation. D-bars and cigarettes can have their own kind of value outside the wire.

"But there's more, Handy," Grey continued. "Do you see the missing piece?" I didn't.

"Well, tell me which Americans these two Brits will replace when they get over here. One of them becomes you; he takes your dog tag, your bunk, your Red Cross stuff. But what about the other guy?"

I saw what he meant immediately. "The Brit you switch with will think he's taking the place of an American in good standing. He'd never take the deal to become a guy the Gestapo's after."

"Got it in one," said Grey like a teacher.

"So I have to find a kriegie who's willing to give his identity to the Brit, so he, in turn, becomes you—becomes the man in hiding . . ."

"Right. Even if you weren't coming with me, we'd have to find that American. We'd have to find someone who'd do that to get me out of this hot spot, someone who'd become Grey, the wanted man, the man in hiding—and for the rest of the war."

"Well, if it weren't for my going with you, I'd do it. We've got to find someone else who sees it the way we do."

"Got any ideas?"

"Yes, but here come a bunch of your fans. Let's talk tomorrow." A clutch of prisoners came to get Grey to tell escape stories back in their bay.

Walking the compound myself later on, I was able to think more clearly about all Grey had said. I thought about who might take Grey's place. Meese? He was too valuable to the kriegies here to take it on. Wilkens? Not likely for the same reasons. I thought of Kozikowski. He was a guy who might consider it. He was resourceful, but kept to himself. I decided to ask him when I saw him. Asking another kriegie to become the Gestapo's number one target was hard enough, but now I came to see another sticking point to his plan. Shattuck had come down hard about having to clear escape plans with the White House. It was in that first conversation about the tunnel. He'd made a strong case. The following day, I decided to tell Grey, though I knew he wasn't going to like it.

"Wolf, can we take a walk together?" Using his public name, I was flagging Grey down as he walked fast along 32A's center aisle. It struck me that I'd never seen Grey amble. He was forever a bundle of energy and purpose. Always on the move.

"OK. Let me finish eating my sawdust with your pals. Then, if I'm still living, I'll be right with you." We'd gotten through roll call and were into our meager first meal of the new day.

We decided to walk over to the northeast compound—next to the burial grove. No one knew us over there. His crewmates were in another compound. We'd be able to talk freely.

Barely out of our compound, Grey said, "What's up?" Some saw him as impatient, but it seemed clear to me that he was just a man who did not want to waste any time.

"We need to clear our plans with Dillard, Kurtenbach's security chief," I said, knowing that Grey would want no preliminaries. "Shattuck's made a strong case for it."

Grey was very still. Then he took out a pack of cigarettes from his back pocket. His face was dark. He was angrier than I had ever seen him.

"I don't clear anything with anyone, Handy. You want to go with me, great. You saved me and I owe you, but this is not a group activity. I want out of here and I intend to go where I want, when I want. I waited on the Barracks 29 tunnel and it tanked. We still don't know who squealed. I'd bet my bottom dollar it was one of the Russians, but that's done with. It just showed that prison's no place for bureaucracy or decisions by committees. When you get killed, you die alone." He lit the cigarette and drew on it. I could see him moving with a studied slowness and understood he was trying to make himself calm. Maybe like me in the tunnel he was imagining his own kind of stars. He wanted some breathing room. Coming at him head-on was out of the question.

"I understand. But by clearing this with the White House, Shattuck doesn't mean asking permission. He just means we don't want to hurt others who might be working on something of their own, something close to ours. He wants to be certain that when we go, the decks are clear, that's all."

Grey grunted. As good as a yes, I thought.

I had never met Dillard and he didn't know me. He was cool and so well groomed, I wondered how he managed it in this place. He seemed uninterested when we asked for some time to talk. Grey was more than reluctant and said nothing while I described the plan. He simply looked out the window into the compound and was silent. Dillard listened, asked a few questions and mentioned he thought the swap could get done for a carton of cigarettes. An older, experienced kriegie, he also made it clear he knew how to assess the likely success of any escape attempts. I couldn't tell whether Dillard had little confidence in us or just didn't care, and I was thinking it didn't much matter when he suddenly turned the conversation upside down with his announcement that his security team would take over the arrangements at the gate when, and if, the storm came. We were simply to wait for instructions from him and his team. He would have the two British prisoners ready to come over for the swap. Grey stared hard at me and looked as if he were going to speak. I preempted him:

"That'll be fine. But we'll pick the time we want to go and give you a heads-up." Dillard looked at me and then at Grey. He didn't like the authority of my tone, but I could see he was slightly intimidated by Grey. I didn't know it at the time, but Grey had already established a reputation at the White House as a man who went his own way. Grey had a physicality that was immense and tightly coiled, and men looked to avoid springing it. Dillard measured the moment and backed down.

"Agreed," he said. And that was it. We left, heading back down the hill toward our barracks.

"OK?" I queried, grabbing Grey's shoulder.

He pulled away sharply, muttering angrily. We walked the rest of the way without a word, but on reaching 32A he turned to make eye contact.

"Escape is a one-man job, but I'll do it," he growled. Then he left.

That hurdle was cleared. Naively, I had no thought that Dillard might not be as competent, or even dedicated, as he seemed. It was time to move on to the bigger hurdle. I'd thought more about it and saw Kozikowski as my best option. Finding him on his bunk studying his Spanish, I watched him for a moment, knowing I was about to change his world in the camp. He'd come to be my friend and I trusted him. Underneath his bite he was serious and selfless and sometimes even a little comic. I'd never been to his hometown in Moline, Illinois, but he loved to tell us all how his little Mississippi town had sprung every John Deere into the world, and how the riverbanks were crowded with mills, farm elevators, machine tool shops and foundries. When the train from Chicago came into town, the conductor would call out "Johnny Deere!" and everyone would know right away they were in Moline. Sometimes he would imitate the accents of the town's immigrants who came from all over the world. Even Germany.

"You got Krauts in Moline?" asked Beast, overhearing our talk.

"Yeah, but they're good Krauts, Beast."

"There ain't no good Krauts," Beast answered.

After a while I got so used to talk of his hometown that I would ask him where in town he wanted to go and would try to tell him all the streets he needed to take to get there. He loved that. But at this moment our friendship was of no matter. As with Grey, I had a working link with Kozikowski based on his view of a soldier's job. I told him I had a request to make that came with a big risk attached. Without a flinch, he said, "Let's hear it." I laid out the escape plan and our need for a third team member to make it work. Would he be willing to switch to the role of the hunted man? He listened with great interest, giving no sign of what he thought of the plan. I went over the key part again: the British prisoners would change places with Grey and me, but one would not want to find himself a man wanted by the Gestapo, and we couldn't exactly tell him that after he'd come over. The Brit would have to be given the identity of one of us. Could Kozikowski be that one so that I could go along with Grey?

"So, you would have a new Kozikowski, a new Handy, and a new Grey?"

"That's it."

"And I'd be the new Grey?"

"Right."

"And have to hide out at roll call?"

"Every single one. Getting caught would be big trouble."

"Well," said Koz without hesitation, "I guess I've got nothing better to do. I'm in." It was like him to make nothing of it, but he was grim and there was a note of anxiety in his voice.

Was I putting him in harm's way? Was I asking of him something I did not understand, as months ago, I had asked Sergeant Wolf to assist us? Was this a reasonable request, given the dangers? Worried for a moment, I told him again how dangerous it would be. I explained that he would have to hide during every roll call and not let the guards get acquainted with him. He would basically have to be alert every second to what was going on in camp so that he would never be caught out by the guards. His life would change until he was free.

He looked at me for what seemed forever and then said, "Can you quiz me on my Spanish vocabulary?" I went back to my bunk marveling at the shape bravery could take. The pieces were falling into place. Now it was simply time to wait.

"AT EASE! AT EASE!" THE NEWSREADER waited for quiet. He passed on a lot of news about home. I paid it too little mind, but one thing stayed with me. He said the Germans had a new and powerful kind of rocket that they were launching at London. The BBC said the rockets were coming down like meteors. Though the Allied bombers were targeting the rocket launch sites, London was ablaze. That night I lay awake awhile thinking about the British. My father with his strong ancestral ties to the American Revolution had raised us to despise them. Thinking back on the guts of the Londoners and the Royal Air Force during that first year of the war, I realized the prejudices of my father and my childish assumption of them as my own. I saw the British now as my inspiration—a people magnificently courageous and resolute in their stand against the Nazis.

There were several snows, but they were thin ones and promised very little opportunity. In the meantime, though the cold kept us quiet and hunkered down in our bunks, the night conversations heated up. During a particularly cold night, I chose to tell a story for one of the few times in all my months inside Stalag 17. We were talking about family pets. Animal tales, particularly dog stories, were popular at night. The oldest and best virtues, unambiguous in an animal, inspired memories that strengthened us. Beast described his uncle's black Lab, a dog they called Bodie.

"She'd stand on the bow of my uncle's boat, leaning way out over the water and whimpering, just smelling the ducks, tasting 'em," said Beast. "Then she'd dive into the water after we'd killed a bird and root through the rushes until she brought it back, swimming to the boat or the blind. She was a pretty sight, coming through the water, carrying that bird high in her mouth. One time," Beast said in a voice as close to reverential as he could muster, "Bodie was heavy with pups when we had our big hunt. She wasn't gonna miss a hunt, and surely not the big one, so she come with us. After a real big shooting, she took off into the marsh to get all the birds, dead and crippled. She was gone a long time. Hours. We called her as the sun began to set, and after riding over the marshes firing our shotguns and calling that dog, we gave up. There weren't no sign of her and my uncle just turned the boat toward home.

"I asked my uncle how come we was leaving the dog behind? And he tells me that ain't no dog worth missing supper for, not even Bodie. Well, we was all eatin' on the porch—fried chicken it was, dripping in sauce that my aunt made from tomatoes and a taste of whiskey, and we was lookin' out over the water and I hear someone say, 'Christamighty, lookie here,' and there in the moonlight comes ol' Bodie dragging her sorry ass out of the water and behind her was six pups, each with a dead duck in its mouth."

"Shit," said a voice, "you had me Beast, you really did."

"Well, it's true," he growled good-naturedly.

Thinking back to the dog I'd loved best in the world, I decided to take a plunge into what was, for me, the icy waters of trying to tell a good story. I spoke up and the bay went dead quiet with surprise.

"When my brother Jack and I were kids, we had a scraggly black spaniel. My grandmother had turned him over to our family saying she couldn't manage him anymore. His name was Beppo."

"What kind of a goddamn name is Beppo?" said someone.

"I'm not sure."

"It's the name only a grandmother would give a dog, that's for goddamn sure," growled Beast, lying in the dark, still missing Bodie.

"Well anyway, Beppo was a sad dog. Real unhappy. When he came to us he already had a bent ear, kind of a moth-eaten coat of fur with some little bald patches, and some kind of trouble with his legs that made him move a bit like a crab."

"Christ, Handy, where in the hell did your grandmother learn to look after dogs?" sniped Kozikowski good-naturedly.

"In Stalag 17," cracked Meese with a chuckle.

Disregarding the derision, I bumbled on. "Without a word between us, Jack and I just decided that we were going to save this dog and look after him. We were the first people to pay him any mind and he followed us around and couldn't wait for a chance to go walking in the fields and woods with us. He'd yelp and whimper whenever he got the idea either of us might be about to head on out. Over the years, Beppo got stronger and happier. He lived a pretty good life. He especially liked our summers out of school, back on my grandmother's turf, though the long trip there grew harder and harder for him. One year my father said that Beppo would have to stay behind when we took our summer vacation. We'd have to leave him behind with Mr. McGregor, the caretaker of the family farm we rented during the winter. Jack and I didn't like Mr. McGregor, but neither of us could explain to our parents why, and despite our begging, my father wouldn't hear of taking the dog."

"I got a bad feeling about this story," said Tony Sac.

"Me too," said Kozikowski.

"My brother and I put in a lot of time thinking about Beppo that summer. We wondered a lot about how he was doing but didn't know how to ask. It wasn't until being away from him that way that we realized how much we cared for him. It was agony to have him not there with us. Finally, with school about to reopen, our family made the long trip back to our winter home. We arrived in the late afternoon. I remember the sun was low and the grass a September gold looking back toward Mr. McGregor's farmhouse, and . . ."

"Get to the fucking dog," hissed a listener. "What happened to the dog?"

"Well, looking back over the long stretch of grass that ran to Mr. McGregor's, we stood at our back door and called him again and again. No sign. We started walking, then running toward Mr. McGregor's, still calling. About halfway there we saw him crawling out from under Mr. McGregor's front porch. He stumbled over the stubbly grass moving like a crab, head half down, half starved, but whimpering and yelping like the battered dog we first knew. In a minute he collapsed at our feet, looking half dead. I cried." I was still for a moment and felt a spasm of emotion in my throat. The bay was quiet. "Maybe my brother cried, too, but likely not; he was tougher than I was. It turned out that old McGregor was a drunk and a thief and had beaten the dog all summer long. My brother and I sat with him on the grass and held his head for a while and then carried him to some straw in the shed. A few days later he died." Again, silence.

"Christ, Handy, who taught you to tell a story?" complained Kozikowski.

"The same lady that named his goddamn dog Beppo," snorted Beast. I wasn't sure why I'd chosen to tell the story at all, or in fact any story—I'd long since come to recognize what a terrible storyteller I was—but remembering Beppo at least did me a lot of good. There were no stories after that. I had brought the curtain down on the night's entertainment.

THE STORM WE WERE WAITING FOR finally came. It was early December, after a morning of dark and driving cold, when the flakes floated timidly to the ground. Soon enough they were thick and fast; it was looking to be a big storm. I was sitting on my bunk when Grey passed by our bay. He did not even break stride, but his glance at me told me everything I needed to know: *We are going tonight.* I had to talk to Kozikowski and fast. He was in the next bay playing cards. I stood off to the side and he saw me watching him. He looked at me, and then over to the window. The snow was blinding. He sighed.

"Fellas, I'll never learn this game. Bridge just isn't my style." There were groans and pleading that he should at least finish the hand, but he passed his cards to the guy who had been looking over his shoulder. "You've been wanting to play my hands all afternoon anyway," he quipped. We walked back together to the bay.

"It's the snowstorm we've been waiting for," I said to Koz. "It's now or never."

"Well, it's now then. Good luck."

"Koz?" I said, pausing.

"Forget about it. I'll be fine. You just look after yourself."

I went back to my bunk and began to sort yet again the few things I would carry, mostly cigarettes and D-bars for trading. "We go light," Grey had said when we first walked the perimeter and planned the escape. When I was ready, I hauled my overcoat down from the bunk and turned to find Young standing next to me.

"Be careful," he said. I wasn't sure how he knew. I had said nothing and knew that not a word would have gotten out of Koz—let alone Grey, who by nature trusted almost no one.

"Thanks. You know I will," I assured him.

"Grey understands what he's doing. He's used to the things that can happen . . . ," Young whispered, deliberately leaving unsaid what we both knew: that I had no experience escaping from a prison camp and had no clue as to what might happen. Young seemed anxious, and his great dark eyes shone. I was surprised and moved, and I tried to put him at ease.

"Don't mind me, I'll be fine. I'll follow the master and just do whatever he does." I punched his left shoulder with a couple of playful right jabs.

"Handy," he said, taking my elbow as I was turning to leave. "He works alone. And he knows that he'll always do whatever he needs to do to survive. You do the same." Before I could answer him, he took something from his pocket and pressed it into my hands. It was a crucifix. "I made it for you." The detail was stunning; the Savior's face looked up at me in anguish. I didn't have much of a relationship with Him, but I was immediately grateful for His company.

"You should have told guys what you were making at that stove. They might have shut up and cut you some slack . . ."

"It was nobody's business," he said quietly, and then he turned away. I was moved by his concern and would never have predicted it. With the crucifix firmly in hand I went back to the far corner in our bay, where Grey and I had decided to wait for Dillard's signal that all was set at the gate. Grey was already there, sitting on the lower left bunk.

"Dillard says they've started." He was agitated, immensely impatient. "I'm not sold on that guy, Handy. If you hadn't saved my life, I might never have listened to you," he growled.

"How long ago did they start?" I asked.

"I don't know. Shattuck got the word to Dillard that we'd settled on today—that the snow looks as though it'll thicken up enough to blind the guard tower. He came back here a few minutes ago to tell us it was under way. You were talking with that guy across the aisle."

"Well," I said, in the calmest voice I could muster, "let's give them time. They have to make the bribe and somehow get the two Brits down to the other side of the gate."

"Oh, Christ, they don't know what the hell they're doing!" he complained. "Never put your own safety in the hands of strangers. Never."

"Sometimes you have to," I said, knowing that I was doing just that at this very moment. I respected Grey, and his high adventure of espionage and ingenuity behind enemy lines gave him all the credibility he needed with me. The fact that the Gestapo had determined to send him on to Buchenwald—was willing to turn Stalag 17 upside down to find him—was incredible to me. Yet I felt I knew what the right move was at this moment and I was going to make it happen. I hoped that our bond was forged with something more than gratitude for the tunnel that had saved his life. I had repeatedly underscored that it took a team to hide him and the others and that Meese, Wilkens, Tony Sac and Kozikowski—but especially Wilkens and his air ducts—were the drivers of that team. But he chose not to forget that Shattuck had introduced me as the leader.

Grey got up and walked over to the window to look out at the heavy curtain of snow that closed over the camp. With his overcoat collar already up around his neck, his wool cap pulled low and his boots laced high and tight, he was ready to walk out the door. I was struck by his uncanny ability to manage his physical presence; despite his size and capacity for anger, he seemed always in control of himself. Sometimes if you were talking to him, he could disappear even before the words he had spoken reached your ears. You would turn to answer him and he was gone. Later kriegies would call him the "Grey Ghost." Even now, despite his mounting fury, he stood by the window in a stillness that was almost serene.

"It's perfect," he growled under his breath, looking out at a winter storm that seemed to be getting stronger by the minute. "It's goddamned perfect." Except for Joseph, sitting up in his blue heaven, no one was in the bay. They all had to know what was going on—certainly

Koz did—and it struck me they were giving us both some breathing room. The minutes passed. I went up to our front door and looked out. The main gate was only a hundred yards away, but I couldn't see it through the snowy gloom. That was good news; the snow was shielding our crossover turf. I went back and told Grey this. He grunted. There was a long silence. Finally he spoke. His voice was calm and determined.

"Something's wrong, goddammit. It's been nearly an hour. You don't need that much time to bribe a guard and line up the two Brits on the other side. They're screwing it up and we have to get up there now. We have to go. This storm is just what we need. The tower guard won't be able to see into it more than a dozen feet. He'll be jumpy up there by himself and won't care a damn about the main gate. I know how to do this, goddamn it, I know how to do this! We have to go now!"

I was taken aback. The idea that we would break ranks with Kurtenbach's team—ditch the plan we were told they would carry through for us—ran against the grain of my thinking about the White House. Grey's wisdom was beyond my reach. I dug in.

"Listen," I preached, "as Americans in this prison we've got to stand with our elected leaders. We've got to stick with their plan, which is for us to hang in here until they're ready to get us through the gate. They put the whole camp at risk to save you from the Gestapo, but that's not even the point. We can't now do something that might risk their necks." He looked at me for a long moment. I could see the snow whirling behind him outside the window, though night had already fallen. Then he spoke quietly, calmly:

"Fair point, Handy. I understand." He thought for a moment and his demeanor changed. "You're right. How about you stay here to meet with whoever they send to get us. I'll go up to the gate for a few minutes and try to scope out what's going on. OK?" That was workable for me; the solution met both our needs. "OK," I said, and he was instantly out of our bay, out the front door and into the dark. I retreated into my thoughts for a minute or two and then turned to see Joseph looking down at me. He must have taken in every word, but he had said nothing. For some reason, I knew he had something he wanted to say.

"What's on your mind, Joseph?" I asked.

He did not speak at first but continued to watch me, as if deliberating. Then he spoke softly but with great solemnity. "You should have gone with him. He was the leader of this plan. It was his call. Now he is gone and I do not think he will come back. You cannot blame him. He does what he must do because it is in his nature. He has a wolf nature. His name is no accident. You are a stubborn man. Very stubborn."

"I'm just doing what I think is right," I answered, only just beginning to wonder if I had thought this all through properly.

"Yes, of course," he said and turned away.

As I was retying my boots, a guy came bursting into our bay like a sprinter. "Your name Handy?" he blurted, out of breath. For a split second I agonized: was this going to be good news or bad? His voice suggested it wasn't good. Had Grey run into a trap and been caught?

"Yes," I said.

"Wolf wants you up at the gate now," he shot back. "Right now. He said to tell you that everything has gone to hell and you gotta hurry. Hurry!" I pulled on my well-stocked overcoat and followed him—we were both almost at a trot—up the center aisle and outside into the snow. It was gathering fast, already three or four inches deep. We headed toward the lights at the main gate that separated us from the Russian camp. What could have gone wrong? When I got close enough to see, I understood. It was a disaster. There were thirty or forty people milling around on our side of the gate. The snow was hiding the main gate from the tower, but bribes don't get made in crowds. I pushed to the front and saw Grey already on the other side. Only he could have bribed a guard in full view of dozens of men and gotten away with it. I saw him looking at the guard and then back at me. He called to me—the noise from the other kriegies was loud. "Handy," he said hoarsely in a half shout, "a dozen men went through before us." The snow was so heavy I could barely see him, but his voice was clear and furious. "A dozen guys, Handy. Your goddamned White House. A dozen guys and none of them have come back. That guard isn't going to let you through until those guys come back. He's scared half to death and he should be. He's already finished and probably doesn't even know it yet. He's still ready to let you through, the poor sonofabitch, he took half my cigarettes for Christ's sake. There are just too many guys over here." I couldn't see him anymore, but I could hear him calculating.

"Stand as close to the gate as you can. We'll wait for these assholes to come back; curfew is only forty minutes away and they'll all have to get back by then. As soon as they cross, he'll let you come through. I'll be waiting."

"Great," I said. "Good work," I added weakly, not certain what to say. We were quiet for a bit and then he called me again, his voice strained, even a little apologetic.

"One more thing. You got to get out of there, Handy. You got to get over here tonight. The guys who are replacing us? They were here. Dillard did something right. The guard let a New Zealander go back in my place. A Brit's waiting for you to come over. Understand? We want to make use of that. We have to get you out tonight."

"We'll make it," I said. "Those kriegies are just over there trading. They'll have to come back soon." My spirits were high, yet he seemed agitated. What did he know that I didn't?

The minutes passed—five, ten, fifteen, twenty—with no sign of the kriegies who had gone over. I began to get angry and to pace around a little, and every minute that passed I grew angrier. There was no sign of any of the men. What were they doing over there? How did they all get there? If they didn't get back, what was going to happen? The minutes passed, the snow fell and still no sign of them. I couldn't see Grey, but I knew he'd be hovering on the other side working on the guard. My watch said ten minutes to curfew, then five, then three. No one came back. The guards would be starting to walk the barracks now, looking to shoot anyone outside. I had to go back.

Grey's voice came again from out of the storm. "It's blown, Handy. Those bastards blew it for us. Meet me at the Barracks 29 fence tomorrow at noon and we'll figure out what we're going to do. And remind Kozikowski he's now me. His dog tags go to the New Zealander."

I double-timed it back to the barracks. The lights went out before I got there, but no guard saw me.

Back in our bay it was black as pitch. No starlight, no moon tonight. There were a number of conversations going, but I stayed out of them. I needed to think about all that had happened. But as I started to climb up to my bunk at the top, I heard Meese's voice quietly saying, "Handy, hold it. Koz and I need to talk with you."

I could now make them out in the dark. "Right," I said, leaning against the bunk and only now realizing how cold and exhausted I was.

"What happened?" Meese said.

"He got through. I didn't."

Meese knew better than to ask any more questions. "Get warm," he said simply and returned to his bunk. Kozikowski stayed and asked, "What's the drill now?" I knew it was not fair to him to go into hiding as Grey, and I thanked him for his willingness to help me. Circumstances had changed, I said, underscoring that he was off the hook, at least for now. I would take Grey's place as the man in hiding. The New Zealander, wherever he was, would get my dog tags.

"I'm sorry for you, Handy. I really am. I know you're disappointed. Maybe you'll get through later. If you do, I'll take your place then." In hushed tones, Koz went on to tell me the New Zealander's name was Ray Bernie, already assigned to my bunk and up there now, maybe sleeping.

Ray Bernie was in fact asleep when I got up there, but I had to shove him over and that brought him to, though groggy. "My name's Handy," I muttered. "Get back to sleep. We'll talk in the morning."

"Right-o," he muttered back, with an accent new to me. We cut it off, but not before he insisted I reclaim half my blanket.

Sleep would have to wait; thoughts about my changed life were racing. There would be a new Handy and I had to become the new Grey and find a way to disappear. Where would I hide for tomorrow morning's roll call? I'd never talked to Koz about what he'd planned to do. The tunnel was one place, but getting in would take a lot of time. Maybe under the bottom bunks. That might work for at least awhile. I'd talk with Koz about it early.

That settled, my thoughts swam back to the tumultuous events of the past few hours and where they had left me. For a moment I felt as alone as I'd ever felt in my life. The men I had worked and lived with in this bay suddenly seemed far away from me, as if my decision to try to escape with Grey would now make me an outsider with Meese and Wilkens and the rest. Replaying what had happened at the gate, I began to grow angry again. Again and again I went over the scene and the characters, trying to determine the villain. Those men who went through? Dillard? Grey? No, certainly not Grey. In every way he'd done exactly the right thing. The one key goal was to get him out, save his life. For him to have waited another five minutes for me to show up might well have—likely *would* have—killed his chance to strike while the iron was hot. He did it right. But what the hell had happened?

I thought of the men who went through. They couldn't know their escapade was spiking our escape plan, so where was the fault in that? I came to focus on Dillard. He hadn't liked our plan or us and had treated us with indifference, as if he had had better things to do. I was a new kriegie, and perhaps he looked down on us. Maybe he used our plan for his own purposes and sent the kriegies through. I thought again of the moment in Peg Leg's office after Max had ambushed me. I'd had a sense then that I was a pawn in some greater game and that feeling returned. Did Dillard have another reason for gumming up this escape? Yet somehow he had gotten a Brit and a New Zealander ready to switch with us; he did that right. I didn't know who to be angriest with, and before too long, I realized I had only myself to blame. Grey had used his instinct and skill, the men who went over could not have known they were wrecking our plans, and just possibly Dillard's failure was not his doing. I was the one who could have acted differently. All my life I'd bucked authority when I felt it was right to do so and not a risk to others. This time I'd thought it would be wrong, but Grey had thought otherwise and his experience far outdistanced mine. Joseph had a point. My own inflexibility may have cost me.

Lying there in the dark I thought of my father. A charming and self-effacing man who had a gift for people, he was also a man who always knew exactly what he wanted to do and did it, whatever the consequences. I remembered one fall morning walking down to the stables with my father. He was to ride in the biggest steeplechase of the year. Having learned to ride in World War I as an officer in the Field Artillery, he used to tell my brother and me how he would be tossed off the surly army horses. We knew him to be an expert rider and it comforted us both to know that someone who rode so beautifully could have once been clumsy. Though he was master of the hounds and went fox hunting on the weekends, it was the steeplechase he loved best. That fall morning there was an excitement in the air; everything suffused with a sense of urgency and anticipation. My father placed his hand on my head as he spoke with authority to the groom at the stables: "Ed, bring out Brillo," he said, "I'll be riding Brillo today." The groom was carrying a pile of blankets and said nothing to my father until he had carefully placed them over the paddock gate.

"Mr. Handy," Ed said in a voice so solemn that I stopped trying to catch the stable cat and listened, "you must not ride Brillo. Brillo is not right for a steeplechase; he's a great hunter but a little crazy and a steeplechase will throw him. Please, Mr. Handy, take Comet," referring to my father's smallest but most intelligent, reliable horse, with a record of having won him many races. The cat crept up to my shoe and scratched at my laces. My father walked to the paddock fence and looked over at the grazing horses. Ed and I stood still waiting. Then he turned toward us.

"Brillo," he said simply and walked away. Ed stared after him for a long moment and then turned toward me, rubbing his hands absently.

"This will be a bad day," he said, passing me like a ghost. The stable cat was gone. Later, at the steeplechase, I was standing with friends right behind a stone wall that lined a dirt road in front of an angled jump. I saw my father and Brillo careening toward us, out front, but sandwiched between two other horses. They were moving fast and I could hear the horses snorting, their hooves all thunder. And then, to the astonishment of everyone, Brillo ran right into the jump. He was killed instantly, and the collision sent my father soaring over the jump headlong into the wall in front of us. There was a terrible cry from the crowd. I pulled myself up onto the wall and looked down at my father in a tangle of limbs with a small pool of blood gathering near his head. Ed was the first one to him, whispering in my father's ear words I could not hear. It would be a long time before my father recovered from the accident and my family's circumstances changed dramatically as a result. My mother had to sustain the family and nursed my father for years. My father's headstrong refusal to at least consider Ed's advice had brought him and his family to near ruin. Headstrong, too, I had been blinded to Grey's logic that we should ignore the White House now that they had ignored us. I realized that given Grey's experience, I should have listened to him, should have shadowed him as I had promised Young I would. Life, as it had that October day when I was ten, headed south in an instant.

Roll call the next morning went off without a hitch. Long ahead, I had worked my way under Wilkens's lower-bunk workspace with his OK and then was screened in by the Red Cross boxes he slid back into place in front of me. Koz broke in Ray Bernie on roll call procedures on our side of the wire. Later Koz and I shared breakfast with him.

"Glad to meet you both in the daylight," he ventured, after getting down a crust of Nazi bread. His New Zealand accent was strong.

"Likewise," I countered. "I hadn't really planned to meet you, but that's my problem now."

"Or is it my problem? You're still here! So who am I supposed to be? How can I be you?" asked Bernie with an earnest curiosity and concern.

"You are and you will be," I said, trying to stay as calm as I could. "I'll explain that later." The New Zealander broke out in a wide smile. "Your friend here told me what happened. Tough luck for you, old man, but I'm delighted to be on the other side of that bloody fence." He was a cheerful fellow, and soon enough the rest of the bay joined us to learn his story. He had been captured by the Nazis in 1942. As the men crowded around him, listening, he held forth like an entertainer:

"Call me whatever you want, lads, except British. Do that and I'll bust your chops, no questions asked, no apologies given. You love the bastards, but we don't. I've been the Queen's fodder long enough to go home. Give me a pint and a vote of thanks and we'll call it even. But I'll get no such luck. When we get out of here, you can bet Mr. Churchill will find a field to slaughter some more Australians and New Zealanders. Oh, he has a particular enthusiasm for us, he does."

It was a strange sight watching them all, grinning at a man who was now me, holding forth as I never had nor could. I felt a little lost and began to face the gravity of my situation. I would have to hide at every roll call; I would have to make certain that no one ever discovered that Ray Bernie and I were the same man, and I realized, watching Bernie laugh and recount wild tales, that the problem was all mine.

Later in the morning, everyone was talking about the dozen men who had been caught in the Russian camp. They were stir-crazy old kriegies who had gone over there for an adventure because someone had told them that Russian women were over there. It caused quite a stir, and guys were laughing about it once the twelve had been thrown back into our camp without punishment. The same could not be said of the guard who had stopped me at the gate. He was executed, we heard, without delay. We all felt bad for him, though in varying degrees. He had looked young. Perhaps he had a wife and children in desperate need. American cigarettes were gold in the Krems economy.

That afternoon I met Grey at the fence to the west of Barracks 29. He was looking over at the Russian Chapel while standing on the very ground we had dug through trying to get him into the Russian camp.

He told me that he was in good shape and, as Ray Bernie, was in a position to volunteer for the kind of work detail that could get him near the Yugoslavian border. I wished him luck, and to my surprise he told me that he was not going to go just yet. He was going to wait for another snowstorm so that he could get me through to join him.

"I'll handle it," he said fiercely. "I'll do the whole thing. *Don't* talk to Dillard. Tell nobody anything. I'll arrange it all myself, the same way we would have done if we'd been left alone." I was stunned. We had had a good working relationship, but the point of it all was to get him out of the Gestapo's reach. The Russian Camp—we called it that even though all the Nazis' victims were in there—could be even more dangerous for him than ours. Tongues could wag for an extra food ration.

"You mustn't do that," I said. "If I hadn't been so stubborn I'd be over there right now getting ready to chop wood down near Yugoslavia."

"If you hadn't been so stubborn," he said with a rare smile, "I wouldn't have asked you to come with me. Don't worry. We'll wait. Another snowstorm like that will come." A bunch of guys were walking toward us. We broke it up, agreeing to talk again tomorrow. On the way back I thought about Young's steely assessment of Grey. Did he miss something?

Every day we talked through that fence. And no snowstorm came. Every time flakes came down, I would go and stand at the door and will a storm down upon us. It was all to no avail. There were just wintry dustings, and visibility was never compromised for the dark watchers in their towers. Every night I was back in the barracks. Days became a week. I told him not to wait, to just go, though I still hoped for the snow that might give me another chance.

I BEGAN A NEW LIFE. I was now a person always on the alert for a roll call, ready to hide in a number of places along my daily beat. I couldn't go very far afield, so that beat was small. It consisted of our compound, and to some extent the compound where the White House was, given that they knew my predicament. There weren't many places to hide in our compound other than in our tunnel, and I couldn't just go there on the spur of the moment. Many times in the morning I would again wedge myself under the bottom of Wilkens's workspace. It was tight and my cheek was pressed to the floor. I could see the boots and recognized the black ones that moved with a slow purpose as the ones to avoid at all costs. It was sometimes only a short wait, but sometimes the wait was unendurably long. I would struggle not to sneeze as the dirt filled my nostrils. Very occasionally I would see a small mouse move under a far bunk, no doubt as startled by me as I was by him.

Soon enough, though, the hiding spot of choice became a place scarcely used by the kriegies. It was the camp library inside the White House, a cubicle with bookshelves that went up about seven feet. The floor space inside this little cubicle might have been about six feet on a side, and to get into it I had to climb over the top of a partition. A table up against one of the cubicle's outside walls made that workable. The door was padlocked, which gave the guards walking by an immediate assurance that it was secure and required no further examination. I'm not certain why the door was padlocked. The books, poorly bound and falling apart, circulated freely, but usually hand to hand, bay to bay. No one ever unlocked the door and came in while I was there during those weeks in January and February, so I found myself tucked away during roll calls with nothing to do but read. And I did, becoming less and less aware of roll call's windup or even of the time of day.

I learned in that library to remember a life when books had been close friends and mentors to me. At six, I had begun with the likes of Dick Tracy, Orphan Annie, and the Hardy Boys, and they were my heroes. On discovering this, my father said he'd get me more books, and I thought he meant more of what I liked. A week or so later two large book crates came to the house—the Great Depression was still a year away—and they were addressed to me. It was a boys' library that went well beyond comic strips and the Hardy Boys. Books like Thornton Burgess's seashore and wild-animal yarns for youngsters, Thomas Bailey

Aldrich's *Story of a Bad Boy* and Dickens's *David Copperfield* became valuable allies, summoned under the glow of a bedside lamp. Some of them I even set aside and reread each summer, like Ernest Thompson Seton's *Wild Animals I Have Known*, which had moved me deeply.

I had read no books while in the service. Just getting the job done and staying healthy took all my time. But here in Stalag 17, living the life of a hunted man, hiding out in that brave library, the chance to learn from books once more unexpectedly reemerged. I read like a man possessed and was reminded why, as Pages had said, books were like deep wells in the desert. Many books tumbled down into my hands and befriended me during those isolated hours, odd selections that contained hidden messages to a hungry loner.

I had never heard of Evelyn Waugh until I saw his *Handful of Dust* and marveled at the doomed circumstance of the fever-laden hero, forced to live out his days in the jungle reading Dickens aloud to a mad recluse. I could understand the hero better, reading and reading as madly as I was. While wading through Lamb's *The Child's History of England*, I came across the adventures of Richard the Lionhearted. Strong and restless, the son of Henry II was determined above all to go on a crusade to the Holy Land. I read of his wars, the fierce and bloody battles that raged back and forth. How Richard carried his heavy English battle-axe and slew Saracens with such gusto that even Saladin, Richard's enemy, admired the English king's courage. When Richard lay with a fever, Saladin stood his troops down and sent him fresh fruits from Damascus, along with snow from the mountaintops. When Richard recovered they took to killing one another again. How odd war is, it seemed to me tucked inside the cubicle of a Nazi prisoner-of-war camp. On his return from the Holy Land, Richard came through Austria and was captured by agents of the Emperor of Germany. It was said that his troubadour Blondel walked across Europe singing the first verse to a song that only his King knew and that, before long, he heard his master's voice singing the missing verse from a tower window. He had been imprisoned in a castle along the Danube, above a place called Dürnstein. I heard again the voice of the German guard in the boxcar and realized I had seen that very castle ruin from the boxcar door.

The library's small collection of books also included some poetry. Years before, my father's selections for six-year-olds had included poetry for roughneck kids—kids for whom only war was glorious. Poems like Tennyson's "Charge of the Light Brigade" and Colonel John McCrae's "In Flanders Fields" had grabbed me and held me in a spell. Kipling's "If," though it had none of the clang and glory of war, offered me a glimpse into the man's world that I longed to inhabit. These were poems with a message, and now, hiding in the stalag, they came to me as comforting helpmates. So, too, the poems about the simple beauty of the world quickened me: Frost's "Stopping by Woods on a Snowy Evening," Keats's "The Grasshopper and the Cricket," Yeats's "The Lake Isle of Innisfree" and Byron's "Roll on, thou deep and dark blue Ocean—roll" all tumbled out of a browbeaten collection of the world's favorite poems. The poetry had the strangest effect. It offered me the deepest kind of companionship at that lonely moment and made me feel like a swimmer in clean water. I was refreshed from the daily ordeal of survival. Once, I came across lines from Wilde's "Ballad of Reading Gaol" that I had read at Milton Academy a lifetime ago. These words had new meaning to me:

> *I never saw sad men who looked*
> *With such a wistful eye*
> *Upon that little tent of blue*
> *We prisoners call the sky,*
> *And at every careless cloud that passed*
> *In happy freedom by*

When I'd read them years ago in a classroom I had had no idea what that little tent of blue might have meant to a soul imprisoned. I would have barely noticed the carelessness of clouds or recognized what

I knew now was the most precious of all gifts: happy freedom. Allan Seeger's poem "I Have a Rendezvous with Death," though written from an earlier war, said everything I felt in this present one:

> *It may be he shall take my hand*
> *And lead me into his dark land*
> *And close my eyes and quench my breath—*
> *It may be I shall pass him still . . .*

I read those words and remembered the rendezvous my two crew-mates had, the twenty men in our wing planes, even the kriegie on the wire. What might my next rendezvous be and when? I wondered in the confines of that makeshift library. I read over and over the end of Seeger's last verse:

> *And I to my pledged word am true,*
> *I shall not fail that rendezvous.*

Was my rendezvous ahead? I knew if it was I'd keep it, but I hoped—like all of us—with something worthwhile accomplished in the bargain.

I PASSED WILKENS ON HIS BUNK. He was busy polishing some tin cans. He had loved those cans when we were digging, but what did he want them for now? "I pound 'em till they shine," he said, "and polish 'em for pleasure. I made some mirrors, you know, though looking at you, Handy, I think you don't want one." He reached over and showed me a can with a wooden handle. "It's for Meese," he said proudly. "I've made dishes, candleholders, small containers." He looked around for a moment and then dropped his voice. "I work for you fellas by day, but by night I work for myself." He leaned back and pulled out what at first looked like a shiny box. It was a suitcase. "I've been collecting the best cans for months, the least nicked and shiniest." He handed it to me and

I was stunned by the smooth silvered beauty of it. The metal hammered flat, the cans as seamless as Meese's hatch. It was a mirror, and I saw my thinned-out, grizzly face looking back at me.

"I aim to carry it back home. Folks tell a lot about a man by the things he carries, that's a fact. Two secrets, Handy. One, like I told you, is mind the things you carry because they tell folks who you are. The second one is to shine the backs of your shoes with a higher polish than the front. Folks will be looking at *you* when you face them, not your shoes. But when you walk away, they'll take another look and will be sure to see the *backs* of your shoes then. Sounds crazy, but mark my words, it's the truth." Clearly, Wilkens was getting ready to go home.

SEVERAL DAYS BEFORE CHRISTMAS, ONE OF the guards at roll call told Tony Sac, who was sorting the last of the Red Cross materials, that the war was turning; the German Army was winning a great battle. We ignored their idle boasts. After all, the guards were becoming as hard-pressed as we were. They were hungry and cold and browbeaten by the same fortunes of war that bore down on us. We may have been the prisoners, but we all knew that that was going to change, and sooner all the time, it seemed. Then one day a news reader came to 32A. He reported that a German counteroffensive had achieved a stunning, unexpected success.

"The Jerries have counterattacked Allied forces," said the reader atop his stool. "Bad weather has limited Allied air power and Patton's assault has stalled. Some of the American forces have been transferred to Montgomery."

"Now you Yanks will get a taste of what I mean," said Ray Bernie quietly.

"The city of Bastogne is surrounded and Allied troops are regrouping. That's it for the moment, fellas, we'll tell you when we know more."

Men drifted back to their bays like zombies. No one spoke about it, but the meaning was clear. None of us believed the guard's assertion that this was the reemergence of the vaunted German Army. We knew better. We heard the bombers night after night, saw the draining of energy in the faces of the men who guarded us, recognized that they had as little to eat as we did. All it meant to us was that it was going to take longer to get out of here. The war would continue its ravenous consumption and our skin would tighten around our bones.

The news shocked all of us into a low-grade despair, but I was devastated as I lay in my bunk. Although Grey and I were still meeting daily and I continued to hope for the return of blinding snow, I'd also begun to let myself believe that the war was nearly over. I was angry with myself for the hoping. The war was just going to go on and on.

"HANDY. HANDY, WAKE UP." IT WAS Tony Sac, standing on the bunk below me, reaching up to shake me. "Boy, you must be tired—you never sleep later than me!"

I sat up. "What's the matter?" I said in confusion, "What's going on?"

"What's going on? Jesus! It's Christmas Eve day, Handy. It's Christmas Eve! The guards are gonna let us pipe some music through the camp. Merry Christmas!" He seemed to have the right idea, but at that moment I felt this was not a day for merriment or even joy. In a different life I would have been happy to take part in one Christmas ritual or another, but here, in this place, it seemed almost hypocritical. I wondered what Jesus would have said to a world at war, to a world engaged in just the kind of madness that he had died to rebuke. I ignored the general merriment all day. In the evening Meese came to me as I was back on my bunk.

"I'd like you to come with us, Handy," he said, looking kindly. "There's a Christmas Eve service being held by Father Kane at the chapel. There will be music and everyone is going."

"Thanks, Meese," I said, "but I think I'll just stay here and sort of have my own service."

"You know," he spoke out, leaning closer to my bunk, "there are some days when what others want of you is more important than what you want for yourself. We want you to come with us. It will be good for us all."

Those were powerful words. I missed my mates but had no way of asking to join them. Meese kindly made it easy for me, and though I did not say so, I was grateful.

I followed the crowd from the bay across the compound. It was dark. No searchlights. The stars were brilliant above; the air crisp and cold. Right away the crunching of the snow reminded me of nighttime treks to the hills we used to sled on in the hinterlands of my boyhood. My friends and family spread along the path ahead and behind. The sense of promise, of excitement, and always the adventure of night.

I'd never been to the chapel. The interior, as in our barracks, was of rough-cut, unfinished wood. The length of the building was filled with crude benches but with enough room left on one side to have an altar and a place from which a service could be conducted. What stopped me as I entered was the light, the glow of dozens of candles. It was a kind of soft glow quite different from the weak electric pulse in our barracks. It was different even from the butter wicks we'd used in the Barracks 29 tunnel. It was warm and safe, and the quiet flickering flooded me with memory. From the age of five to thirteen I had gone to a tiny school near a beautiful little church. During Christmas seasons there had always been a tall tree to the left of the altar, candles nestled throughout its boughs. These tree candles were not lit until Christmas Eve, and once or twice I was given the chance to light them. I remember the leaping of light as I moved from one candle to the other.

We walked down an aisle and took our seats on a bench.

"That's Father Kane," whispered Meese, pointing to a tall man who placed something over his shoulders like a scarf. "He's a captain, an Irishman who carried a Bible and a .45 automatic. He said he was tired of the Krauts using the cross on his helmet as a target and decided to give as good as he got. He's something." Meese fairly beamed. Kane stood patiently in the front, waiting for the men to gather until the shelter was overflowing with bodies. I had never seen most of them before, so there must have been prisoners from the other barracks and compounds.

"Father, I know you will excuse me language, but I need to speak to me boys with the words we all share at Stalag 17."

"He loves to say that," whispered Meese with a smile.

"Well now, 'tis a fine thing to have such a full house," he said in his thick Irish brogue. "Nice to see your shinin' mugs it is. And I know that not all of you are here just to celebrate the birth of the Savior, but everybody's got his own memories of this night, whatever your faith. And if God don't mind your reasons, who am I to argue? So welcome." Men shuffled and coughed and made room for one another on the benches.

"You know, we're as cold as Mary and Joseph were, maybe even a damn sight colder."

"And they had cows and goats," someone cracked.

"Yeah, 'cause the Germans hadn't found them yet," said another voice. Laughter rippled through the candlelit space.

"True enough, boys. True enough. Well, this special evening puts me in a mind to tell you a story about two women and the children they brought into this world. Both were utterly bewildered by the miracle of motherhood. Both were told by the Archangel Gabriel that their sons would change the world. One of them you know as Mary, mother of God. But the other, I'll wager you a D-bar you don't know. Her name was Elizabeth and she was Mary's cousin. Elizabeth was long past the age when she could have had any children, and when she found herself pregnant, she hid in her home for five months. In the sixth month, Elizabeth's cousin Mary came for a visit. Mary was herself five months pregnant with the Lord Jesus. When Elizabeth heard Mary call her name as she entered the house, the baby in Elizabeth's womb leapt. Elizabeth was filled with wonder and the Holy Spirit filled her heart. She cried out, 'Blessed art thou among women, and blessed is the fruit of thy womb.' Imagine shy, shamed Elizabeth, who had been hiding in her home, greeting Mary in a voice that everyone could hear with such a message! And then it was Mary, inspired by her cousin's voice, who was herself filled with the Holy Spirit. That's something to consider, boys. Elizabeth's baby leaping at the sound of Love, at the presence of the sacred, and sparking mothers toward holiness. Faith is a simple damned thing, as simple as dominoes. One topples the other and down they fall all around the table.

"Anyway, these two women would have their sons, but it was Elizabeth's child who came first. He was called John and he began to preach from the start. He told the unbelievers that light would come to those in darkness, wisdom to those who lived in ignorance, kindness to those in pain, peace to those who suffered. He knew the Word was coming and he knew that he was a witness bearing witness to that light. 'I am but a voice in the wilderness,' he said. 'Prepare ye, the Kingdom of Heaven is at hand.' He promised that we would be delivered from our enemies so to serve God without fear. Service, boys, service to others. John served. But service was only a part of John's message. Remember what John told believers at the water's edge? 'The axe is laid at the root of the trees and every tree that brings forth bad fruit shall be hewn down and cast in the fire. I may be baptizing you, but he that cometh after me is mightier than I, whose shoes I am not worthy to bear. He shall baptize you with the Holy Ghost and with fire.' The Holy Ghost and with fire," Father Kane repeated, very slowly and with great feeling. Then he paused. When he started again, his voice was no longer that of a storyteller. It had a breathless quality, a mounting urgency to it that all of us heard. There was no sound in the chapel except the spit of the candles.

"My boys, there's a cleansing fire burning across Europe, and it is coming toward us even now. We are of that fire but we came before it, like John. And like John we herald its coming. Every day that we walk this camp with our heads up, we grow stronger. We are messengers, voices in the wilderness. We tell our enemies that those who bring forth bad fruit will find the axe laid at their root. Theirs will be a vengeance that they cannot escape. Our message is as clear as he was: the Truth is coming and you cannot stop it."

He smiled and his eyes shone.

"You know the truth I mean, boys, so do the Jerries. It's a truth that looks like a Sherman tank, like an American GI, boys, and that truth, that homely looking sonofabitch from Des Moines or Texarkana, is coming to set us free. Don't mind what you hear about the setbacks of war, freedom is coming closer every damned day, and the Germans know it. You can see it in their faces. Hear me about this, boys, and hear me close. That fire will come and it will burn away all the madness. And after it passes over us, another kind of walking will start. A long hard walking that will last you the rest of your lives. And because of what you have learned here, it will be a different kind of walking than most other fellas you know. Because," and here he looked at each of us so closely that each of us might have thought he was the only one being spoken to, "we're the sons of John here at Stalag 17. We call out beyond the wires that hold us. Deep calls unto deep, my boys. You are soldiers and you have fought like men, but in these holy, hellish months, you have learned something else, something deeper than the strength of the mighty. You have learned concern for others. Bless you, boys, for deep calls unto deep. And you have studied at the feet of Love. You may not know it now, but I swear to you when you get back and start your lives again, you will realize that you learned to love your fellow man in Stalag 17."

And here Father Kane looked up as if he were seeing something floating over us and understood more about what was coming than he could say. As if he saw our future. And right then, we started to believe that we were beginning our long journey home.

"Let's sing together," he said softly, and with that, Father Kane began in a low, rumbling voice the familiar words to "Silent Night." We all picked up the melody and joined him. I felt like a child. The words came easily, the melody deeply comforting, and for the first time in longer than I could remember, it was Christmas.

On the way back from the chapel to our barracks, men were still singing the carols, some with a good natured burlesque ("Oh, little camp in Austrrrriraaah . . ."). Someone else was laughing over the comment made by a fellow from Louisiana who had said, "Ah ain't felt so good since ah tripped 'n' fell into my daddy's watermelon patch!" but I struggled, and memories of home filled me with both joy and sadness. I rolled Father Kane's words over in my mind. What would I take from my experience here? What was life asking of me? When the fire burned over us and set us free, where would I go and what would I do?

That night, I dreamed I was wandering through my father's house and could hear someone crying. In my father's study I found my younger sister, Virginia, who we called "Tinker," curled in an oversized chair, sobbing. I put my arms around her as she wept and wept, shoulders heaving, inconsolable. I kept trying to talk to her, to ease her somehow, but it did no good. It seemed I spoke to her all night long, but the crying never ceased. I woke up in a sweat. It was dark, though first light was not far off. I thought of my grandmother from Ohio—my mother's home—and the oft-told family story of a similar dream she had had about her youngest son who was on a bike tour in Germany after the First World War. She had woken and said to my grandfather: "Franklin is in terrible trouble." They set about trying to track him down only to learn that he was indeed gravely ill. My grandmother wasted no time, sailed to Germany and nursed him back to health. I could only hope that I did not dream with the prescience of my grandmother. I tossed and turned for hours. I did not go back to sleep.

A FEW WEEKS LATER, I SAW Grey for the last time. He had now waited thirty days for the snowstorm I would use to go over. The weather had continued bitterly cold and brought a number of snowfalls, but none that came close to hiding the main gate from the nearby guard tower. All the same we'd meet every day—at different places along the Barracks 29 fence and at different times to lessen the risk that guards in the tower at the fence's north end might take an interest. We'd talk for a few minutes, exchanging news from each of our camps and then setting the next day's time and place. Not once did Grey give me a hint of impatience—he must have been missing one promising work trip after another—and I just went along with it. I wasn't thinking of him or what he might need to do. I was blinded by my own determination to get to Yugoslavia with him.

Sometimes moments of truth come to us in life as clear and bright as the moon. You feel something still and sure inside you, and you know at last the thing you must do. So it was for me then, by that fence with Frank Grey in mid-January of 1945. What should have sunk in weeks before was finally to grip me as we stood there once again trading news across the barbed wire. The day was icy cold but the sky was blue, graced with snow-white clouds and a warming sun. Something about Grey caught my attention that day. I could see him shifting from foot to foot and remembered how impatient, how fast he was. It occurred to me that this tireless, almost fearless man of action was standing almost like one indecisive, uncertain. What was he still doing here? And then I saw it. He was waiting for me. He wasn't waiting for another opportunity. He could spin that opportunity out of thin air and be gone to Yugoslavia anytime he wanted. The White House may have pegged him as a solo operator who did what he wanted, but I knew better. Grey figured I had had a hand in saving his life and he owed me. He was not complaining, but I was continuing to hold him back, waiting for a snow that was not likely to come. I now understood that he had to escape, and every day lost put him in more danger of being caught. He was stubborn. He'd keep waiting for that snow unless I forced him to give it up.

"Frank," I said—I'd never called him by his well-known first name before. "You've waited long enough—too long. You've got to go. You've got to get on the next crew headed south to the border."

"Handy, thanks, but let's hang in on this one. The winter's got a ways to go. We'll luck out yet." He was firm.

"Frank. Listen to me very carefully and do as I say. Go," I said, watching the journey I had dreamed of so often melt away. "Do that for me. It's the biggest thing you can do for me. We'll meet again in better days."

He looked at me for a moment and started to speak. But he stopped. "Look after yourself," he said, and then he was gone.

Several nights later I awoke to the sound of Joseph's insistent whisper.

"Handy."

"Yes? What is it?"

"I had a dream. Do you hear me? I dreamed about the Wolf. I saw him."

I was quiet, barely breathing for listening to Joseph's voice.

"He was in his wolf form. You know he is a wolf, don't you? His four legs were galloping through the woods like a horse, his ears pinned back. Trees bent at his passing. There was fire in his eyes and his breath came like smoke. He was free. And Handy?" Joseph leaned out over his bunk to be certain I heard him.

"Yeah?"

"He thanks you." And then Joseph turned to look out his window, his shadow, as always, a study in stillness. And I wondered if it was true that Frank Grey had escaped Stalag 17 once and for all.

WE WERE STANDING IN THE COMPOUND midmorning. It was cold; the trees in the grove were bony fingers scolding the wind. Men stood in groups, arms folded, talking over the rumors and outrageous fictions that swept through the camp. Out of nowhere, with a howling so loud and sudden that men ducked or dropped to the ground in fear, four American fighter planes shot across the compound. We barely had time to see them before they were gone.

Men started running after them, calling them. "Come back," they shouted, and as if in answer, one rose out of the formation and curved back around.

"He's coming for another pass!" men cried. "He's coming. Here he comes. Oh, what a beauty. Come to Poppa. Here he comes." Only a couple of hundred feet above us, a fighter plane with a bright American star freshly painted on his wing—a P-47 Thunderbolt—lifted the dust on the compound. They must have been briefed we were here as they planned the attack on the Krems industrial area.

"Shit!" someone shouted. "Look at the markings. That's a plane from the Fifteenth!"

"I thought they were based in Italy. What are they doing here?" The plane curved back to the south, occasionally dipping below the tree line altogether, but the sound of his engine enabled us to track his approach. When we saw him again he was headed straight at the camp as if he were on a strafing run. It was an awesome sight. The guards were startled and yet, instead of scrambling for cover, they stood as we did and gaped. As he passed over he waggled his wings. We were grateful and men waved wildly, cheering. Whether the pilot was as surprised by us as we were by him or whether he had a deeper purpose in mind, he banked once again and began to circle over us, looking down from his cockpit. Three times he circled. Then, on the final bank, with a formality that made me hold my breath, he saluted us. He rose up over the trees to catch up with the formation that had gone on without him. Meese came up to me. His eyes were moist.

"Comrades," he said, watching the empty horizon that would soon fill with smoke.

OVER THE NEXT MANY WEEKS, I thought about what it was to have and not have comrades. My new life cast in the role of the wanted "Wolf" worked more and more to split me from our bay. I had begun the hardest days I was to have at Stalag 17. The playing out of winter corresponded with a rising of cabin fever, a fraying of the edges between men. We had had experiences that had bound us one to another, but the weeks now were giving way to a listless waiting. Escape plans were utterly shelved; news of the war was an obsession. *Where were they? When were they coming?*

During that time, I managed to be nimble and resourceful about not being caught, but the cost was steep to my own sense of comradeship. My link with the others, the men in my bay, my tunnel colleagues, all seemed to slacken. They were indifferent to my watchful planning for understandable reasons—we had all stared down the challenge of survival and it was getting harder. We had all wrestled with our circumstances, and months of imprisonment had frayed our capacity to help others manage what we ourselves could barely contain. My problems were not theirs, and shared problems were an essential bond at Stalag 17. Time hiding was like my time digging. I was alone, only now there was no team above, no sense of a shared goal. The unspoken rule that escape activities weren't to be talked about was well observed. Not many knew where I went, or even really why I went there. My detached life made others uncomfortable, maybe even a little jumpy. Ray Bernie, who we'd moved to Grey's empty bunk, became an affable and popular newcomer to 32A—his relationship to the Grey escape, and now to me, fading from everyone's memory. Never exactly affable or gregarious, I became increasingly occupied with my life on the run—my responsibility to protect both Grey and Bernie. Like Young in the opposite bay, I was now a loner, too, largely insensitive to the group's interests and needs. I must have grated on my fellow kriegies.

It was only a matter of time before this grating came to a head. It happened one night in the bay. If I had a best friend at Stalag 17, it had come to be Kozikowski. I admired men like Meese and Wilkens, and they had taught me much, but my relationship with them was more formal, marked more by respect than friendship. Kozikowski, on the other hand, had brought me all the quiet collaboration of friendship. Quick to criticize—and always in his humorless, dogged manner—he was not an easy guy to get along with, but somehow we managed. Perhaps it was because we each saw a lot of ourselves in the other. I was a man on the run, but had I not insisted that it was my obligation to be Grey, he would have assumed the role himself without complaint. That night, before curfew, I had come in from walking the perimeter and the men had been talking. They lay about their bunks, and it was as if I had come into the middle of the conversation. The laughter ebbed as I sat to untie my boots.

"What's got up your backside, Handy?" sniped someone. I didn't know what he meant except that, as I had less and less skill at joining a conversation, I may have seemed more of a loner than usual. I no longer felt a part of the bay and had no clue how to address that fact. So as a result, I stayed quiet. My silence made others feel awkward, and I remembered what Meese had said about Young. And then Kozikowski, lying in his upper bunk where he could look down on me, said with a cutting edge:

"Well, Handy, if you didn't have such an unpleasant personality . . ." Whatever came after that, I can't remember, if I heard it at all. It didn't matter. Ill equipped as I was to tease or banter, an even worse deficiency now surfaced. I couldn't tell the difference between casual and definitive judgments. I didn't even recognize that there was such a difference. It was my great misfortune to grow up that way. It was built into me to assume that Kozikowski had given me a definitive judgment—the equivalent of "get out of our lives, we don't want to see you around anymore." Any other guy in our bay, had he been on the receiving end of that dictum, would have said—with a smile and a voice to match—something like "Yeah? What the hell got up your backside, Koz? Somebody piss on your D-bars?" He would have known, of course, that Koz may have meant it at the moment, but a friendly rejoinder would have set it aside and the long-standing friendship would have emerged intact. I was to walk a long road before learning that. As to learning that your critics can become your best friends, that would take even longer.

Instead, I glumly said nothing. Nor for a few seconds did anyone else. My own fumbling of the moment then extended to believing he spoke for all the bay, since no one had contradicted him or defended me. I now felt fully and finally alone. Continuing to say nothing, I climbed to my upper bunk and decided to press on without the men I'd shared my life with at Stalag 17.

NO DOUBT THERE WERE OTHERS WHO also woke at the first approach of the engines. We were increasingly used to Allied aircraft overhead, and as they neared, I suspect many of us lay there doing the old calculations, identifying the aircraft and their number, weighing their direction, altitude and possible targets, waiting even for the camp air raid signal that would roust some of us out and into the trenches by the latrine. This morning, though, the engines did not pass and fade as usual but came on, growing louder until the roof above us seemed to shake. We tumbled out of our bunks and spilled out into the compound. Night was still on the ground, and above the sky was a blue heaven patterned with hundreds upon hundreds of planes, silvertipped, gleaming. There were so many squadrons that you could not distinguish their formations. All around the slow-moving bombers were beautiful birdlike fighter planes playfully rising and diving, putting on a show. Eyes skyward, we stood in awe. Some cheered, some cursed, some wept. This was a raid of such immense scale—we had not seen its like over Stalag 17 ever before—that each of us remembered again what it was like to be part of such an armada.

"Those are P-38 Lightnings," said a guy next to me, pointing, like a boy at the circus. Their vapor trails were brushstrokes backlit by the sunlight. And the bombers kept coming on, relentless, inevitable works of God, dazzling new creations as beautiful as any bird. *Can you see me?* I wondered, knowing they could not. But I saw them; I could hear them calling out to one another on their intercoms, checking their instruments, gazing distractedly at an alien landscape below. There were engines and equipment to monitor, charts and timetables to follow. They were as preoccupied with their tiny world as I had once been a thousand years ago. Their bellies filled with Air Corps grub, their heads still aching from last night's beer, they were determined, focused and asleep to the mysteries of their own meaning. I knew those men up there and remembered the clean, hard clarity of my own heart. They could not see us, did not even know we were here. They could not see farmers at their plows or the peasant women who had saved my life. The ground below them was the seedbed of the enemy, and though it could be neither seen nor known, sadly it might finally have to be destroyed to win this just war. And I understood them. I, too, had ridden with those airborne angels. I thought of that last moment before our two wing planes burst into flames when I had witnessed the vast airborne armada coming to liberate Europe. As for the people who were soon to be terrified by the same overwhelming roar that even now made us cheer? Though our targets were arms plants, they would see death rain down like rice. Blind to what they had called down upon themselves, they would hate us. In that moment, I felt as if I could see what neither the airmen above nor the enemy would consider in the moment of drama both were about to engage in: that life was precious and fragile and mysterious. It was as if there was a difference between the doing, which seemed the work of man, and the seeing, which belonged only to God. For that brief moment, we were ragged watchers, half starved and worn, but armed with sight and understanding about the power, the humiliation, the horror and the hope. We saw it all, felt it inside of us with wordless certainty. Father Kane was right: we were the sons of John. We were the witnesses, and watching them fly over us we understood the shape of things to come. As Joseph had said, it would not come without great and enduring grief, but the world was changing before our eyes. I have no idea how long we stood there, but it was long enough to last a lifetime. I was washed clean. No longer an airman or a prisoner, I was simply a man looking up into a sky filled with meaning.

When the wide blue chased away the last of the bombers and their trailing fighters, I closed my eyes and listened to them leave, the sound still humming in my ears long after they had gone. Then I woke to myself, a barefoot dreamer standing outside in the compound. I was not dreaming, and looking around, I thought for a cold instant that it was a dream turned nightmare. No one was anywhere to be seen. I looked down the east side of the fence that ran between the old and new kriegie compounds and saw the prisoners neatly stacked up, standing there for roll call. I knew I was now in danger and had no one to blame but myself. Not keeping up with the crowd was for me an experience with deep roots. Before I could turn to run inside, I felt a hand on my shoulder and heard, from behind, the familiar barking: "Rolll Calll. *Schnell, Schnell, SCHNELL!*" After months of hiding successfully, I'd blown it. I was in big trouble.

Turning around, I pointed to my bare feet, and with gestures and some pidgin English—I'd learned almost no German—I got across to the guard my need to get my boots and that they were inside. If I could get him to let me go back into the barracks, he might walk on down to the roll call and let me follow after getting shod. He had to let me go back: it was the morning of March 1—too cold to make me go down barefoot. But he didn't move. I looked at him more closely. It was the sad-eyed soldier who had warned me to take my things during the search for Grey.

I walked the cold ground back to 32A's front door—the opposite direction from the roll call—and down the center aisle to our bay at the back. He followed me all the way. I sat down on the lower bunk and—knowing he had a grasp of English—kept saying, "It's OK, I'll be along. I'm coming. Don't worry." I made out that I couldn't find one of my boots—it was on the floor well under the lower bunk—and fiddled around hoping he would go, but he stood right at the edge of my bay and made clear to me he was going to wait until I got my boots on. I stalled as best as I could. I thought that if I'd been Grey I might have talked my way out of the whole problem, but the only thing I could think of was to stall. Making out that I'd finally located the missing boot, I began to put the two on with exaggerated slowness. I kept looking up and motioning that I would come after him, promising to follow. He didn't move. I felt a spasm of fear and then a spreading sense of peace, perhaps the residue of earlier thoughts while watching that armada in the sky. I didn't tie the laces. I just sat there motionless and looked straight into his eyes. It might have been smart to smile, but I didn't. The message was "You've got me; so what are you going to do about it?" He looked back at me just as hard, his face without expression. It was as if I had never looked so long and so hard at another human being. I could see the crow's-feet at the corners of his eyes, a faint childhood scar on his cheek. Of medium build, he had a large head, unkempt hair and blue, expressive eyes. I had always known him to be a guard who possessed no malice. He had warned me about the impending confiscation of our personal effects during the Grey search and I had been grateful. If he could shout and order us around like the other guards, he maintained a certain dignity to it, as if to telegraph his own reluctance to play the part. I realized, as I looked at him, that he was a good man and I liked him. At that very moment, I saw his eyes soften. He looked at me with the hint of a smile, as if he had figured something out. Then, to my astonishment, he turned toward the washroom door and walked out. I waited. Had he left to get help? After a few minutes, prisoners filled the aisle, laughing, talking and utterly oblivious to my small, momentous drama. The roll call was over.

From that time on, I took every opportunity to give that guard a sense that I was thankful for what he had done. The next afternoon, I found him standing just inside the barracks door, to get out of the wind. I gave him a D-bar that he quickly put in his pocket. Some days later, I found him in the same place. We spoke awkwardly at first; he watched the door nervously, but after a while he relaxed. I learned his name: Franz Schubert. He rolled his eyes and repeated the name when I offered him a quizzical look. Yes, he seemed to say, like the composer. He talked of a wife who was far away and of a family he had not seen in more than two years.

After listening to him, I came to believe that it was not fear of retribution that kept him from turning me in. I think he simply understood that I was a man not so different from him, a man fighting a war that never should have happened, and that that was hard enough on us both. His eyes had too much suffering in them to want another man to suffer as well. Was he also, like me, becoming a human being?

PART V

SPRING AGAIN

> *For we have made an end to all things base*
> *We are returning by the road we came.*
>
> —SIEGFRIED SASSOON

THE ARTILLERY HAD been getting steadily closer over the past week. The Russian guns were a little over thirty miles east of us, closing in on Vienna. Off and on the artillery thundered like heavy machinery rolling across a wooden floor. The ground shook. Dirt from the tunnel hidden in the crawl space above our bunks drifted down, remnants of a memory that no longer mattered. Each night the great animal pounded closer and closer, the sky lit by dueling artillery. Kriegies increasingly sought the zigzag of the trenches dug along the latrines where they could wait until the guns ceased. Muddy and wet as the trenches were, they afforded a sense of comfort.

The air raids were relentless. When night targets were close, we crowded the windows to watch. Sometimes we could see the British bombers caught for a moment in the dazzle of a searchlight and we all winced, imagining a darkened plane filled with a blinding white light. They would twist and dive, trying to elude the bursting flak that closed quickly on them. When an unlucky bomber would torch and fall like a meteor, each of us remembered our own last moments up there in our bombers, the confusion, the smoke and the fire. As the British bombing intensified, the night guards let us go outside to the trenches, an eerie change in our relentless routine. The daylight raids by Americans were bittersweet. Kriegies cheered as the bombers crushed the rail yards at Krems or flew overhead toward the military-industrial targets outside Vienna, but we were reminded in low voices that many guards had families nearby and that a guard's retribution might well come at a kriegie's expense.

I was walking the perimeter when a particularly loud crack of artillery surprised me. German guns near Krems firing back. *Close,* I thought. *Very close.* One of the guards standing in the tower looked away from the camp, his hands on the railing. The machine gun, its muzzle pointed skyward, seemed suddenly meager, unthreatening. His profile was worried, vulnerable. A boy frightened by the approach of thunder. We always felt that the gunners in those deadly tree houses were very different from the guards who rousted us out in the morning or shouted at us during roll call. Barracks guards had personalities, however rough or awkward, and you could see in their eyes or their body language aspects of their natures. We knew nothing about the dark figures behind the muzzles that were always trained on us. The tower guards were like judges, those who could neither be reasoned with nor managed. If they saw you and you weren't where you were supposed to be, they would kill you. We all suspected that they itched for the opportunity, if only to show their determination or break the monotony. We didn't matter to them. The sight of this guard's small white hands anxiously rubbing the tower rail, his chin lifted as if listening or trying to see a great distance, sparked a moment's pity in me.

"They are on their way from Vienna," said Franz Schubert, who stood several feet away and looked as though speaking to the air.

"How close?" I asked.

"Thirty kilometers. We hold them now. They will soon break us."

I said nothing.

"We are afraid," he said, raising his voice a little.

"Of the Russians?"

"Yes. And the end of the war. We will lose the war and we do not know what will happen. Some are even afraid of you prisoners."

"There's enough fear to go around," I answered.

"You know that when the war is over, the Germans and the Americans will have to fight the Russians together," he offered.

"Well, it's the Russians you better worry about right now. They're likely to kill a lot of you before this war is over." The moment I said those words, I regretted them. He seemed frightened.

"Maybe a lot of us, too," I added, trying to ease the sharpness of my words. We both knew better. Risky though these days were for the kriegies, we knew we were winning the war. Our comrades were coming for us. Who was coming for him?

"Yes," he said, as if he had not heard me. "The Russians are cruel and they hate the Germans." I thought of the dead Russians, propped in the lines for food. The tables were turning.

"You know I am not German. Czech. Not German. I want to go home, too. Like you."

It was common of Germans to try to distance themselves from the Nazis. Wilkens said that there were no Germans left in camp, that all the guards were really from Southern California and just wanted to go home. Schubert had a quality, however, that had always set him apart from the others, and it occurred to me that he might be telling the truth. He had saved my life at some risk to his own. I had thought he had helped me as part of his own growing humanity, but perhaps it was simply an act of defiance against the Germans or the Nazis. I wasn't sure. I knew that, Czech or German, he and the other guards were in trouble. Prisoners and guards were jumpy; wary conversations were taking place all over camp. What do you know? Did you hear? All rumors hailed from a credible source: a guard stationed in the commandant's office saw the order himself; the kriegie heard it with his own ears on the BBC; a reliable Frenchman ("he's a goddamned doctor, so why would he lie?") overheard two guards by the wire. Everyone was scavenging for rumors to trade, and fantastic stories sprang from mysterious sources. Though guard and kriegie had long worried about the activities and intentions of the other, we were now aware that we were both isolated from a war that was coming at us like a bullet. Everyone was at risk. The shells fell closer and closer, and sometimes we thought we could hear small arms fire. Fear was in the air.

"What will you do?" I asked Schubert.

"I don't know," he said quietly, moving closer to me but still looking off to the woods as if he were not speaking with me. "Some of the guards say they will kill themselves and their families before the Russians come. They say the Russians will torture us and do terrible things to our women. The children, too. One of our soldiers comes to our barracks in search of food yesterday. He is fighting for a month—every day. He says he kills one hundred Russians. Some he kills with his knife. He has big hands and many bruises and cuts. He says you can cross the Danube on the bodies of the dead without wetting your feet. He sees it with his own eyes." Schubert rubbed his elbow like an old man. His gun hung over his shoulder and it seemed worn and utterly useless.

"I broke my arm as a boy," he said with a faint wince. "My father carries me to the doctor in his arms, three miles. I am heavy but he does not complain and he makes stories all the way so I do not think of pain."

"Why don't you just go?" I asked. "Just get out of here? I heard that one of the guards took off."

"Yes," he said, startled that I knew that. "Not one, but four. If we speak of it with anyone," his voice dropped to a whisper, "we will be shot." He was quiet for a long while before speaking again.

"I have nowhere to go. I am safer to stay with the Americans than to try and go home." He moved even closer to me.

"We heard that Hitler ordered all the Allied prisoners to be shot," I said, telling Schubert something I had heard on the grapevine last month. I wondered if it was true.

"It is over. It does not matter what Hitler says. Do you think we

take orders from him?" Schubert snorted in disgust. "The Nazis are finished. It is a matter for us to stay alive now. That is all we think about.
How we stay alive. The best way for us is to be with the American prisoners. We cannot let anything happen to you." And now Schubert
stood so close to me I could smell his rancid breath. "They say that we
are to take you out of the camp, we will march west and surrender you
to the Americans. They say other camps all over Germany are marching
west even now. We must not wait for the Russians to come first. They
have no interest in you," he said glumly, "but they are happy to kill us."

Someone shouted beyond the barracks and Schubert stiffened. "I
must go," he said and walked off.

"PACK IT UP, BOYS. THEY ARE taking us out tomorrow morning,"
said Pappy, standing alongside a big-boned kriegie with a face pocked
by teenage acne and a mouth of ruined teeth. The kriegie had come
directly from the White House; I had never seen him before. Despite
his attempt at efficient calm, he was terribly agitated and shifted from
foot to foot, impatient to get moving. Kriegies gathered around Pappy.

"We don't know where we're going, but it is sure to be west and it's
damned sure to be long," said Pappy. "Get together everything you can
carry. What else do you know?"

"Damned little," said the lumbering kriegie. "Dillard just sent us
out to all the barracks to get the word to you as quick as we could. The
Jerries are scared shitless. The Russians are getting close to St. Pölten.
That's across the Danube and about twelve miles east of us. They are
killing everyone with a German accent." It seemed Schubert had told
me the truth. Maybe he really was Czech.

There was a huge excitement. Everyone was hustling between bays
and conversation was shouted, like passengers preparing for a journey. I
took no part. Mine had become a loner's life more, perhaps, by habit
than desire, although I continued to tell myself that Koz had spoken
for all of them, that I was no longer a close member of the group. As
they got their things together and talked of the coming march, I stayed

clear, not wanting to risk having someone for one reason or another invite me along. They were all ready to go out together, and that was fine with me.

We began packing up what odds and ends each of us had scrounged or saved up over the many months. Tony Sac, who had a big journal now filled with Shattuck's drawings, was trying to work out how to hide them so that they could be gotten later. I gathered my few possessions. Though I'd never had a real interest in possessions, several things had begun to take on an almost talismanic power. My last American dog tag—Ray Bernie had my other one, along with my Stalag 17 tag—was an emblem of the world to which I'd first belonged. The D-bars that I'd saved for trading represented my ongoing faith in someday making an escape. I wasn't much of a trader in the camp, though I'd recently given chocolate to Franz Schubert for the gift of his silence. The journal and the stubby pencil contained the thoughts that mattered to me; the watch my mother had given me reminded me of her and, strangely, the young mother who had refused my offer that first day on the ground. As for Young's crucifix, I prized this above all, not so much for its value as a religious object but as a keepsake from the loner who had made it and given it to me. His was a gesture as close to friendship as he could manage, and I treasured it. I understood something of his isolation now in a way that I had not when I was part of the tunnel team. Digging, I had felt the joy of belonging to a group's effort, but Young's crucifix reminded me of the power of solitude, of the work done alone, within the confines of your own spirit.

At some point, I found myself alone in the bay with Wilkens, who stood with his hands on his hips like a foreman surveying a finished job, and Joseph, who sat on his bunk, high in his Indian heaven. Joseph was looking out the window as he had on our first day in camp. Though an immense amount of confusion roiled out there, guards and prisoners shouting, horse-drawn wagons rolling by, he was still as a leaf, dreaming with his eyes wide open. Wilkens spoke:

"I'm not one for rumormongering, fellas, but there's a plan cooking at the White House that says we have to be ready if the Germans decide they want to kill us and hightail it out of here."

"If they so decide, what plan of ours would change their mind?" asked Joseph in a formal voice, one almost detached of fear or anxiety, as if he were simply curious.

"If it becomes clear, there will be a signal and a group will rush the German guards closest at hand. Any rifles captured will be turned on the tower guards. Others will scale the towers at the same time. We get the machine guns and we can defend the camp from the Germans outside the camp. Lots of guys would die, but that's the plan." I thought of Pappy's story about the Russians dying in waves along the wire. I mentioned Schubert's comment, that they were safer staying close to us.

"They will not shoot us," Joseph sighed. "Handy's guard is right. We are brothers to the guards for the moment, because we are both at risk. They know that we keep them safe if they keep us safe. The trouble will come when we no longer need to be brothers. Like before all this started. Only then it is the Germans who must worry."

Wilkens smiled. "You're a damned special man, Joseph. It's like you got yourself an extra eye in that Indian head of yours." Joseph's mouth twitched in faint acknowledgment of the compliment.

"Hey, Wilkens," someone shouted as we settled for our last night in Stalag 17, "you think that Flame guy is out of smokes? Think he'll oversleep tomorrow?"

"Maybe so," said Wilkens in his easy drawl. "Maybe so."

THE NEXT MORNING IT WAS STILL dark when the guards came in. They were nervous and louder than usual. Some banged their guns on the floor, others stood along the aisle shouting, paying no attention to whether we were minding them or not. Noise seemed a particular comfort to them this morning. It had rained the night before, and as the dawn broke, it looked as if it would continue. The last roll call was different from any we had ever seen because the Germans were also on the move. Horse carts were loaded, soldiers carried heavy packs, officers were dressed and moving outside the gates like annoyed fathers hustling their children off to the first day of school. Even in the dark I could smell spring on the wind. My second spring in Germany. All I really knew about time at Stalag 17 was measured by the seasons.

We were told that we were going to go out in groups of five hundred. Mostly the men organized themselves by bays for the journey. I was leaving Stalag 17 as I had entered: a part of a group and yet not at the same time. On the last day I had agreed to team up with a kriegie from a nearby bay named Hill. Like me, he was looking for someone to go with. Solitary by nature, a man of few words, he recognized that in the days ahead it would help to have a teammate. We had little in common and rarely talked, but we both understood that a buddy system would help us keep our eyes out for opportunity and trouble.

The Russian Camp—about ten thousand prisoners of many nationalities—was closest to the main gate, but the Americans were taken out ahead of them. Our group of five hundred waited while most of the others went ahead of us, and there was much understandable impatience. Finally we began to move in fits and starts toward the front gate.

"It is Sunday, April eighth," said someone in a clear, calm voice. "I'm going to remember this moment for the rest of my natural born days. I can hear them bells ringing. And I don't mean the kind that tolls, like for a dead man, but the swinging kind, like when someone just got married."

"Ain't no broad dumb enough to marry you," piped up someone behind us.

"It don't matter what you say," the speaker said defiantly. "This is my wedding day. As God is my witness, this is my wedding day."

Coming out to the gate, passing under it, some of us said little while others whooped and hooted, but everyone shared the elation of the open gates. We would soon be on open roads walking west. We stepped out like boys to a long-awaited holiday. We were excited, impatient; even the danger was appealing, our caution behind the wire now thrown to the wind. The bombs dropping closer, the shaking of the barracks, the assault of rumor and anticipation had worn many of us down. Now with legs moving, at least something had to happen, good or bad. It was a relief. I looked back to the east to see if I could catch the last sight of the grove of trees, but I could not see them for the barracks and all the bodies still on the move.

Soon out of the camp, we were led onto backcountry roads. On either side were woods and fields shedding their winter fetters. The tightly budded trees were just as I had seen them from the boxcar door the spring before. The tall dark pines crowded the road, and the heavy green branches rose and fell slowly on the wind. Unseen animals skittered through the corridors of trees and squirrels leapt from branch to branch. Looking up for the last time, I saw the red-tiled roofs in the hills beyond. It had been a year of Sundays since my Easter mission to Tutow, when we had just missed the small plane that swung the heavy stove. A year of five seasons. The second spring welled up within me. Stalag 17 was fast disappearing behind with every step.

THE GUARDS SHOUTED AT US TO maintain a six-man-wide column, and more from habit than obedience, we settled into the routine of walking. Conversation was alternately colorful and monotonous, but not as prevalent as silence. Most men knew they had to keep moving, and it was fast becoming a chore. They focused on fighting the fatigue and the fear, and there was not much room for talk. The travel was west, always west. The sun rose at our backs each morning, a relentless prod, and at evening it shouldered its way through the forests ahead of us, urging us on. The narrow roads were scenic and wound across forest floor and hilltop vistas alike. I had been a relentless walker of our compound's perimeter and had become attached to its northern vista of hills. But out here was a whole new world, a changing landscape, fresh air and trees, the smell of grass and the occasional breeze.

We went for many hours without even seeing a guard, but we kept moving. Pappy and others had reminded us repeatedly not to take off, no matter how tempting.

"We are a good deal safer all together than any of us would be on our own, so I don't care if a blonde whispers from the woods that she's got a bed and a good meal waiting, stay with the group."

"If that blonde calls me, you can bet I'll catch up to you later, Pappy," offered a listener.

"I'm serious, fellas. We're in more danger out here than we were in the camp."

We understood their logic. The Germans wanted to get us as far west as fast as they could. The option to take off if there were really serious trouble was always whispered among us. We were not going to stand around if we heard a lot of machine-gun fire or we saw guards preparing to do us harm as a group. Even so, I soon heard rumors of prisoners taking off. I didn't know any of the ones who did, nor did any of us realize then that almost all of those who left were never seen or heard of again. As for the guards themselves, each day fewer and fewer took to the roads with us. They were slipping off in the night, knowing that their odds of survival were narrowing, as ours bettered with every step. The ones who stayed were most likely the ones with nothing to gain by leaving. They were the farthest from home and were not likely to survive heading east back into the bloody jaws of the Russian advance.

THE FIRST NIGHT ON THE ROAD, we broke off into a field next to a farm. There was a horse and wagon with food. The Germans had promised it would be there, but none of us had believed them. The old stalag slop. It was good if only because it was warm enough to remind the stomach of soup. Almost twenty of us stood around a small, stoked fire. Not far away was another group, including the guys from my bay. They were laughing and talking and I listened to them with a kind of regret. In the middle of the din, a voice rose above the others. It was the unmistakably clear voice of Kozikowski and most unusual given his typically quiet nature.

"Well, you know, I'm the one who should feel bad. I took a shot at my best friend and wrecked a friendship. I'm sorry I did that."

I heard him and knew he was talking to me. It would have been a simple matter to cross that dark field and join him. He had opened the door wide and called me to walk through it. A warm handshake could itself have been the reincarnation of our friendship. We could have sat together as in days past and listened to Wilkens's drawl, to Meese's quiet, steady conversation, or to others who, like them, talked well. Sitting by our fire, though, I had time for thinking back to the reasons why he and the bay were over there and I wasn't. Ignorant as I was that harsh words among friends aren't final judgments, those reasons still seemed sound. All the same, what he had now said was getting to me. Should I at least let him know I'd heard? A slow thinker about that kind of question, I decided to sleep on it. And so I made a mistake I would remember the rest of my life: I made no answer to my friend's voice across that dark field, and the chance never came again.

The next morning I woke as stiff as if I had slept in a B-24 tire. There was no time for a fire or hot water, and they began to move us out. Shuffled into lines, pushed forward, ordered to stop, inching forward again, it took a while before we swung out onto the dirt road with enough distance between us to walk with ease. We did not know that we were beginning a pace that would not let up. It was a pace the Germans required in order to save themselves. I lost track of the men in my bay and would not see them for many days.

The days blurred. I don't remember much about the march except that nature was close, the air fresh and invigorating. I watched for birds and listened to their ever-present song. Talk was limited; everyone seemed intent on dragging one boot over the next. Men shuffled like hobos. Chaff hung in the trees, testament to the endless Allied bombing runs. The ditches on either side of the road became receptacles for the things that men could no longer carry. Sometimes I saw items that might be useful but I moved on, knowing that my own endurance depended on lightness. One time I saw an overcoat.

"Poor sonofabitch," said Hill. "By the time he needs that, it'll be too late." Hill was right, and the poor kriegie who tossed that coat would have needed it that very night. It rained and rained and the wind blew. It was early April but it felt like November. We huddled around a small, sputtering fire in a field crowded with kriegies. Guys were talking about the march.

"We're gonna have to go hundreds of miles," said Hill glumly. "And there's some guys who aren't gonna make it."

"Yeah, I saw some guy helping Miller," said the kriegie next to him. "He was damn near carrying Miller on his fucking back now and we ain't gone but thirty, maybe forty miles." I had no idea who Miller was, but I felt for him.

Another man with a long jaw and narrow, suspicious eyes spoke up. "You guys hear that some of the kriegies are taking off for Stalag 17?"

"What?" said Hill incredulously.

"No shit. I know it for a fact. Two guys from my bay went. There were dozens that took off. They figure it is safer back in camp hiding out 'til the Allies catch up. They say this is a death march and that if the walking don't kill us, the Jerries will." Going back to the camp? I thought that crazy but did not say so.

"Sometimes the fear you know is better than the fear you don't," said Hill. "I guess some guys can't take any more of the fear they don't know." We slept that night huddled against a barn wall, our coats over our heads and our arms wrapped around our knees.

WE WOKE COLD AND DAMP. JOINTS were stiff, backs ached and men groaned in exaggerated complaint. As we hit main roads we were shocked by our first glimpse of the world outside Stalag 17: the chaos and traffic, the military vehicles, jeeps, wagons, men marching, prisoners herded, refugees everywhere. The soldiers were always in a hurry, the jeeps and trucks honking and nearly running people over. When we got back onto the country road the walking was quieter, more pleasant.

"Wow," said Hill. "Almost like downtown Mobile."

We lived off farms commandeered by our guards. The farmers must have grieved at the scourge of hungry prisoners foraging for anything they could find, but at that point, sympathy was dulled by the need to survive. Separated from one another by the chasm of war, the tension between us was unspoken but clear: the Nazis were commandeering their farms, but it was still the American prisoners they blamed. We were rowdy and, no doubt, ungrateful guests. They made good hot porridge for us, but most of them treated us with a grudging indifference. At the end of the day, we slept wherever we could: under big trees if it was dry, inside outbuildings and barns if we got there before others. Once, a gang of us stumbled onto a large hayloft and were able to dig ourselves into a great spread of hay for a sound night of sleep. It was the first time I had felt anything remotely resembling comfort. My bones slipped into ease and I groaned with pleasure.

"Ain't this the life?" someone said with a laugh.

"The fucking Ritz," came a voice in the dark.

The next day we started all over again. Mile after slower mile. It was not long before many among us began to suffer. The traveling was not particularly hard, the roads wound pleasantly through forests and over hills, like an invigorating day hike, but the problem was that the road never ended and the walking barely stopped. Men who had not eaten well for months and had even less food now, found their stamina draining away. Most kriegies were simply not fit for travel at such a pace and for such a distance. Blisters ruined the feet of men who had been wearing clogs for months. One kriegie was sitting by the side of the road and peeling away what was left of his sock from a bloody foot. The sores had burst and pus edged the wound, a grisly study in crimson and green. He grimaced as the sock, still stuck to the wound, tore away a fresh piece of flesh.

"Jesus," someone whispered as we passed him.

"Jesus ain't got nothin' to do with this unless he's got a new pair of socks," the man with the bloody feet snapped.

Dysentery was another problem. Men could not stop to crap in the woods, the guards would not allow it, and so they squatted on the road as the prisoners filed past. It was humiliating but necessary. We averted our eyes, held our breath and walked on. Soon enough, the weak needed the support of the strong. Men leaned against one another, but always there was one who pulled while the other sagged.

Occasionally we would catch sight of a sudden patch of whiteness in the brush, a contorted, frozen form that was hypnotic to us as we passed. The dead. Were they Russians? Germans? Civilians? It was too hard to tell without looking closely, and there wasn't time for that. The clothing was shredded or blackened. Only the marble-blue skin, tightening or torn, reminded you that once there was life in those twisted figures. I never saw any of the Russian prisoners along the road. I wasn't sure whether they marched ahead of us or behind. For the moment, the road offered the same kind of proximity we had found in the barracks. If the straggling line of prisoners stretched miles ahead and behind, we knew only of those who walked alongside us.

I saw Franz Schubert again. We were resting by a long ditch off the side of the road. It was late afternoon and the sun had just broken through the clouds. Men had just fallen out and dropped along that ditch, some using the steep embankment as a backrest. Schubert was standing alone at the edge of the woods. He barely acknowledged my nod. I rose and walked near to him.

"How are you?" I asked. I was genuinely glad to see him. He had saved my life.

"You did not believe me when I told you I was a Czech," he said, acting almost hurt.

"No, Franz," I said, deliberately using his first name. "You're wrong. I did believe you."

"You think I enjoy the work of the guard. You are wrong."

"No," I said. "I know you don't like it. Neither of us likes any of this."

"Your president is dead," he said abruptly. "I heard the guards talking about it. They are hoping this will change the war and that maybe the Americans will want peace now." He looked at me hopefully and then his face fell. Roosevelt had been president most of my life. I did not believe him. The rumors of war.

"Your guards told us that Hitler was dead, too, and that wasn't true," I shot back.

"Bad for us all that he didn't die," said Franz in a whisper, looking suddenly miserable. "He was born in Brannau, you know," he said, easing his manner slightly. "We are going there, I think."

I said nothing and wondered again if Roosevelt were really dead. What would that mean? It would be yet another blow to all of us. Schubert, as if sensing my mood shift, spoke again more formally.

"The walking is hard. A guard has died on this march."

I was startled to think that a guard had found this journey so physically taxing that he could die.

"It is true," he said defensively, as if reading my skepticism. "The officers make us carry this heavy equipment on our backs. Many of the guards still here are old and they cannot bear the load."

I knew that what felt like a hard but welcome hike for me was wearing other kriegies down, but I simply could not believe that a man could die as a result of the march. Certainly not a guard, though the oversized backpack, thick overcoat and heavy rifle gave me pause. Roosevelt, a dead guard, who knew what to believe? Was he looking for sympathy? I did feel sorry for him.

"Perhaps he did not die. Maybe he just went home."

"Yes, some have gone home. But not him. I saw him. It was Schmidt. Did you know him? He had a wife. She was a seamstress in the village. She was a big, fat, happy woman, but she will cry when she sees Schmidt again. He was thin and broken. You all are lucky. You are young."

"How long do we have to go?" I asked him.

"They tell me nothing," he said. "I know nothing."

That night, the death of Roosevelt was confirmed. Reliable guards confirmed it and the news moved through the kriegies like a great wind. Everyone was talking about him. Men were sad, scared, as if their father had died. It was as if he had held all the pieces of the net that bound all things American together and his death loosened everything, tipped us into uncertainty. Outrageous stories circulated that foretold a terrible chaos: the Germans had gone trigger-happy and were going to try to murder us; Russia had declared war on America and already the Red Army was killing American POWs; jumpy American fighter planes, uncertain of our nationality, were likely to strafe our column. It was as if Roosevelt's death were a sudden swerving into a landscape filled with a new menace. Still, we walked on the next day as we had the day before. The march was becoming a way of life.

WE HAD BEEN ON THE MOVE for a week and a half. The Germans were leading us west, and before long we knew we were going to have to cross the Danube. The Luftwaffe selected the bridge that led right into the city of Linz. An industrial city of some importance, Linz had rail yards, river docks, factories and a number of roads running through it. The Allies had targeted it for destruction, and as we came along a winding road that opened onto a view of the city, we confronted a city of hollowed buildings. The streets were so rubble-strewn that many seemed impassable. It was a terrible sight. The Allies must have bombed the place around the clock.

Word spread back along the line (originated by the guards themselves), a whispered caution that traveled over four miles of bony shoulders: *Say nothing. If they learn you are an airman, they will kill you.* Stay alert and keep quiet. I thought of the crowd in Hanover and the Luftwaffe guards who protected us. The stalag guards were as worn and tired as we were; they would be little help backing off a crowd who thought we had destroyed their city. Many of us were wearing our regular Air Force clothing, including my own shirt with an Eighth Air Force insignia on it, so there was some anxious folding and tearing of cloth. I had no desire to pull my own insignia off; it had come this far with me and I determined that it should go the distance. I turned my shirt inside out.

We crossed the bridge, marched to a small park at the city's center and were told to stop for a brief rest. We were there no more than fifteen to twenty minutes, but it was long enough for us to attract the attention of a group of German soldiers. They were mostly young, their uniforms new and unused, their hair blond, with squared jaws. I saw them watching us, and to my unease, they nudged one another before coming toward us like a street gang. You could smell their wildness: soldiers worried that war was fast leaving them with nothing to show for it. They sensed our fatigue. They had about them a menacing gait. Like Max at the showers, they were bullies with time to kill. Five or six swaggered up to us. Behind them others gathered, as if preparing for some kind of amusement. Hill and I were standing along with two or three others under a small tree seeking a sliver of shade.

"They're SS," said Hill quietly as they approached.

"Hitler youth," said another.

"Keep quiet," whispered a third.

A tall one came forward. He barked at us in German. We shrugged. He barked again, more sharply. Then another came alongside. He had piercing blue eyes and reminded me of the little boy in the field the day we were shot down, only now grown up. He spoke in French. His stare was hard and challenging; our silence was fast becoming more trouble than help. So I answered in French. The one who had spoken in French looked at the others in triumph and they, in turn, seemed to egg him on.

"You are prisoners, American prisoners," he said. "Yes?"

I nodded.

"What unit were you with?" he asked with a snort. I noticed the tense of his question but ignored it.

"What are they saying?" asked Hill and someone shushed him. I kept my eyes on the German soldier. I was careful not to challenge him too directly but was trying to read his intent. The others had unslung their guns and their smiles had faded. Prisoners around the park were poking one another and staring over at us. There was nothing they could do. I was uncertain. Never given to lying or even bluffing, I remembered how my father had always said, "The good thing about telling the truth is that you don't have to remember what you said." His advice would do me no good here: truth was simply not an option. I could not say we belonged to those who had turned their city to dust.

"Did you hear what I said?" he said, moving closer to me. He poked at the insignia turned inside at my shoulder. "What unit were you with?" He was getting angry, more keenly aware of his own comrades than of me.

"Handy, whatever you are saying or not saying, you are pissing him off."

I began to sweat. The other soldiers closed in, a coliseum crowd famished for entertainment. I knew virtually nothing about American ground troops and their individual units and anything I said was likely to be hopelessly wide of the mark. Then it occurred to me that during one of the late-night bull sessions, someone had mentioned a unit I had never heard of before. The unit's name had caught my imagination. I took a breath.

"The Green Berets. We are with the Green Berets," I said nonchalantly, having no idea who the Green Berets were and hoping like hell they weren't a French or British outfit. He repeated what I had said to his comrades in German and, in an instant, everything changed.

"Green Berets!" he said admiringly. "Were you at Monte Cassino?" The other soldiers had begun to come in close, crowding us with respect, almost admiration. I had no idea what Monte Cassino was or where it was, but with a kind of Latin ring to it, I presumed it was in Italy. So I stepped boldly toward my second lie.

"Yes, we were there," I said, becoming war weary and experienced.

He flooded me with questions, the other boys shouting in German questions of their own from behind him. He spoke quickly and I had trouble following his French. Other men from Linz had fought there, he said, and they had told them of the fierce fighting and how well the Americans had fought, too. I could feel the need for lies I simply did not have in me—I had no idea of what fighting on the ground required—but to our great relief a whistle blew, our break was ended and the guards were calling us to our feet.

"We know you were brave," he said in a grave tone, "because the soldiers from Linz are lions and they spoke well of you." He was not ready for us to go and I saw him look back to the others. They were weighing the possibility of challenging our departure. I realized, looking at their boyish, eager faces, that they knew nothing of war.

"We want to hear more of your fight at Monte Cassino. You wait here," he said stiffly. I sensed more trouble. These fierce boys were not done with us and were not intimidated in any way by our bedraggled guards. We were as close to the war as they had ever come and perhaps as close as they would ever be if the war ended before the Russians came to Linz. With an instinct I did not know I had, I startled us both by extending my hand to him.

"We must stay with our comrades. You understand. One soldier to another. Good luck."

He stopped and looked at me. Then, as if recognizing that I had spoken in some secret code, he straightened up and raised his chin. Even the others stiffened in respect. He took my hand with great solemnity.

"Yes," he said. "One soldier to another."

We fell in with the other prisoners and started out of the city. "What the hell did you say to that guy, Handy?" someone whispered. I looked back over my shoulder at a gaggle of boys whose war had been made more real than all the bombs and burned-out buildings could ever be. They had been touched by the Green Berets. War may have its profound purposes, I thought, but at its core it is tragic theater.

"I just told him," I answered, "what he needed to hear."

AFTER A FEW MORE DAYS OF walking, we found ourselves on a little country road that ran along the bank of a river. The wildlife became everyone's entertainment. Foxes, hedgehogs, rabbits, and whirls of birds were everywhere. Men pointed with growing gusto and admiration, exaggerating the size, color and speed of everything they saw. Soon enough, stories were launched of greater wonders at home, where everything was bigger, brighter and faster. Fishing tales were popular and kriegies bragged about how, given ten minutes with a rod and reel, enough fish could be caught to feed the whole camp. A light drizzle, refreshing at first, soon caused grumbling and discomfort. At about the same time that the drizzle gave way to a downpour, we found ourselves coming out to a bold confluence where the river we had followed was joined by another. We were at the edge of an immense forest filled with ancient, stately pines, spruces and hemlocks, many rising so high I could barely see their crowns.

At first, I was aware only of the cover as we stepped under the canopy of branches that broke the driving rain. It was an incredible relief. We had been on the road for over two weeks and had worked our way through some beautiful Austrian countryside, but this pine forest was like nothing any of us had ever seen. We would not have been surprised to come across Hansel and Gretel's cottage or to catch sight of Grimm's woodcutters and witches threading their way to fairytale destinies. Was this place the Black Forest that I had often read about as a boy?

A short distance into the forest the guards stopped us and spread the word that we had reached our destination; this was where we would be staying. The march was over. Fall out, rest and wait. The guards went off and left us on our own.

"I don't like this," said Hill. "These woods are spooky and I can't see much of anything. It could be a killing ground. We gotta keep our eyes open." Hill had a point. I remembered that last talk with Wilkens and Joseph in the camp. Was this the moment Joseph had predicted? But he had said it was the Germans who would have to worry. I hoped he was right.

The forest began to fill up as prisoners came stumbling out of the downpour and into the woods. The more kriegies that came in, the bolder we all felt. We were something of a wet and bedraggled crowd, but we were becoming a small army in our own right. As men flooded in, so came a pressing need for shelter and warmth. We went to work. Dead wood lay scattered about on the carpet of browned pine needles and ample supplies of damp leaves and twigs were soon coaxed into kindling. Men tore away low-hanging branches, and the sound of scavenging was loud and purposeful. Among the wilderness of tall pines we found a clearing that suited us perfectly and we set out to make a fire. The kindling caught flame, and though our fire started small, men kept coming with armfuls of fuel. In minutes, we had built up a massive bonfire, the biggest I had ever seen. At least a hundred of us, three deep, could crowd around at any one time.

Men who had lived together and had managed scant resources as long as we had wordlessly developed a collaborative system: one third of the guys would be out getting wood, another third would be putting together or improving their shelters for the night, and the final third would be taking their turn getting warm and dry around this giant and beautiful blaze. Then the groups would rotate after about ten or fifteen minutes. It moved like clockwork and without any confusion or complication. The rain never let up, but the fire had grown far beyond any kind of intimidation—as had we. The pulse of the heat and the smell of the burning pine were intoxicating. As each of us took our place in the front row, standing first with our backs to the fire and then turning toward the front, our spirits quickened. There was a good deal of laughter, and soon stories flowed like wine.

A man spoke up, his face bright with firelight. He was handsome and I could tell from his bearing that he was thoughtful, intelligent.

"Did you guys see those folks along the road with the star of David on their clothes?" he asked. Several men nodded sadly. Others looked on, ignorant of what they were talking about. I was one of them.

"Go ahead, McKenzie, tell us," said someone.

"The guards stopped us and had us fall out into a ditch. We all leaned against the embankment and rubbed our feet, glad to get a break. In a moment, we heard a kind of a hum, like a bunch of people all talking at once, and we saw a column coming down the road. When they got closer we realized it was not talking, but a kind of droning moan. A terrible sound." McKenzie was quiet. A twig snapped and hissed with flame.

"They looked like old men, stooped, ragged old men, but as they passed I could see they were men and women, young and old. They shuffled and hobbled, some walked like they were blind, others like their feet were made of wood. Some had little pillbox hats and woolen caps. Their skin was so tight I could see all their bones. All of them. Ribs and shins and hips. They had wrapped clothing around their feet and the cloth was bloody and filthy. The Wehrmacht pushed and growled and butted them. They had yellow stars on their clothes and they were being marched east, back the way we came."

"Why are they going east?" someone asked.

McKenzie was quiet. Another piped up, "They'll put 'em to work making tank traps and blockades with logs and stones."

"Sure," said another, "that'll hold the tanks for about a minute or two."

"It was the saddest sight," continued McKenzie. "We were helpless and watched them pass. Seeing us, the moaning got louder, as if they were begging us for help. We couldn't understand what they said, but they reached out to us and pleaded. Our guards pointed guns down on us for the first time, in case any of us got ideas. We could do nothing. Several said 'Cigarettes' and a few guys tossed what they had to these skeletons. There was an awful scramble for the cigarettes and people shoved and fell over one another. The guards kicked them away and took up the cigarettes themselves. It was awful.

"And then I heard these sharp cracks, short bursts, coming inter-mittently from down the road. I could see Germans standing over the same ditch we were in and pointing their pistols down. Small bursts of flame and then the sound, but we could not see who or what they shot. When they came alongside us, we saw they were SS men. They had the death's-head insignias. One in particular, with a flat nose and a square jaw, looked down at me and gave me a little salute. I stared back. He was so close I could smell the leather of his pistol holster. A few feet beyond me, he pulled his pistol and shot an old woman in the head. He looked back at me for good measure and smiled." Again, McKenzie went quiet. "After they got us up and walking, we passed dozens of bodies in that ditch, their faces looking startled, their mouths wide open like baby birds."

We all sat quietly. Some men hugged their knees; others lay back with their arms beneath their heads. The fire snapped and winked and the branches glowed above us with the light of the flame and no one spoke again that night. We were all glad to be alive.

I WAS OUT ON ONE LAST trip foraging for firewood when I came across Wilkens and Thompson. They were headed to another fire, their arms filled with kindling and branch scraps. We laughed at the sight of one another and spontaneously dropped our piles at our feet. Seeing Wilkens reminded me of how deeply I had come to respect him, and Thompson made me think again of Tedrowe and our crew. There was warmth in the greeting and the handshakes.

"Damn, Handy, how the hell can you carry such a big pile?" said Thompson gleefully.

"Handy's always been able to carry a heavy load," said Wilkens with a warm smile. "Always."

I felt a sense of gratitude I couldn't express, particularly to Wilkens. Speaking was not my strong suit, but I tried to say what I felt.

"Thanks for all your help and support, Wilkens. I learned a lot from you. And Thompson, I'll always remember how you came through on that catwalk that day."

"Don't mention it," said Thompson. Wilkens put his hand on my shoulder. "You were quite a digger, Handy," he said.

"Have either of you seen Koz?" I asked.

"No, not for a while. He'll turn up before long, though," said Thompson, beginning to gather up his load.

"Well, say hello for me," I said, sensing the opportunity was gone.

"You bet. And Handy," Wilkens took my arm, "you did fine. Real fine." I didn't know what to say. I was thinking it was he who'd done more than any of us. I watched them move off into the forest and called out good luck one last time, but they didn't hear me. I thought about Koz and, walking back to my campfire, arms loaded with wood, resolved to find him and start again where I should have that first night on the march.

One by one the men had peeled off to find comfort and sleep in the flimsy but welcoming "lean-to" shelters made out of broad pine branches. I stayed up long into the night, gathering the wood, stoking the fire and warming myself. By the time I found Hill and one or two others in the shelter we had made, they were fast asleep. I lay down and before my head hit the ground of pine needles, I, too, was gone.

The next day broke gray and drizzly. The woods were full of men, and though some tended the scattered, smoking campfires, most lay under their makeshift shelters, their muddy boots poking out like the feet of the dead. There were no guards around at all, and we seemed under no instruction from anyone. Hill and I decided to set out and try to scavenge some food. There would surely be farms along the edge of the forest. We came out of the trees and began to follow the river until the ground opened up and we could see fields and fences. It was an astonishing sight to be in the open countryside with miles of horizon, walking free of columns and guards, moving like animals wherever we wished. I almost wanted to run. Down the country road, with the dark forest receding behind us, it felt as if we had been cut loose. We did not think of ourselves now as escaped or even at risk. It was so rural and quaint and quiet that the war, the Germans, even the forest filling with prisoners we had just left, quickly seemed part of some other place, very far away.

More than a little hungry, we had agreed we would ask for food at the first farmhouse we came to and, after only a few minutes walking, we saw one, perched at the end of a winding road, on the top of a small hill. Standing out in the field at the base of the hill were several farmers watching us. We paused and talked over whether or not we should detour around them, obeying a primitive instinct that men who stop to watch you are often trouble. We chose to walk on toward them. We were experiencing a renewal of our own power and a sense that we were returning to a world where our will and authority had meaning. We were simply two bold, confident sightseers, traveling the countryside, taking in the local color. We waved. They waved back, though theirs was uneasy, almost timid.

One of them was a French prisoner who had become a farm-worker—Austria was packed with them, we soon learned—and when I told him who we were and what we needed, he seemed almost relieved. We followed him to a barn where he left us, only to return with milk, eggs and bread. He handed the milk to Hill, who handed it to me. The bread he gave me, I offered first to Hill. The habit of kriegies to share and safeguard one another's food had become almost a reflex. The milk was warm and rich, and while it did not taste like the milk I remembered, it coated my stomach with warmth. Nothing powdered here. Accustomed as I was to the kriegie's brick-hard loaf packed with saw-dust, I was amazed at the soft sweetness of the farmer's bread. As for the eggs, we ate them raw and they slid down our throats like oysters. We lay stretched out in a small barn and slept away the morning. No one bothered us at all.

When we woke, the farmer was nowhere to be seen. We turned back out onto the road and walked for hours. Late that afternoon, we stood at the edge of a very large, well-maintained farm. There were workers in the fields and they leaned on their hoes and, again, watched us come down the road. One of the workers came forward alone to greet us. He spoke with an impeccable French accent and, when he learned we were Americans, insisted we come to the main house and meet the owner of the farm. The owner, a broad-faced, pink-cheeked woman, swept out the front door and greeted us in German. She stood with her hands on her hips and her eyes were clear and blue, beautiful, reminding me of my mother. The worker—apparently her farm manager, a former French prisoner—translated for her. She welcomed us to her home; she could not give us the kind of welcome she might have offered us only months before, she said, but times were hard. The war was stripping her of most everything. Hill and I looked around, stunned by the opulence of her home. What exactly had the war taken from her?

She led us into a wide mirror-lit dining room where gold drapes spilled like bunting over the bookshelves, and for a moment the mirrors gave us both a glimpse of how disreputable we looked. We seemed so out of place, so utterly unfamiliar to ourselves. Through the back doors I could see a garden teeming with spring. There was an empty pool filled with plants.

"Sometimes, in the old days, I would have a winter party and we would dig out the pool and sit on the bottom, wrapped in our coats and watch the stars. Like being at the bottom of a great well," she said wistfully.

"Helluva place," Hill mumbled.

She seated us at a long mahogany table and we were joined by a young Austrian woman who spoke fair English and served as her interpreter. In spite of our filthy appearance, the young woman treated our words with great formality, gravely translating as if we were dignitaries from a distant land. It must surely have been the strangest luncheon that dining room had ever sponsored. Servants appeared with china dishes and silver cutlery on costly trays. Though the wartime menu was simple—a motley root vegetable soup and hard bread—for us it was a banquet. We went at it like wolves. They both watched us eat with a kind of horrified pleasure, and we made no apologies as we helped ourselves to seconds. After months of dreaming about fruits and vegetables, meats and desserts, eating at a table with other ordinary men and women felt like the first step back into a life I had almost forgotten. When the meal was done, the matron took us for a walk about her house. Curtains swept across the edge of the glass-framed tall windows. The walls sported fine pictures of horses and leaping hounds. There was a glass painting of a Chinese woman with tiny, delicate hands and a most quixotic smile on her pale, melancholy face. I stood before that image for a long time.

"That is my favorite," she said, coming alongside me and speaking with a maternal kindness. The young Austrian woman, standing behind Hill, continued to translate.

"I bought it in Vienna," she said. "This Chinese woman has become a great friend to me in these dark days. She is serene. Always so serene. See here," and she leaned forward to point at the painting, "these tiny flecks where the paint has fallen off and left the dull glass beneath. So she is like me. I am not what I once was." And then she turned her beautiful eyes on me and made me think of my mother's own lost dreams I thought of her singing at my bedside: *I lived for art, I lived for love; why, why, oh Lord, have you brought me to this.* But it was the young translator who took my breath away. I had not been so close to a comely young woman for several years, and she had my blood running strong.

We continued on the tour. The halls were long and wide. We passed the doors to many rooms, each a different color, each suggesting almost a different mood. She had the elegant toughness of a woman who understood the demands of land and sweat, yet she managed to cup and hold a most delicate beauty in her home. She seemed so like her paint-flecked Chinese woman.

"You may stay here, if you like," she said as we gathered again downstairs in her living room. The young Austrian woman had left us and a French household worker was brought in to translate.

"She says we can stay here," I told Hill, certain he would welcome the first chance to sleep in a bed for over a year.

"Tell her we appreciate it. She's got a beautiful house. But we're dirty and the barn is a better place for us," Hill said with a sudden dignity.

When I told her, she nodded and for a moment a touch of emotion lit her cheeks. The French worker led us out to a barn.

"Rest here. In the morning we will bring you food," he said before leaving. We settled into the hay, grateful and a bit proud of ourselves.

"Unless we want to try and make a run for it on our own," said Hill later that night, "we best be getting back to the woods tomorrow. If they start moving and we lose them, we haven't a clue where to go." He was right, though I was not worried. When in doubt, walk west. Look for the sunrise and start walking the opposite direction.

The next morning we bid the mistress farewell, and I could see that she was relieved by our friendly departure. It was hard to know what these Austrians really felt. They seemed readily willing to dissociate themselves from the Nazis, but did that come easier now that this war was nearing its end? Were they as troubled by the war when they were winning? I had to remind myself that while we were starving, our hostess was drinking cold milk and eating roasted meat. Yet, different as she may have been from Hill or me, she was also very like us. She was waiting to resume a normal life and, like us, had a long way to travel before that was possible. As we walked down her drive, I thought of the other stragglers who would pass by that glass painting soon enough. I hoped they, too, would leave it intact.

We did not turn back to the forest just yet. The sky was blue overhead and spring was all around us. Instead we followed a little farm road into a small valley filled with wildflowers. The ground was awash with color. At the base of the valley, like a still life, was a collection of covered wagons. We had eaten well that morning and we were not hungry, but we were certainly curious, so we went down to take a look.

We came down a grassy slope to the nearest wagon. Coming around the corner we surprised a small family similar to the kind I had met the day I was shot down: there was a grandmother and a young mother holding a baby, and a number of small children running about a tall man with a limp. Unlike a year ago, however, this man was not a soldier-son home on leave, but rather the young woman's husband. He spoke French and he kept looking over my shoulder as if expecting more of us to come along. I could not tell whether we worried him, but he was distinctly wary. We talked a bit about our circumstances and then he explained they were Hungarian gypsies trying to stay out of the way of the military and the civilians.

"People hate gypsies," he said resignedly. "We live a life too free for them. The soldiers want to kill us and the civilians want us to leave." His children ran about the wagons with their little friends, stopping to gather in knots to watch us and whisper. The man told us of their journey, trying to move ahead of the guns that every day seemed everywhere.

"We know the Germans are losing and are scared, because they pay us no mind. When they come we get out of their way and they pass us as if we are not there; in the old days, they would stop us and take what they wanted. They were," and here he stopped speaking for a moment and watched his wife, weary and thin, begin to make a lunch in the wagon's tiny galley, "hard on us. Hard on our women. The Nazis are dogs," he said grimly.

Soon the family gathered around a rectangular table with benches built into the wagon floor on two sides and they asked us to join them. Our bellies still full from the farmwoman's lunch, we refused with as much grace as we could muster. They had a small bowl of porridge, barely enough for one. There fell over us all an awkward silence, and to break it I pulled a D-bar out of my pocket and handed it to the grandmother. She looked at it—they all did—as though it were pure gold. I thought she would immediately take the chocolate and divide it into six pieces. Instead, she called for a knife. A big-boned woman with powerful arms and large boots on her feet, she was, without a doubt, the head of this household. She took the D-bar with the knife and leaned over toward the two smaller children who sat before their small mounds of porridge. And then, with a deliberate solemnity, she scraped the D-bar's surface, creating a kind of chocolate dust. The children were delighted and looked up at her first and then us with sweet, tender smiles. We were astonished by the restraint of all of them, the discipline. I thought of the way we had eaten in the Austrian farmhouse and winced. Even before our stalag life I remembered the Air Corps mess halls. The food had been awful, but the eating was mostly a matter of speed and appetite: you ate fast and sought more. An embarrassment of plenty. The gypsy grandmother dispensed that chocolate dust as if in a ritual of celebration. She took none for herself, gave none to her daughter or her son-in-law. When the children ate, they seemed so happy that it was as if Hill and I were tasting the chocolate right along with them, and for the very first time. Transfixed by what seemed almost a ritual, we sat there watching until Hill nudged me:

"We'd better get our asses back to the forest." The good-bye among the adults was formal, poignant, but the children hugged our knees and smiled. I wondered what would become of them.

We walked for many hours, the day giving way to a gloomy night as we retraced the roads we had traveled. When we arrived again at the forest, the fires winked; men were busy moving around talking, laughing. We had been gone for two days but had not been missed.

The next morning I went out for a walk alone. Being away from the forest for those two days had worked to somewhat broaden the horizons of my mind. I wanted a chance to think beyond the limits that the long, hard months inside the barbed wire had imposed. As I started out, it struck me that for the first time in years I had no immediate obligations or concerns: this day was my own. The woods were formidable and dark, but sunlight speared through the topmost branches. The bed of needles made the walking soft and easy, and I must have walked for miles. Climbing a hill, I came out into a meadow full of wild grasses greening with spring. The sky above was a magnificent blue, and around me there were many wildflowers. The meadow ran to a base of higher hills with forested slopes and far-apart red-tiled roofs. I had taken along the blue notebook and pencil with the intent of finding a good place to sit down in such solitude—if it could be found—and think about my coming new freedom. I wanted to think hard and deep about its meaning, think about what I should do next, in what direction I should go from there. There were snow-covered mountains in the far distance. A more beautiful place to sit down and go about that thinking could hardly be found.

So I flopped into that wild grass and for a while just let the surrounding beauty wash over me—as perhaps with surf on a sunlit beach. Then thoughts began to take shape. Out of the sunshine and crisp morning air came an overwhelming sense of having been given my greatest gift ever, the gift of having come to the end of the war—with all its life-threatening minutes, hours and days—alive, well, and able to go forward into a new life. What should I do to return this gift of survival and, more important, to honor those brave men who were cut down a year ago while we, the Luftwaffe's target of choice, had miraculously survived? I didn't know, but looking out over the green grass leading to the hills, I resolved to try from then on to live, in their honor, a life that would serve others rather than me.

That resolve might have been made in the dark of the night, or in the bowels of our Barracks 32A tunnel, or elsewhere in the grimmest of surroundings; but the way it was, I was making it in—perhaps drawing it from—the heart of this extraordinarily beautiful meadow. Thinking about that, I was reminded of something that had been coming back to me little by little as we had hiked along the country roads of Austria during the past three weeks. Perhaps foolishly, perhaps wrongly, I had long since cast my lot with the world of nature—long since sought inspiration from the beauty nature seemed to give me as a framework for doing my best thinking, such as it was. Struck now by the force of that uncertain tie to nature, I resolved to no longer doubt its wisdom or justification but rather, in the rest of my new life now starting, to openly seek inspiration from nature whenever possible.

Chewing a piece of grass for a while, I turned, for the first time in over a year, to thinking about America's flag. I thought of what it had always meant to me and it was victory—victory in battle against America's enemies. I now came to see that the flag meant more to me than victory in our wars; it stood for the *heart and soul* of America: the freedom to speak out or write about whatever was in your mind without danger of harm to yourself; the commitment to justice in the courts; the unsurpassed concern for the needs and rights of the underdog and the downtrodden. I resolved to try to make a big part of the rest of my life the defense against whatever forces might look to weaken or kill that heart and soul, and to begin that effort by volunteering to fight in the Pacific war still under way.

Looking at a cluster of nearby wildflowers for a few minutes, my thoughts turned to the prospect of being once again in a world where men and women could live together. From a very early age I had thought about, written about, what might be called my vision of a life with a woman of great heart, soul and beauty who would share with me—in a bond that could withstand all vicissitudes and onslaughts—the common goals of my life and hers, and the hard, unrelenting work to turn them day by day, little by little, into substance. I resolved to search, whenever and however possible, for that great and beautiful woman.

Sitting in the grass I wrote these resolves down as best possible in the school notebook. They were overwhelmingly important to me at that time and in that setting. I decided to call them, altogether, my green grass resolution. Then I stretched out in the grass again and watched white cloud ships drift across the cobalt sky. Before long, I fell into a deep sleep.

The sun was beginning to slant in from the west when I woke. Light and shadow in the grasses had taken on a changed beauty. The morning's resolves for the future took shape again, but then something stirred in me to move from thinking about the path ahead to going back over the long road traveled since taking the train to war more than three years ago. In the solitude of that meadow, elusive truths came to mind. I had come to the Air Corps, to the war, to the stalag itself, it struck me, with my own stubborn ideas of duty, of right and wrong, of good and bad. I had thought I knew precisely who I was and was sure of what I knew. Yet from the moment the German peasant women had elected to save my life, I was faced with a mysterious sense that there was more to the world than I had ever known. There was much I could not know or explain: why I was alive and the poor Jews shot along the road were not; where Frank Grey might be now and where I would have been if we'd gotten out together. All I knew was that I'd been part of a group of men who had endured and had done so by teaching, collaborating and helping one another. The chance meeting under the pines with Wilkens and Thompson had reminded me that comradeship was one of the stalag's lasting lessons. The men with whom I'd endured Stalag 17 had, in my year of five seasons, become my teachers, my partners in learning. Their lessons in ingenuity, essential know-how, humanity, even humility had offered me new models of wisdom and insight. If I was no longer certain of who I had been, I was growing to understand who I was becoming. And I knew that I owed my kriegie comrades a great and lasting debt.

But now the sun was low in the west and the hill's shade was moving down the hill like a dark tide. Something in me quickened at the change of light, an animal instinct. *Get back*, I thought. *Get back now.* As I hurried down the hill, weaving between the pines like a skier, I felt a growing sensation that I was isolated, cut off. At the base of the hill I came to another, smaller clearing, still bright with the afternoon. The animal in me was fully up now and I stopped to listen. Something was moving through the bushes. Another deer? I saw bushes tremble and then heard the heavy crack of a branch. This was no deer. And then, out from the clearing's edge stepped a man. A German soldier. Like me he was aware that he was not alone, his head lifted as if sniffing the wind. I saw his face. It was Max. He stopped when he caught sight of me and, at first, not seeing clearly (the sun was in his eyes), he looked as if he were going to step back into the woods. We were separated by not more than fifteen feet, and it took him only a moment to recognize the kriegie he had struck outside the showers, the one who had cost him the commandant's reprimand. When he did, a cruel smile spread over his face and his hand fell across his pistol holster.

I might have rushed him right then and there ("Always make your move early," Frank Grey had once said), but that thought came only later. More animal now than man, I pulled my body up as straight as possible, stood hands on hips, and locked eyes with him. We stared at each other. Perhaps he was weighing the merits and risks of killing me, measuring the value of my life, calculating how he might kill me and not endanger himself. *Are there other prisoners with him? Where are they? Will they hear the shot?* I didn't know. All I did know was that I held my gaze on him and began thinking "Go ahead and shoot, Max, if you think that'll help you live better. Go ahead and shoot. But you'll be making a big mistake. Your revenge will cost you dearly, most likely your life." Standing there close enough to hear each other breathing, neither of us blinked or twitched a muscle. We both knew it was his move. Time stopped. I could smell the wind off the pines around us, pungent and sweet. The forest might be my only move if he chose to shoot. I could get to cover if his first shot missed. But now it struck me that if he reached to pull his gun, a zigzag sprint right at him would likely make that first shot miss. His hand rested on his holster and I waited. The hoarse cry of a hawk startled us both as it crossed the clearing, heavy, slow wings taking it up and over the treetops. Max looked up at it and then, in a gesture as simple as the one Franz Schubert had made that morning in the barracks, he turned away. No final look or acknowledgment, no mercy asked or given. He just walked off into the woods and never looked back. And with him went Stalag 17. I did not know it then, but at that moment, my war was over.

WHEN I GOT BACK TO THE bonfire, it was a gray, smoldering heap. Everyone was gone. There were several guys poking around the debris of the campsite, last stragglers to a finished banquet. I did not know any of them and they seemed surprised by my appearance.

"Where is everybody?" I asked.

One of them, a lanky fellow leaning on a walking stick, waited while the others tied their boots.

"Gone," he said. "Most to the aluminum factory, some down to the village."

"Why? Are we on the march again?"

"On the march?" The man looked at me like I was crazy. "Ain't you heard? Where you been? It's done. We got liberated. We was all standin' around when Patton's Thirteenth Armored rolled in. The Jerries gave up. It's fuckin' over."

"Where's the village?" I asked, not at all certain what to say.

"I ain't sure. Bunch of guys headed down there. There may still be a few guys back that way," he said, pointing into the forest behind us, "waiting for American trucks to come in later this afternoon. Take your pick." The others called to him, eyeing me impatiently. Old kriegies, they saw me as an interfering stranger.

"Let's go, Billy," one said, looking like he wanted me to get lost. They got their stuff and walked off without saying good-bye. I had to get my gear and wondered whether the guys still in the woods could tell me more, so I headed back the way the kriegie had pointed. At the next clearing there was another handful of men gathering up their things, getting ready to leave. Right away I saw Tony Sac, and when he saw me, he rushed over with a look of such joy that his whole face shined.

"Isn't it the greatest?" he said, grabbing my shoulders.

"What happened?" I asked again.

"Oh man, it was great! What an encore for yesterday."

"Yesterday? What happened yesterday?"

"Handy, you're always out of it. Do I have to start looking after you, too? Look, I gotta get a move on, you should, too. Come on with us to the pickup."

"Tony. What the hell happened?" I asked one more time.

"It was the best. We were standing around and all of a sudden we hear the sound of big engines. Someone shouted 'That's a goddamned tank. Let's get the hell out of here!' But we had no time to run before three big Shermans come busting through the bushes. The most beautiful machines you ever saw. They sit there for a minute, engines idling. I'm not sure what they're gonna do, almost like maybe they was gonna start firing or something. Then the hatch opens and this captain, I could see his bars, pops his head out. 'What the hell is this?' he says, and man, we start cheering and crowding his tank. For a moment he don't know what to do. 'Whoa, whoa,' he says, like we were going to wreck his tank. 'Who the hell are you?' he asked us, and somebody shouted, 'The best goddamn airmen in the Eighth Army Air Corps!' and the captain says, 'You gotta be kidding. Sweet Jesus. We heard the woods were full of Germans. We were going to blow these woods to kingdom come. Oh, thank God.' And I thought to myself: you are damned right, mister. Thank God. I mean, can you believe that, Handy? We come this far only to get blown to smithereens by our own guys? Anyway, he gets on a field phone and calls back saying, 'Hold everything. We just liberated American prisoners.' And then he is quiet for a second and then he says, 'Listen, Colonel, I'm sure as hell. It's the goddamnedest bunch of guys I've ever seen,' and all the kriegies let out another cheer. I mean the place went wild. We started laughing and crying and hugging each other." Tony looked at me oddly for a moment.

"Handy, where the hell were *you*? Why are you always in the wrong place at the wrong time? The greatest moment of the whole goddamned war and you missed it!"

I could not speak. I knew that my own moments had their own meaning, but there was nothing to say.

"Well, like I said, he was from the Thirteenth Armored Division, Patton's Third Army. He told us where the army was, but none of us paid him no mind. We were too happy listening to that beautiful American accent. Guys just kept rubbing that tank like it was the goddamned family dog or something. He says, 'Don't move, fellas. Stay right here and sit tight. Our men will come up and take care of things, but probably not until tomorrow. We won't be able to deal with your guards until then, so meantime watch yourselves.' Somebody shouted,

'Hey Captain! Where you from?' and the captain grinned and said something I couldn't hear. 'Where's he from?' I shouted at a guy who shouted back, 'Who the fuck cares. He's American, ain't he?' Then they left. Just like that. Somebody told me later that a Nazi staff car with two officers, one German, one American, stopped on the road over at the edge of the woods and that they told everybody that all the Stalag 17 officers and guards had surrendered. The American, a colonel, repeated what the tank captain had said: we'd have to wait at least a day before troops could come up to take over. Meanwhile the guards were supposed to stay on and wait, too." Tony Sac's smile ebbed and he looked away. I could tell by the sorrow in his face that something else had happened, and I thought that I knew already what it was.

"Middle of the morning," Tony Sac continued softly, "two American jeeps came up the road and stopped outside our clearing. I'm over there with my brother. A bunch of GIs with rifles jump out and start shouting at the Jerries. They were some of Patton's boys. Mean-looking, too. Most of the guards had already taken off and headed for home, but there were a few who stayed with us, waiting like we were. They kept to themselves mostly. That captain had warned us not to hurt the ones who waited to surrender. 'Don't do anything rash, fellas,' he said, 'these guys ain't got nothing left.' He was right. We gave them no grief and they gave us none back. But those GIs were looking for trouble. They quickly rounded up all the Germans they could find and started to beat the shit out of them. They took one of the ones who fought back out into the woods and shot him dead." Tony Sac was quiet. "They were good enough guys. They did what they did because looking at us—I think we look lots worse than we think, Handy—they got the idea that the Germans hadn't done right by us. They figured the Jerries should pay for it on the spot. Those guys thought they owed that to us. It don't make it right," he offered soberly, "but that's the way it went."

"Did you know any of the guards who got beaten up? The one who was killed?" I asked, already knowing.

"They beat the shit out of quite a few and woulda killed 'em all if not for some of our guys putting a stop to it. Some of those guards got pretty beat up," he said, watching me carefully. "The one you knew, the guard you told me saved you. What was his name?"

"Franz Schubert," I said. I could see his blue eyes and the way he talked with me by the wire, his body half turned as if he were looking the other way.

"Yeah, well, they worked him over pretty rough. Somebody must have stopped 'em before he was killed, but by the time I saw him your guy was pretty well done. He had no teeth left in his mouth and one eye was swollen shut." I thought of Max moving easily through the woods, a loaded pistol in his holster.

"Anyway the trucks are coming and we're going home. But first we have to go and stay in some aluminum factory. Hey, there's Sanford. I got to tell him something . . ." and Tony Sac turned away. I walked back into the woods a ways and found a spot under a tree. Scrunching a pile of pine needles under my head, I lay down and thought of Schubert. I was sorry that I had not been there to help him. I knew that if I could have told those guys that he had saved my life, that he was no German, that he was a Czech . . . Did it matter that maybe he wasn't? Maybe he was Austrian or German, but he had been a human being when I needed him to be and I had not been able to return the favor. I would have to think on all of this when there was time.

The sun was beginning to set and I had to get moving. Our fir-branch lean-to was empty save for my gear; Hill was gone. I hoped he was OK, as I hadn't seen him since leaving on my spring-morning hike. Gathering up everything and heading for the road, I encountered a lone guy who told me that they had just now loaded a truck and left. It was getting dark. As far as he knew, there would be no more trips today.

"Got any suggestions for me?" I asked, not surprised at having missed going with all the other guys.

"Sure. There's a village down the road a ways, at the bottom of the hill. Some of the guys disobeyed orders and went down there; a night at an aluminum factory didn't sound so good to them. Or me. I'm going to the village myself."

"I'll go with you," I said.

"Suit yourself," he answered, not looking my way.

We hit the narrow country road. Twilight was setting in so we walked briskly, without conversation. Before long the road wound down into the village. It was small, quaint, filled with brick buildings and shuttered windows. We came into the village square and there, in its grassy center, with an American infantryman standing guard, was a huge pile of guns. American soldiers must have reached the village and disarmed the Germans, and every imaginable kind of rifle was piled high. The guard let us sort through it looking for weapons that were loaded or had ammunition beside them. He wasn't sure what to make of us, but he knew we were Americans and needed to be armed. In the pile were mostly rifles, all of them old. I found one that held a clip of several large bullets.

"You know what that is?" the guard asked me, knowing I didn't. "That's a rifle from the Great War. Austrian. It's been around."

I was now armed, and it gave me a strange, almost unholy feeling. Four other kriegies had been scavenging for guns and they fell in with us. Finding that none of us spoke German, but that I could speak French, the group asked me to lead the way. We needed to find ourselves a place where we might get some food and a bed.

Others had had the same idea. Walking the village streets, we could tell that a number of families had already taken in our comrades. Also clear to us was the brutality some Americans were dealing out to Austrians still in the streets. We were later told that it had been worse the day before, that some men had been badly beaten by a few American soldiers. Some of the houses appeared to have been looted: windows were broken, objects were scattered about the streets. Curtains were drawn; there was no sign of life. We walked through the landscape as if in a dream. It was eerily quiet.

"This is a bad scene," someone said angrily.

"Let's agree if we see more of this," I added, "we'll stop it. Raise our guns if we have to. It's bound to be a few thugs if they're still around." Everyone agreed. We walked on and soon came to an imposing house.

"Let's ask these folks if we can get some rest here, maybe a bit of chow," said someone. It was a good idea. The place looked prosperous.

"You all wait here," I offered. "Look presentable." Everyone laughed at that. "And don't make a show of your guns." Responding to my knock at the door, an elderly gentleman opened up. French wasn't needed; he spoke English with a thick German accent. I explained our situation, and without hesitation, he welcomed us in. We shuffled up the walk, sheepish with our dirty boots and stolen guns.

It turned out that once again I found myself—as I had the day our plane went down—in the home of a burgermeister. As we lurched, one by one, through the open door, we found inside and waiting, as if in a receiving line, the entire family. There were perhaps a dozen people, from grandparents to children. They had been about to sit down to their supper. We were led into a large dining room where they made places for us, and we sat down to a family supper of vegetable stew and, of course, the dark, hard bread that they told us was their own wartime staple. The elders asked us in broken English where we were from, how we had gotten here. They seemed distressed that we were former prisoners and apologized, as if they themselves had been responsible. We all conducted ourselves with an exaggerated formality, a politeness that seemed almost competitive. At the insistence of the most elderly lady, perhaps the burgermeister's mother, we downed one generous helping after another.

After supper we were shown to a room with two giant beds and, dead tired from our nights of little sleep in the forest lean-tos, we thanked them and said good night. Too excited to sleep, we lounged around and talked like brothers. It was like being at a kind of childhood sleepover. Then we heard a hiss from one of our group. He was beckoning us to follow him. We crept out into the hallway and found ourselves looking down into the living room below. There was the whole family on their knees, praying. They were oblivious to us. We watched in silence. I felt Young's crucifix in my pocket and wondered what had happened to all of us these past dark years.

There were no sheets on the beds, just billowing comforters, top and bottom. Three to a bed, we sandwiched ourselves between them and found surprising warmth and comfort—a far cry from nights on hard wood and, for the last month, on hard ground. We slept like teenage boys. When we woke, the sun was high in the sky and the day well along. We came downstairs and the children laughed and pointed at us. We were sleepy and embarrassed by our lateness. A breakfast was now laid out for us with coffee and eggs and buttered slices of thick bread. We ate with gusto and, with a fever to be out and around, said our thanks and, rifles in hand, headed for the door.

As we were getting ready to leave, the family grandmother stopped me and asked me to accompany her to a larger village down the river. She had a horse and wagon. The others were tumbling out the front door, indifferent to one another's plans in this strange, shiftless time. Thinking back to those dangerous streets we'd seen the evening before, I understood her request and agreed. They brought the horse around and hooked up a handsome carriage and she and I began a clip-clop ride over country roads. It was a long ride—nearly an hour—and we said very little. I sat shotgun with the gun cradled in my arm. We passed many men who stared at this odd couple. Many were hauling off things they had looted, and all were aggressive and loud.

We stopped to let the horse drink from a spring. Three American soldiers came ambling along the road and stopped.

"What the hell do we have here?"

"I'm an ex–prisoner of war," I said somewhat harshly, thinking of Franz Schubert and the brutal treatment of some of the Austrians in the village. Some Americans had seemed to have learned all the wrong lessons from this war.

"I'm seeing to it that this woman gets home safely."

"What is she, your fucking grandmother? That would make you a Kraut, too," said one of the others ominously.

"U.S. of A., mack," I said sternly. "This woman and her family have helped a bunch of us. She's getting the same treatment her family showed to us. You guys got a problem with that?" I added, feeling angry. He eyed me for a moment and shrugged.

"Suit yourself, sonny. Play nursemaid if you like." They walked on.

We rode into the larger town where she got her foodstuffs. I stood somewhat warily by the carriage, rifle in hand, ignorant of the real danger I was in. The town was quiet, the streets were largely empty, but armed GIs were prowling around. Soon enough we were on our way back and made it safely past dozens of others looking for local treasures. I was riding shotgun through a wild, lawless country where the source of the danger was American GIs. It shook me that a few of our troops would bring the very danger and brutality to this woman and her village we had associated with the enemy.

Late that afternoon, after all of us were back in the house, we sat around the upstairs rooms talking about the day's events. Someone said that an American officer had gone through in a jeep, using his bullhorn to tell former prisoners they should stay put, that they were going to get us all out of here very soon. I told Tony Sac's version of the last two days' action in the woods.

"That ain't how I heard it," said another. "I heard it was Bill Clarke swimming the river."

"What are you talking about?" asked somebody else.

"You guys know Bill Clarke?" he said authoritatively. "He's a kriegie from 29B. I know him. He was an engineer–top turret gunner on a B-17. Brave bastard. I just heard the story this afternoon. He went with a buddy down to the river couple of days ago looking to fill a water container. The Jerries had a guard posted down at the river's edge."

"Yeah, they want to shoot kriegies trying to swim the river, and everything that floats down the river they shoot, too, in case there's a kriegie hanging on to it," added an eager listener.

"I'm gettin' to that, dammit," said the storyteller, annoyed at the interruption. "Well, Clarke figured he was a good swimmer and he might try and get across the river. The plan was to have his buddy distract the guard long enough to let him slip into the river without being seen. They didn't need to because the guard turned away to light a cigarette 'cause the wind was fierce. Clarke went in with his clothes and boots on. The current was a bitch—two rivers colliding make it hell—and though it made the swimming hard, it carried him out of the guard's sight right quick. Damned if he didn't swim the fucking river. Truth, I swear I heard it from the guy who watched him. He said that a couple of times it looked like the current had pulled Clarke under and he was gone. It was ice-cold water, too. I don't know how he did it. By the time he got to the other side, he was damn near frozen to death from the swimming. Not knowing whether German troops were over there nearby, he got into some riverbank bushes and rested until dark. Then he worked his way along the riverbank north toward Brannau."

"What did that kriegie tell us? That he walked with one foot on the bank and the other in the water so he wouldn't step on a land mine?" said the same kriegie, looking to share the story.

"Who the fuck is telling this story, Marty? You or me?" said the first kriegie, agitated and menacing.

"Don't get sore," sulked the other.

"Well, after moving north about a mile," the kriegie continued, sure of his authority to tell the rest of the story alone, "he could see troops around some kind of construction site. He took a chance that they would be Americans and found out they were GIs from Patton's Thirteenth Armored Division. They were building a pontoon bridge because the Germans had blown up the bridge that crossed the river. The GIs he spoke to thought he was a crank—we all look like goddamned hobos. And the poor bastard didn't have any American Army clothes on him. All he had were some RAF duds he'd gotten back at camp. They took him to a master sergeant who was skeptical, too. Still, in the end, I guess the story was crazy enough and Clarke was enough of a mess to make some kind of sense, and the master sergeant told Bill to hang in until the officers came back the next morning. So the next morning the C.O.—a major—comes roaring in. He's got a jeep with a silver-plated shotgun on the backseat. Like Custer or somebody. Well, the major is more than skeptical, he's pissed at all this fuss for a guy who looked like shit. Clarke pressed the point that there were thousands of GIs in the woods.

"The Major eyed him for a bit. It was normal procedure to shell the shit out of the other side 'wide and deep' for as long as forty-eight hours before a crossing and he wasn't going to let some spy looking like a soaked GI throw him off the plan. Anyway, he asks Clarke to name the Yankees' catcher and Clarke tells him 'Bill Dickey last time I knew— we've been out of touch for a while, sir.' So the major ups the ante. He says 'O.K., who was fucking Blondie last time you knew?' When Clarke shoots back 'Dagwood,' the major says they'd hold off on the shelling. Clarke rode with the Thirteenth Armored until the next day, when he rejoined us again."

"That's the best. One of our own kriegies saves our hides. And to think, us getting killed by our own guys after all we've been through . . ." said the kriegie called Marty.

No one talked for a while; then someone said "Amen."

Shaken, I got up and went downstairs and out into the yard. So many near misses. Every step of the way. For me, for all the kriegies of Stalag 17. Outside in the yard I came upon a woman who was stooped over a washbucket, busily scrubbing clothes. Startled at first, she looked at me with a kind of fear, relaxing only when she discovered that I could speak French. I introduced myself and learned that she was the family's maid. We stood in the warmth of the afternoon sun, and before long, she began to talk. In these days around the war's end, it seemed everyone had a story they needed to tell. Some were tales of survival; others were narratives that amounted to an intense witnessing. Everyone needed to speak, as if only in talking with one another could these strange days be managed. She was Hungarian. She spoke of the disappearance of her brothers and father, the incarceration of her cousins and the long, terrible death of her worn-out mother. Her journey had its own terrible course and she recounted it without self-pity or sorrow. She had endured her own kind of Russian compound, and even now she barely understood what had happened to her. After a moment of quiet, she brought our conversation to an end. She asked for my socks, saying that she would wash and darn them for me overnight.

WE STAYED ANOTHER NIGHT AT THE burgermeister's home. The next morning, eating another generous breakfast, we heard a banging on the front door and one of our guys went to open it. When he came back he said that the kriegies were gathering at the aluminum factory north of the village.

"It is not far," said the elderly gentleman. "It is near the main road and there is a lot of space there." I finished my breakfast. We had to go.

One of the littlest girls, a bright-eyed, wide-smiling child, came right up to me and asked me if I knew how to tell time. I said I did and she said that her grandmother did not think so. We slept when we should be awake and talked when we should have been asleep. I showed her my watch and she looked at it with amazement and a kind of awe. I tried to hand it to her, thinking that my mother would like it to go to a sweet child.

"It is yours," I said.

She put her hands behind her back and shook her head, though her eyes had already taken it. Then she looked up at me.

"I am Anna," she said. "I am eight. I am not afraid."

She was a shoot of green. There had been fear in the eyes of her parents and older siblings; her grandmother had kept me close on the ride, though perhaps fearing me as much as the roving men who terrorized her village. But there was no fear in this child's eyes. Her gaze was steady, wise beyond her years. I saw many things in that little girl's eyes, things she could not yet have known but must already have felt. Her house was filled with exuberant American prisoners, her family and her village were under siege. Yet she was not afraid. It was as if she knew we were leaving; that the dead would be buried and everything would begin again with the new spring. Looking into her blue, fearless eyes it occurred to me that though the world no longer belonged to those who had brought it to its knees, the world was still much the same. Tyranny would come again; the rights of humankind would be at risk again and again. History would always teach us its hard lessons: Mintz and Orlando in a burning plane, the kriegie hanging along the wire, the dead Russians and Jews sprawled along the road, these were written chapters, with more to come. And yet, if tyranny had denied millions of good men, women and children the chance to stand at the dawn of their own lives as Anna and I did now, we still had the choice to set ourselves against it now and forever. If the old world, with its tangled alliances and brutal consequences, was still with us, then all of us who had endured this war would shoulder the choice of where we carried the world next. And that must have been what Father Kane meant. For now the walking must begin, just when I thought it had come to an end. Now the burden must be raised to do the things every day that demanded doing. And the question that had come back to me again and again throughout my war—why had I survived?—seemed to have its answer: to live a new and better life, the life I wrote of in the meadow. And I knew that Anna, wherever she went, would go with me and I with her. I touched her head and she smiled up at me—as if we both understood we were the redeemers of that old and weary world.

EPILOGUE

NEARBY, THE COUNTRY
CALLED LIFE

> *I have come by the highway home,*
> *And lo it is ended.*
>
> —ROBERT FROST

W̶E ASSEMBLED AT that aluminum factory and began a new journey as American soldiers once again. Trucks led us to an airstrip where DC-3s packed us up in groups and flew us to northern France. New trucks carried us to Camp Lucky Strike, an American encampment for prisoners of war set up near St. Valery-en-Caux, a French village on the Channel coast. Americans of all ranks who had been recaptured by Allied forces were brought together, fed, clothed and sheltered. They did not know much about how to feed us, and many soon got sick from all the rich food that was endlessly supplied by well-intentioned army chefs.

The first morning I was there, General Eisenhower arrived to meet us. He shook our hands and spoke to us as fellow warriors. We were thin and mangy, and yet he acted with great humility as if we had made a sacrifice that humbled him. Later I would learn that the Russian prisoners who had marched from Stalag 17 would reach their own country only to be tossed into another prison where they languished for many more months and many died. Having surrendered or been captured by the Nazis, they had been immediately branded collaborators upon return to their own country. After enduring years of brutality, starvation and sickness, they had to be "cleansed" of their treason.

I met many comrades in those few days at Camp Lucky Strike. All had brief, vivid answers to the question that each of us had for the other: how did you manage to survive? There was a flier named Houchard, one of the only two men who got out of Lieutenant Brand's plane on the 466th's first mission—a devastating run to Berlin. After they were struck and their plane was burning, he and Frank Pheiffer, Brand's other waist gunner, had watched each other helplessly as the centrifugal force of the bomber's downward spin pinned them to opposite walls. At the last minute Houchard had gotten out by inching himself along the plane's skin, rib by rib, toward the waist window. With the window finally within reach, he'd torn open his parachute pack, yanked free the little pilot chute and pushed it out into the roaring slipstream. The next thing he knew, he was regaining consciousness in a chute nearing ground. Somehow the pilot chute, once out in the slipstream, had ripped both his main chute and him past the twin machine guns and out the window, breaking bones and knocking him out along the way. But he recovered and now here he was, alive and well. I thought of Pheiffer, who had not survived. He had not been assigned to that first mission. A sudden illness on the way over had left him behind for several weeks in a Brazilian hospital. Reaching our 466th base the day before, he was told he'd have to go through several days of orientation before rejoining his crew. Such an order was an easy way to stay alive for at least a few more days. But Pheiffer insisted that his temporary replacement as right waist gunner be sent packing. His crew was flying the group's first mission. Wherever the target, whatever the consequences, he was going to fly with his buddies. Captain Bryant, our tough-minded operations officer, had softened a bit and, meaning well, let him do it. One of so many good men gone.

On that first morning out there listening to Ike, I felt a hand on my shoulder and turned around. It was Tedrowe. His smile was broad and warm. As always, he made no small talk.

"Thanks," he said quietly, broadening that great smile. Nothing more. We just shook hands—a long, warm shake if there ever was one—and took each other's measure. Hopefully my face hid how deeply I was moved. His one word of thanks had said it all: flying on the last, failing engine, he'd needed an engineer to help him understand the key facts and what to do about them. To me it was just another entry in the log of pilot-engineer teamwork, but all the same his thanks dug deep. I knew they covered not just that last mission but all our earlier work together up to that day. We talked then about his experience and mine—the journey behind the Nazi wire—and traded information on crewmates. Then he began to talk about getting back to flying. He had decided to switch to the A-26—the highly thought-of Martin Marauder, a twin-engine fighter-bomber—and to fly it in the Pacific war. The Marauder had a two-man crew—pilot and engineer/ gunner.

"Would you go with me?" he said.

"Great" was all I could get out, thoughts swirling in my head about how much his question—his magnificent offer—meant to me. We shook hands on it. We talked about the Air Force being able to help us locate each other stateside, and then we went our separate ways—neither of us aware that we would never see each other again. A few days later, some of us were flown back to London and were given a place to stay. I'm not sure why, because most everyone stayed at Lucky Strike for some weeks. The London group was to report in every day at a certain address because people were going to be put aboard boats and sent back to the United States. After the sixty-day furlough granted us upon our return home to New York, the Pacific war came to an end and with it, the end of my military life.

·   ·   ·

I WAS TO SPEAK TO TEDROWE twice more. Shortly after the Pacific war ended and the GI education bill was signed, I decided to try to get into MIT. I'd been accepted before the war, but they said that was too long ago and I'd have to start all over again. After we'd talked about this by phone, Tedrowe wrote a great letter of support. Then on April 11, 1969, the twenty-fifth anniversary of our last mission, I found myself in Chicago's O'Hare Airport, back from a day's work in Oklahoma. When I realized the date and the anniversary, Tedrowe was the man I wanted to speak with. I went to a pay phone and, after several calls, managed to reach him in Tampa, Florida. We spoke of the old days for nearly an hour. He had married, started a family and made colonel. Now, at fifty-three, he was going to begin teaching at the University of Tampa. I had become a city planner, married and started a family of my own. We spoke as two men in midflight, trading the details of the lives we had chosen, lives that kept us both preoccupied and busy. Neither of us knew that would be our last conversation. He died several years ago.

It would be fifty years before I would see any fellow kriegies again. In 1999 I attended my first Stalag 17 reunion—though only for its last evening—it being held in easily reached Valley Forge. Why did it take me so long? Back from the war, like so many of us I decided to stay with the Air Force, but the pull of the GI bill changed all that. Instead I went to MIT to become an aeronautical engineer, but during my second year I became interested in a newly developing field I hadn't known about called city planning. The pay would be small but the work would be far more one of giving back—far more keeping faith with that green grass resolution—than building better aircraft. The decision to change fields led to five years of tough academic work—for me, engineering would have been much easier—and then to a very demanding fifty-year national and international career of city planning assignments. There was time for little else than work and family. I have no regrets, though: working to improve living conditions was good for the soul and, more vital, my first job as a city planner had me reporting to an extraordinarily beautiful woman seven years my junior. Margaret was that great woman I'd dreamed of in the Austrian meadow. Her career as an educator became as demanding as mine. We retired together only two years ago and in 2002 marked our fiftieth wedding anniversary with extended family at the home of our daughter, Jenifer, and her husband, Steve Pittman. Since retirement I've had the great experience of getting to all the Stalag 17 reunions and to reconnect more and more with the men who had taught me so very much.

Brief as my meeting with them was at the 1999 reunion—just for the banquet—the forging again of those now-rusty bonds began apace that evening. Waiting for me in the lobby was Gene Meese. He looked the same: handsome and tall, his handshake as strong as ever. We traded stories. After the war, he had returned to Plainville, Ohio, east of Cincinnati on the same Little Miami River that had flooded his beloved mother's home. He married and returned to his job with Western Electric, retiring after a long and successful career. We walked into the hotel bar and there I saw Tony Saccomanno. After great shouts and bear hugs, I learned that he and his brother had given their mother her greatest day by coming home safe and sound together. They teamed up in the restaurant business and eventually Tony moved to the clothing-manufacturing field and became a very successful plant manager. Both now live in Florida and are grandfathers. He rattled off information about others as fast as I could ask: Pappy Barksdale had returned to his family farm in Gray Court, South Carolina, where he still lives in the house his father built. Now retired from a forty-five-year career as chief financial officer for a nearby firm, he manages his farm and enjoys the frequent company of his two daughters, five grandchildren and three great-grandchildren. All the family are rugged horsemen. Chet Shattuck had returned to his home in Greenfield, Massachusetts. He died several years ago after retiring from a career that involved extensive work in Africa. Harry Sanford also returned to Massachusetts, where he earned a bachelor's and master's degree while working for the Union Pacific Railroad. He had a long career with Campbell Soup in Toledo,

Ohio, retiring in 1982. After his wife's passing in 1994, he moved to Nevada, where he lives with one of his daughters. Bob Watson, who was so badly wounded by flak his last mission (and saved by Pappy Barksdale), made it back to his father's farm in northwestern Pennsylvania, near Meadsville. After a long business career, he retired with his wife to Mine Hill, New Jersey, and lived there until her death from cancer in 1987. He stays close to his two daughters, five granddaughters, one grandson and one great-granddaughter. To this day, Pappy Barksdale is his dear friend. Ed McKenzie, who recounted to us that night in the forest the story of the Jewish prisoners along the road, returned to his native state of New Hampshire. He served his country again in the Korean War before beginning his business life. He retired several years ago as chief financial officer of a group of utilities in New England. Since retiring he has written a wonderful book—*Boys at War, Men at Peace*—centering on his recent reunion with the Luftwaffe pilot who shot down his crew's Flying Fortress. It includes a great account of our collective experience at Stalag 17. He coauthored a World War II book in German, served as Stalag 17 historian and continues to write a newsletter for combat fliers. He and his wife live on a wooded hillside near Conway, New Hampshire. Their son and fourteen-year-old grandson live nearby. Later someone told me about Clarke, who had swum the Inn River and saved us from "friendly fire." After getting home, Clarke had stayed with the Air Force (Maguire Field) for thirty-three years, and in the late 1950s—while applying for Veterans Administration help with health problems—he met again the Thirteenth Armored major, now a colonel, and asked him to vouch for his swim in the icy water. At first the colonel failed to remember the incident, but when Clarke asked him whether he'd gotten his silver shotgun home, the colonel was stunned and agreed that Clarke had to be telling the truth. After retiring, he and his wife Mary settled down in Levittown, Pennsylvania, where he continues to serve as a highly effective volunteer claims officer for Disabled American Veterans.

The catch-up continued with Tony. He knew a great deal. I learned that Wilkens died in 2001 and that Joseph had passed away a decade before. It brought me comfort to think that Joseph had lived to see seventy springs on his beloved reservation. Kozikowski, Thompson, Dailey, Young, Hill and many others were lost to me and my fellow kriegies, beyond our ability to track them down. All efforts to find Kozikowski in particular failed me. Like many others, he never joined the American Ex–Prisoners of War or Stalag 17 associations. I still wish I could meet him one more time and thank him for his friendship. I learned that the Germans had buried Irvin Mintz and Alfredo Orlando, our two lost crew members, in a cemetery southwest of Hanover, Germany. We will never know whether, as the Germans reported, they went down with our plane or whether they bailed out and met death in some other way. The Orlando family has made several visits to the gravesite, and Ralph Orlando—a nephew of our tail gunner and himself a fighter pilot who served in the Vietnam War—put together a heartwarming documentary about his uncle.

"And what about Frank Grey?" I asked Tony as we stood at the bar waiting for the dinner.

"Ask him yourself. He's right there." And standing a few feet behind him was Frank Grey. Still imposing, he was talking to a woman I learned was his wife, Dorothy. I came to his elbow, and as he turned to greet me I introduced myself.

"I'm Ned Handy, Frank."

He looked hard at me.

"Hello, Handy," he said softly, slowly remembering, piecing memory together.

"The last time I saw you was at the compound fence. I told you to go."

And with those words I saw memory come back to him as vividly and immediately as light. He smiled.

"I remember you," he said. "You saved my life."

"Lots of us did," I answered, looking toward Meese and Tony Sac. And then he told us his incredible story, filling in what had happened after that last afternoon in 1945 by the wire. He caught on with a work group, escaped and crossed the border into Yugoslavia as he had planned. He joined Tito's partisans and fought for months. After VE Day he returned to Florida and married Dorothy, who had waited courageously through those tumultuous wartime years. They now have three children and six grandchildren, and Frank is a veteran of an Air Force career that included service in the Korean War, during which he was awarded the Distinguished Flying Cross. Most important to us, though, was that he was our "Wolf," our "Grey Ghost," who had a record of seven great escapes and was the only man to escape from Stalag 17 never to be recaptured. We all went to dinner and the stories came back from one and all.

Many of the kriegies had been coming to reunions for years, so I often found myself listening not only to kriegie memories, but also to the retelling of adventures that had occurred during earlier reunions. It was a group that had forged a bond in war and in the years after the war. It had taken me a while to rejoin them, and if at times I felt that old sense of being outside the group, I was still grateful to be among them again. Even if I was not as much a part of them as they were of me, seeing so many kriegies offered me once again the sustaining power of comradeship. There are others I hope to meet again and talk with about all that we lived through together. The reunions, the shared stories, the return of memories long set aside, all are part of a new life for me that has begun with my own retirement. Stalag 17, the place itself, however, is less important to me now than the men I met and learned from there. They reminded me that we had done more than endure, we had prevailed. Those of us in 32A would always remember that we had saved the lives of four men, and that one of those men had escaped to fight again. We had learned to look after one another in that hellish place and, by doing so, had discovered secrets to our own natures that would serve each of us in the years to come.

I remember the moment when I turned away from that grim compound for good and pointed toward the rest of my life. It was late May,

1945. I had come to London and was waiting to go back to the States. I wanted to close the circle and return to the airfield that we had left that last morning. The ground crews may well have rotated, but I hoped that there would be guys who, if they didn't remember Tedrowe or his crew, would appreciate hearing what had happened to some of us they thought had died. I understood that my return would have no particular significance, as there were too many dead and wounded airmen for one returning flier to matter. At the very least, though, I wanted to thank them and finish the journey I had started the year before. So I set off.

The train ride to Norwich was uneventful. Summer had already overrun the English spring. At Norwich I got a cabby to take me to Attlebridge.

"Fly from there, did you?" he asked as we drove along.

"Yes," I said. "I was shot down over Germany. Was a prisoner. I just got back." He was quiet and I was glad of it. My mind was filling fast with memory. I recognized nothing on the way out there and realized how little I had actually seen in my few weeks before that last flight. We got to the airfield and, when I thanked the cabby, he thanked me, too, and refused the fare.

Out on the tarmac, I was startled by the quiet and the emptiness. Planes were grounded; it already looked like an air museum. The day was rare and cloudless. One lone bomber, high up in the blue, circled the airfield but I could not hear its engines. I walked out to the part of the runway where our plane had been parked that last damp morning—a plane I did not know and would live with for only a few hours. I remembered the cowboy who had left it such a mess and noted that I no longer harbored any resentment toward him at all. Men gathered in clusters of conversation and storytelling. I could hear their occasional laughter. I walked up to one group and stood awkwardly at their edge, listening, waiting to be invited in. Several noticed me and their smiles ebbed at the presence of a stranger, but they did not acknowledge me. I remembered the old kriegies. The first instinct of men separated by experience from others is suspicion. You are not one of us. I did not blame them. Finally, during a pause, I spoke up.

"Excuse me. I wonder if you could help me? I was a member of the Four Hundred Sixty-Sixth Bomb Group. We got shot down over Germany and I was a POW for over a year."

"Lots of guys got shot down," said a surly mechanic with a cap cocked over unruly, greasy hair. The war was indeed over.

"Yeah," snickered another, "lots of guys from the Four Sixty-Sixth, too."

"You here to pay us back for all that good equipment you turned over to the Krauts?" said a third man. They all laughed. One fellow looked at me oddly for a moment.

"When did you say you were shot down?"

"In April. April 11, 1944."

"Man, you poor bastards. You were part of that last bunch that lost so many planes. A couple of weeks later the Luftwaffe packed up and went home. But you boys, shit. You threw a lot of hardware away last spring."

"We didn't throw it away," I said, annoyed. "We got shot to hell."

"Yeah, no offense," he said without meaning it. "The guys flying later didn't leave so much equipment rusting in Germany, that's all."

What could I say to him? I thought of bombers in the sky and hand-fashioned saws, of earth and the sound of the Gestapo's rods poking the wooden floors, of the endless days and cold nights, of Wolf standing like a ghost in the snow, the blue, bony foot and the hand through the wire, palm up, asking for help, for mercy, for forgiveness. I thought of Joseph and remembered his dream of me down among those roots, growing toward the sky. We had all been like Joseph's roots in the stalag, we had waited for the sun that would allow us to grow into a fuller life. All that we send into the lives of others comes back into our own. My heart was too full to speak.

Walking back out on the tarmac, I looked up to find that lone bomber again, only to realize it was not a bomber at all. It was a bird, languorously circling as if waiting for something to happen below. At times it seemed to be utterly still, painted on the blue sky like one of Shattuck's bunk paintings, but then it would tilt and I would see its elegant tracing as it banked away on a gust. I had always loved birds, had wanted to be an airman as some kind of kinship with them. Standing out there, I knew that what I might have had in common with these laughing strangers was nothing compared to what I already shared with that solitary bird high above the Attlebridge Airfield. My life was beginning again in a blue silence, as it had a year before. Even now, like the bird above me, my own landscape seemed to stretch out ahead of me, mile after perfect mile.

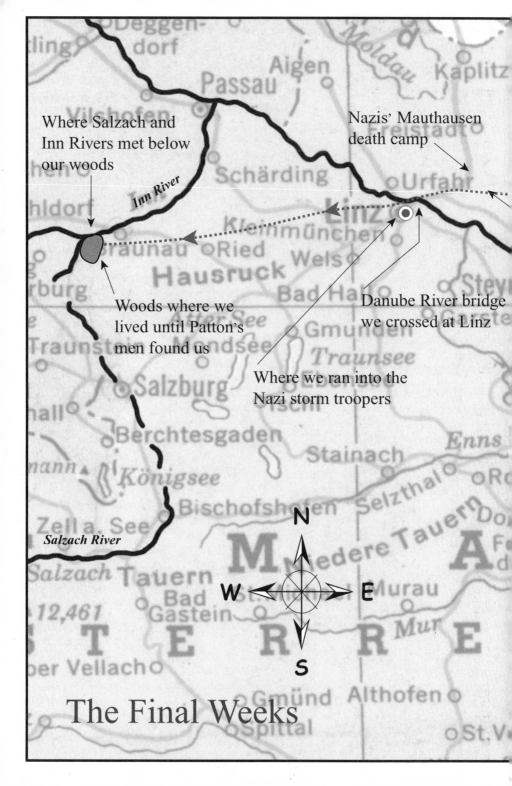

Where Salzach and Inn Rivers met below our woods

Nazis' Mauthausen death camp

Inn River

Woods where we lived until Patton's men found us

Danube River bridge we crossed at Linz

Where we ran into the Nazi storm troopers

Salzach River

N
W E
S

The Final Weeks